SO-CJN-398

PERGAMON INTERNATIONAL LIBRARY
of Science, Technology, Engineering and Social Studies
The 1000-volume original paperback library in aid of education,
industrial training and the enjoyment of leisure
Publisher: Robert Maxwell, M.C.

ATTENTION AND MEMORY

THE PERGAMON TEXTBOOK
INSPECTION COPY SERVICE

An inspection copy of any book published in the Pergamon International
Library will gladly be sent to academic staff without obligation for their
consideration for course adoption or recommendation. Copies may be retained
for a period of 60 days from receipt and returned if not suitable. When a
particular title is adopted or recommended for adoption for class use and the
recommendation results in a sale of 12 or more copies, the inspection copy may
be retained with our compliments. If after examination the lecturer decides that
the book is not suitable for adoption but would like to retain it for his personal
library, then a discount of 10% is allowed on the invoiced price. The Publishers
will be pleased to receive suggestions for revised editions and new titles to be
published in this important International Library.

Some other titles in the series

ATTENTION AND MEMORY

BY

GEOFFREY UNDERWOOD

Department of Psychology, University of Nottingham, England

PERGAMON PRESS

OXFORD · NEW YORK · TORONTO · SYDNEY · PARIS · FRANKFURT

U.K.	Pergamon Press Ltd., Headington Hill Hall, Oxford OX3 0BW, England
U.S.A.	Pergamon Press Inc., Maxwell House, Fairview Park, Elmsford, New York 10523, U.S.A.
CANADA	Pergamon of Canada, P.O. Box 9600, Don Mills M3C 2T9, Ontario, Canada
AUSTRALIA	Pergamon Press (Aust.) Pty. Ltd., 19a Boundary Street, Rushcutters Bay, N.S.W. 2011, Australia.
FRANCE	Pergamon Press SARL, 24 rue des Ecoles, 75240 Paris, Cedex 05, France
WEST GERMANY	Pergamon Press GMbH, 6242 Kronberg/Taunus, Pferdstrasse 1, Frankfurt–am–Main

Copyright © 1976 Geoffrey Underwood

Library of Congress Cataloging in Publication Data

Underwood, G

1. Attention. 2. Memory. I. Title. [DNLM:
1. Attention. 2. Memory. BF321 U56a]
BF321.U5 1975   153.1'2   75−17614
ISBN 0−08−019615−2
ISBN 0−08−018754−4 pbk.

Printed in Great Britain by A. Wheaton & Co., Exeter

CONTENTS

PREFACE

How do we select information from the world around us, represent it to ourselves, and use it to guide our behaviour? Stated concisely these are the questions to which this book addresses itself, but given the refined nature of the apparatus which we use to acquire information from the world, and given the enormity of the amount of information available, then the simplified nature of the questions becomes apparent. The inevitable conclusion of a review text such as this must be that psychologists have only just begun to look away from artificial laboratory situations and towards the human being as an interactive element in a very complex environment. The subject matter of the book is biassed very heavily towards our ability to process verbal material, and that is because this is the major source of evidence when we start to consider the questions of the operation of attention and memory. This operational approach engages discussion of both the structural constraints to our knowledge of, and behaviour in, the world, and the processing strategies used within these constraints. As a review of the psychological evidence available about human memory and its major control process, attention, the book is intended for use in conjunction with undergraduate and graduate courses in experimental psychology. The text grew out of a course of lectures which had the same title as the book, and which were delivered to undergraduates here between 1972 and 1974. Revisions and elaborations were performed both in Nottingham and at the University of Waterloo during 1974 and 1975. My own views on the nature of the attention process, on the unitary trace theory of memory, and on the automaticity of word recognition have been influenced by a number of colleagues, many of whom despair at the conclusions reached here. These influences will nevertheless be apparent to the reader.

Deserving of particular thanks for commenting upon discussions now contained in the text are John Brown, Phil Bryden, Chris Darwin, Ian Howarth, Doug Mewhort, Neville Moray, Joel Singer, and Dave Wood. Especial thanks should also go to Jean Underwood for her assistance in the task of organizing the bibliography and indexes.

We wish to thank the following publishers for permission to reproduce figures in the text:

Human Factors Society for Figs. 1.2 and 1.4; the American Association for the Advancement of Science for Figs. 1.5 and 3.6; the American Psychological Society for Figs. 1.7, 1.8, 2.2, 3.2, 3.5, 5.4, 3.8 and 4.2; the North Holland Publishing Company for Fig. 1.10; the Canadian Psychological Association for Fig. 1.11; Academic Press for Figs. 1.13, 1.14, 1.15a, b, 2.3, 2.5a, b, c, 2.8, 2.9, 3.4, 3.9, 4.4 and 4.5; the Experimental Psychology Society for Figs. 2.4, 2.10 and 2.15; the University of Illinois Press for Fig. 2.7; the Psychonomic Society for Figs. 2.12, 3.1; and the American Institute of Physics for Fig. 4.2. Thanks also go to the authors concerned.

Geoffrey Underwood
Nottingham

ERRATUM

p. 144   The caption to Fig. 3.4 should read: "Mean percentage of words recalled over trials for lists repeated with the same or with changing quartet groupings. (From Bower, Lesgold and Tieman, 1969.)"

p. 145   The caption to Fig. 3.5 should read: "Mean recall errors over four trials for noise items and for items repeated with the same grouping or with different groupings. (From Bower and Winzenz, 1969.)"

CHAPTER 1

IMMEDIATE (SENSORY) MEMORY

A resilient view in modern psychology is that human memory can best be described as comprising two systems, short-term and long-term memory. However valid or invalid this distinction may be, we are now compelled to add at least one other system, and this may be described as immediate or sensory memory. The justification of this addition is the subject of the present chapter, together with the consideration of the separation of processes within the concept of sensory memory. The division and sub-division of memory is more than an academic exercise, even though this purpose alone has its merits in the assistance of the development of psychological science. In the description of the representation of knowledge by human memory we shall necessarily draw conclusions about optimal presentation and retrieval procedures, which should be transferable to non-laboratory situations where information processing is presently inadequate. The model-building approach to the investigation of memory, prevalent during the last ten years, is not without its limitations however. Not the least of these limitations is that model-builders have tended to lose sight of the *purpose* of the components which they have been satisfied to include in their flow-charts. Although the present approach will attempt to keep sight of the purposes of the processes to be described, the reader should be aware of this fault with this and with any description of memory and its control processes.

Immediate Memory of Visual Events

One of the earliest experiments performed on human memory processes has been revived over the past few years, with a corresponding updating of its interpretation. The amount of visual information which we can apprehend at any one instant was considered by the Scots philosopher Sir William Hamilton (1859). He noticed that if we look at six objects or less we can say how many are present without much difficulty. If the number is increased then increasing difficulty is experienced in judging how many objects are present. This would suggest a limit on the amount of information which we can perceive at a time, and Hamilton's remarks were tested empirically by Jevons in 1871. Jevons threw beans into a tray, never knowing in advance how many would have to be estimated, and quickly judged the number landing in a pre-defined area. When three of four beans were present no errors were made, but when more than this fell into the test field then errors became more frequent as the number of beans increased. When 10 beans were estimated Jevons was correct about 50% of the time, but with fifteen beans he was correct in his estimate on only 18% of trials. As recently as 1954 Woodworth and Schlosberg described these results as indicating the upper limit to the span of attention, that is, the amount of information which we may perceive at any one time, and hence suggesting a perceptual limitation explanation. Use of the tachistoscope, giving accurate and short exposures of visual displays enabled replication of the span of attention result for the case of written material. Erdmann and Dodge (1898) found that 4 or 5 unrelated letters could be reported when the letters were exposed for 100 msec.These data have been used traditionally as support for a theory of behaviour in which information is said to be perceived, stored in memory, retrieved from memory, and used to guide the response. Hence the profusion of compartmentalized courses in Psychology under the headings of "Perception", "Memory", "Skills", etc. That perception and memory are interrelated rather than serial processes has been demonstrated convincingly by Sperling (1960), in an experiment which challenged the traditional interpretations of Hamilton, Jevons, and Erdmann and Dodge. Sperling pointed to the fact that subjects often claimed that they saw much more than they could report in these experiments, and went on to show that the subject can perceive almost all of the items presented in a short exposure. The limitation to the "span of attention" must occur at some other stage than the layman's notion of "memory". In this experiment subjects were shown three rows of unrelated letters with four letters in each row, a typical stimulus array being shown in Fig. 1.1. Displays of this type were shown for 50 msec. and shortly after termination of the display the subject

S N T R

P K L A

D Q J M

Fig. 1.1. A display of the type used by Sperling (1960).

heard a tone. This tone indicated which one of the three rows of letters
the subject was to report. A high tone instructed the subject to recall the
letters from the top row of the display, a medium tone the centre row, and
a low tone the bottom row. The important feature of the experimental
design is that the tone is presented after the display has been removed
from sight, so the subject must attempt to remember all 12 letters until
the tone is heard, at which point a part of the display is reported. From
the "span of attention" data provided by Erdmann and Dodge we might
have expected that subjects would only have 4 or 5 letters available from
the 12 presented. As these letters would be distributed over three rows
then only 4/3 or 5/3 letters, on average, would be reported from any
one row. However, Sperling found that subjects were able to remember
about 3 letters out of the 4 required on each test trial (i.e. about 75% recall, on average). They could report about 3 letters from any of the 3
rows, and since they did not know which row would be cued for recall
then this must mean that they could have recalled about 75% of any row.
Hence the subjects must have had 75% of the total display available for
recall after the presentation had finished. That is, about 9 of the 12
letters were in some form of memory after the display had been terminated and before presentation of the tone which cued recall. Whereas the
early experiment had suggested that the span of attention is 4 or 5 letters,
the Sperling experiment shows clearly that this is not the case. It is this
sort of counter-intuitive result which distinguishes Psychology as an experimental science.

An explanation of the discrepancy between results from the 'whole
report' procedure of Erdmann and Dodge on one hand and the 'partial
report' procedure of Sperling on the other hand is provided by recall
data when the tone, whichever the row required, is delayed. With a cue
which follows immediately after the display we infer that about 9 letters

are available, but if the cue is delayed for 1 second then only 4·3 letters are available from the whole display — a figure similar to that reported by Erdmann and Dodge. What is happening in this 1 second interval that affects recall to such an extent? Sperling has argued that his experiments provide evidence for the existence of a visual memory system in which items decay extremely rapidly and are lost from this system within 1 second. This decay function can be seen in Fig. 1.2, which shows the result of an experiment reported by Sperling (1963) in which the total

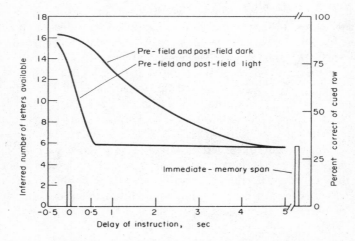

Fig. 1.2. Recall of briefly presented visual displays with whole and partial report cues. The immediate memory span corresponds to the number of items recalled from the whole display. When the subject is instructed to recall part of the display, and the cue follows with a short delay, then a large proportion of the target set may be recalled. This implies that for a short period a large proportion of the whole display is available. (From Sperling, 1963.)

numbers of letters in the display was 18. As the delay between termination of the display and onset of the tone is increased from 0 seconds to 0·5 seconds the number of letters reported drops from about 75% of the number presented to about 30%. Thereafter the delay of cue makes little difference to the number of letters reported: the partial report had been asked to recall items anywhere in the display. The proportion of items reported would be the same for any row, cued or uncued.

Sperling explains this result by postulating the use of a memory system in which all of the visual display is stored in the form in which it is presented, that is, as a series of visual images rather than a series of meaningful symbols. This visual representation, which Neisser (1967) described as the "icon", has a very short life and so information must be extracted from it very quickly if the original stimulus is exposed for a short time. In very general terms, Sperling considers that estimates of a span of apprehension of 4 or 5 items reflect not the capacity of the first system of storing information which is presented to us, but the number of items which can be extracted from this visual memory before the icon has decayed. In support of this notion a number of experiments have been reported which suggest that physical cues may be used to advantage in the partial report situation, but that semantic cues give no advantage if items are sorted in visual memory prior to being processed for meaning we would not expect their meaning to be of any use in selecting which items from the total set are to be recalled from the visual store, and this is the case. Clark (1969) found that subjects could selectively retrieve from visual memory items of one colour in multi-colour presentations, with the same effect as Sperling's subjects could selectively retrieve items on the basis of their spatial location in the display. Turvey and Kravetz (1970) were also able to use the shape of the items as a basis for selection. Semantic information cannot be used as a selection cue in the same way. Sperling (1960) presented mixed displays of letters and digits, with the tone cueing recall of letters or digits. In this situation subjects were unable to recall the same proportion of digits or letters as they did when recalling items from the whole display, digits and letters. This reaffirms Sperling's view that visual memory is a precategorical store, that information is stored in visual memory prior to being analysed for semantic content. Our ability to select information on the basis of physical rather than semantic features is a debatable issue, however, a number of experiments suggesting that non-selected (and presumably selected) sources of information are processed to some extent and not simply rejected following the analysis of physical characteristics. This particular debate is also a feature of work on the problem of selective attention: given competing auditory inputs (the "cocktail party" situation) and the need to listen to one at the exclusion of others then what cues do we use to select the relevant message? The simple answer is, again, that we use the physical characteristics of the message, but it is apparent that the semantic content of relevant and irrelevant messages may also be effective.

What could be the purpose of a literal memory of a visual scene which persists for a quarter of a second or so? It is a useful facility to have when engaged as a subject in a tachistoscope experiment, but its usefulness elsewhere may be justifiably questioned. Buswell (1922) reported that skilled readers fixate for above a quarter of a second, and Mackworth and Morandi (1967) found that duration of eye-fixations whilst looking at a   picture was not much greater than this figure. Thus, we do present ourselves with a tachistocopic view of the world, fixating briefly on different aspects of the environment to synthesize our perceptions. The purpose of the icon in this process is to ensure that we always have a stimulus representation which persists long enough for us to extract the important information from it.

Sperling, in 1967, described how he evolved a model to handle results concerning the inter-relation of sensory and short-term memory systems. It may be useful to follow Sperling's reasoning here, both as an exercise in the method of theory-building prevalent in experimental psychology, and for the purposes of comparison with other models of memory which are to appear in later chapters. The basic question asked by this series of models was: "Why is there a limitation to the amount of information reported following a brief exposure?". The answer offered by the first model suggests that only 4 or 5 items are usually recalled because after these items have been read out of the visual store the icon has faded, and items are no longer extractable. The limit here is due directly to the fading of the visual image. Figure 1.3a indicates the stages of processing which would be sufficient to describe such an explanation. This model may be rejected quite simply because by the time the subject begins to execute the response of writing or speaking the icon has already disappeared. The icon has a very fast decay function, and the latencies between the end of the presentation and the response greatly exceed the period of life of the visual image (VIS in Fig. 1.3).

The second model postulates intervening processes between visual storage and output (Fig. 1.3b). The major modifications are the introduction of a process of auditory coding and a process of auditory rehearsal. Auditory coding is implicated in memory experiments by the

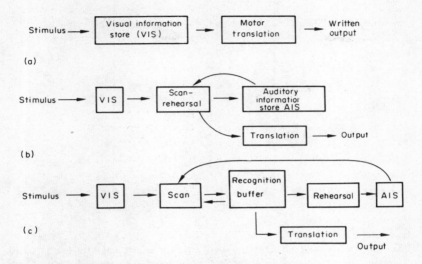

Fig. 1.3. a-c. Sperling's (1967) successive approximations to a model of storage and response to briefly presented visual stimuli.

occurrence of acoustic confusion errors with visual presentations: items sounding the same (e.g. "P,B,G,D,T") are recalled less well than items which are acoustically distinct (Conrad, 1964). Items are said to be transferred from visual memory to auditory memory by means of subvocal rehearsal, and the response is facilitated via the rehearsal loop from a form of auditory storage. As the cued items are read out of iconic memory they are subvocally rehearsed, and thereby stored in auditory memory. The limit to the number of items reported would therefore be a function of the rate of decay of the iconic image *and* upon the rate of reading items out of iconic memory into auditory memory. The problem with this model is that the speed of rehearsal cannot keep up with the speed of extraction of information from the display. Fig. 1.4 indicates the rate at which items can be extracted from visual displays.

In this experiment Sperling (1963) found the number of items which can be reported with varying exposure durations. At the end of exposure a "visual noise" mask was presented, thus preventing the formation of an

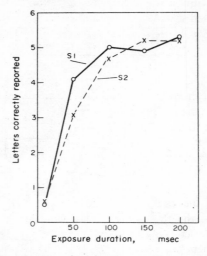

Fig. 1.4. The number of letters reported correctly as a function of the exposure duration. The pre-exposure field was dark, and the post-exposure field was a random dot pattern ("visual noise"). The two curves are for the two subjects.(From Sperling, 1963.)

image which would persist after termination of the display. Fig. 1.4 indicates that the first few items are processed at a rate of between 10 msec and 20 msec per item. Thus the model would have to allow transfer from iconic to acoustic memory at this rate, which may be the same as the subvocal rate of rehearsal. However, it is not possible to rehearse words at such a fast rate, and Landauer (1962) has found that it takes more than 100 msec to rehearse subvocally a single syllable. Hence either the model is inadequate in that subjects could not have been encoding items in auditory memory immediately as they read them out of visual memory, or the supposition that rehearsal rates are identical to read-out rates is incorrect, and so Landauer's data would not be pertinent.

The third model retains the rehearsal process, but gives it several functions (Fig. 1.3c). The "scan" function represents the subject's strategy of acquisition of information from the iconic image available to him, and is evidently restricted to the use of information about the physical properties of that image. The "recognition buffer memory" converts the visual image selected by the scan procedure into a set of instructions for the motor execution of the rehearsal activity. By this differentiation of function Sperling is able to explain the apparent contradictions of data relating to rehearsal rates (one item per 100 msec) and data relating to report rates (5 items per 100 msec). Motor instructions are said to be set up and retained in the rehearsal buffer at the faster rate, but execution of these instructions is much slower. The limit of 4 or 5 items reported might then be due to the limited capacity of the rehearsal buffer or due to a restricted speed of conversion of icon image into motor instruction. The model is otherwise similar to the second model.

This model is not complete, however, for it says nothing about processing of information from iconic memory during the interval between offset of the display and presentation of the partial report cue. The model implies that nothing at all happens, except perhaps autonomous decay of the icon, and this is supported by an experiment by von Wright (1968). When von Wright forgot to present the partial report cue, by accident, his subjects were unable to report anything at all from the display, suggesting that they had waited for the cue before they started to process the letters by setting up motor programmes, etc.

A finding reported by Mewhort (1967) is not consistent with this view, however, and suggests that processing of the icon is not entirely dependent upon the timing of the report cue. Subjects were cued by one of two tones to report either the top row of 8 letters, or the bottom row of 8. The variable of interest here is the nature of the uncued row: it was either another list of randomly selected letters (e.g. "LTAINRVE"), or letters arranged as they would be if they formed a word (e.g. "VERNALIT"). with high transitional probabilities between individual pairs of letters. the uncued row could be read as a word more items were reported from the cued row than when the irrelevant row was composed simply of random letters. Subjects must have been processing the uncued row (and presumably the cued row also) prior to the tone, or this irrelevant information could not have affected recall. The word-type arrangement of letters would have been easier to process, being pronounced in a few syllables rather than the 8 syllables for the random arrangement. Perhaps subjects quickly read the pronounceable arrangement and then started to process what was to be (unknown to them) the cued row, whereas with two rows of random letters chance would dictate which row would be processed first. This would indicate an effect of Sperling's scan facility prior to the information given by the tone as to where to look, and it cannot be said that the subject selectively processes the cued items and ignores completely the uncured items. Indeed, Rumelhart (1970) proposes that the cue serves to focus attention upon the required row of letters, thus speeding up its processing. All elements of the display are said to be acted upon immediately and in a parallel nature when presented, the tone having the function of directing the processor to the relevant items at the exclusion of other items. However, work by Mewhort, Merikle and Bryden (1969) and by Hershenson (1969) has indicated an effect of letter position in tachistoscopic perception. When presented with a row of 7 letters for report after a brief exposure observers tend to report the letters to the left of the display more accurately than those to the right. This suggests that information is transferred from iconic storage in a left-to-right serial fashion. By presenting a masking stimulus shortly after the display of letters the effect may be increased, with the appearance of an advantage for items at both ends of the display (Merikle, Coltheart and Lowe, 1971; Merikle and Coltheart, 1972). This finding has led to the suggestion of an "ends-first" processing strategy, by which both ends of the display are processed into categorical memory before the items in the centre of the display. This strategy, which is by no means confirmed (see Henderson and Park, 1973, for a critique), is not incompatible with Rumelhart's notion of parallel processing, or course, for parallel processing may occur prior to presentation of the cue-tone, and serial processing once the cue signals which part of the display is required for recall.

The possibility of simultaneous processing of all of the items presented, at least up to the time of presentation of the partial report cue, is also supported by data provided by Holding. Never the strongest supporter of the iconic store hypothesis (see his 1970 article), Holding considers that observers' strategies of acquisition of information can more readily account for the data than can the postulated availability of the entire display immediately after presentation. Using a recognition test in which observers compared two 3 x 4 displays of letters for similarity, Holding (1973) found that the interval between the first display and the test display, when varied from 250 msec to 1 sec had little effect upon recognition.

This is claimed to be contrary to the expectations of iconic storage theory, although if the icon has vanished by 250 msec (and all available information extracted from it by then) then increasing the delay of the recognition display beyond 250 msec might not be expected to produce any decrement. Furthermore, observers were able to recognize the presence of a repeated row just as well when it was in a new position as when the letters were presented in the same position. This finding may indicate that on presentation of the first display (which was exposed for 50 msec) the letters from all rows are processed in parallel sufficiently well for each row to gain an identity for the observer, who may then be able to rely less upon the spatial characteristics of the display. In this experiment the observer does not need to use categorical information about the displays, visual symbols could provide the necessary identity, and so the skill displayed by the observer is not necessarily dependent upon naming behaviour.

During their investigations of the classification of visually presented characters, Posner's group have provided evidence that Sperling's (1967) model does not describe nature adequately (Posner and Mitchell, 1967; Posner and Keele, 1967; Posner, Boies, Eichelman and Taylor, 1969). Response times were measured for observers to report whether two letters were the same or different letters could be the same by merit of their physical shape, as with the pair "AA", or by merit of their name, as with the pair "Aa". This remarkably simple experimental design is able to tell us a great deal about the complex processes of recognition and categorization which subjects can perform. To respond "same" to the pair "AA", for instance, the subject may consider only the physical characteristics of the letters — horizontal bar, uprights adjoined at the apex, etc. To respond "same" to the pair, "Aa", however, the subject must name the letters with an arabic notation, a physical comparison is inappropriate and further stage of processing is essential. "Same" responses to "AA" pairs are approximately 90 msec faster than "same" responses to "Aa" pairs if both items are presented together, thus eliminating the possibility that "AA" pairs are also compared on the basis of their names. Now, if the two letters are not part of the same display, but are presented one after the other, then the delay between the 2 letters (the interstimulus interval) has little effect upon responses based upon a comparison of names, but does have an effect upon physical matches. When the interstimulus interval is 2 seconds the difference between name matches and physical matches is minimal. This relationship is indicated in Fig. 1.5.

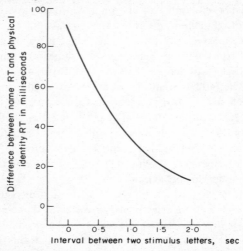

Fig. 1.5. Difference in response latency between a name match (e.g. A and a) and a physical match (e.g. A and A) as a function of the inter-letter interval. (From Posner and Keele, 1967.)

Further evidence for the use of two matching strategies has been provided by Posner and Taylor (1969) who investigated the effects of name similarity and physical similarity upon the supposed name and physical matches. When a physical match alone is all that is necessary to make the decision then auditory similarity between the letter-names should have no effect (e.g. as with "B" and "D"). When a name match is necessary to make the decision then visual similarity (e.g. "F" and "E") might be expected to have little effect. Conversely, name matches should be affected by the acoustic confusion effect, and physical matches by the visual confusion effect. These predictions were confirmed, establishing the psychological reality of the two processes of visual and auditory coding.

Posner (1969) accounts for these results by suggesting that visually presented information can be represented in the memory system by two codes, according to its physical characteristics, and according to its name. The visual code, storing physical information, might be parsimoniously thought of as being analogous to Sperling's visual information store, but this would be incorrect. The evidence indicates that decay of the icon is immutable, but the decay of the visual code appears to be under the control of the subject to some extent. For instance if, when a "same" response is appropriate, the two letters always have the same appearance and the same name, then use of the more complex name code is unnecessary, and the subject may rely upon a physical match. In this case it is advantageous for the subject to increase the life of the visual code for the duration of the inter-letter interval, and in fact, increasing the inter-letter interval up to 2 seconds in this experiment has little effect upon the time taken to make a physical match. This perhaps indicates that the life of the visual code may be controlled by subjects' strategies. It is not easy to conceive of a purpose for the visual code in non-laboratory life, and it may well be vestigial from organisms without symbolic representation.

If iconic storage and representation in a visual code are independent processes then Sperling's (1967) model is clearly incomplete. Current thinking on the problem of how visually presented material is processed and responded to is represented by Fig. 1.6, which is a composite of the views of Posner (1969), Coltheart (1972), Haber and Hershenson (1973), and others.

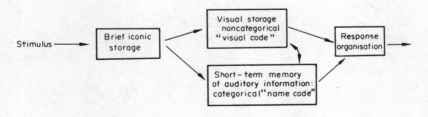

Fig. 1.6. Immediate processing of visual stimuli. Interactions with long-term storage are neglected here.

By this system information from the icon may be processed into visual storage (Posner's visual code) or auditory memory (Posner's name code).

The latter form of storage may be identical with the system generally referred to as short-term memory. This would allow us to describe the short-term memory functions for visual material which is not coded in an auditory form (Nickerson, 1972), and may explain why subjects have such persisting memory for the modality of input of information (e.g. Murdock and Walker, 1969; Hintzman, Block and Inskeep, 1972). The evidence for separate entry of information from iconic storage to visual storage or auditory storage, rather than a serially dependent system whereby the item might be transferred *through* visual memory in order to reach auditory memory, is provided by the data of Posner and Taylor (1969) already mentioned. If visually similar pairs of letters must be processed through the visual system and then through the auditory short-term memory system then a decrement would be expected with name matches. No such decrement was observed, leading to one conclusion that the two systems operate independently and in parallel. The distinction between the visual code and the name code is discussed further by Coltheart (1972).

Immediate Memory of Auditory Events

If we don't see what we look at the first time we can generally have another look. A visual display may be presented for several milli-seconds or several years — it is only when the display has a short exposure duration that we can establish the logicality of a nervous system in which the display persists in its original form, after the stimulus has terminated. So, one of the most important differences between auditory and visual transmission of information is that whereas a visual display may be presented as an entire unit, with spatial features containing the information, the auditory display (e.g. speech) must be presented sequentially. Here the changes of frequency, intensity, etc. which contain the information vary temporally. Spoken words are here and gone, it is only when they are written down that they are available for repeated inspection. Except, that is, in the minds of men, which are liable to error. Errors may occur in conceptual interpretation, or in storage, or in retrieval, but the possibilities of error which concern this section are those of acquisition.

If a word is not perceived and categorized at the instant of presentation then it is lost forever, or at least it would be without preperceptual storage.

The usefulness of such a storage system is intuitively appealing and, indeed we can argue for its existence on logical grounds alone. If listeners are to make use of the redundancy of language then speech analysis must be performed periodically rather than continuously. Given the utterance "the iguana bit the man in the", before hearing the terminal word "zoo", the number of words which could follow is largely determined by the rest of the utterance. The range of words is restricted first by grammar and, secondly, by meaning — the word must be a noun or a noun qualifier, and the listener is aware of this constraint. The semantic content of the utterance also limits the words which could follow to a set which includes "leg", "cage", "wild-life park", etc. This is what we mean by redundancy. The word is not completely unpredictable, some of the information which would have been contained in the word in another situation has already been transmitted to the listener by the rest of the utterance. Identification is aided by the constraints of following words. The word "iguana" is not very common in everyday language and so might be perceived with more difficulty than "dog" for instance. (The effect of word frequency upon recognition is, in fact, very well documented, e.g. Howes and Soloman, 1951; Bruce, 1956). The context offered by the rest of the sentence would be very useful in the recognition of this word, but it can only be useful if the word is retained in some system prior to recognition. The more unusual the word the more useful would be this system of memory. Another use of this preperceptual memory, which Neisser (1967) describes as "echoic memory" would be in a situation where the listener is not paying attention to the speaker. If we had such a representation of what was said we would be able to analyse the message some time after presentation when our attention returns. Given that such a facility as echoic memory would be a great convenience, even if not essential, let us now turn to methods which psychologists have employed in their attempts to establish the validity of this system empirically. The first section will discuss the storage of nonverbal stimuli, on the assumption that if we cannot find evidence of preperceptual storage of the stimuli which go together to form speech then this will question the validity of evidence finding preperceptual storage of speech itself. The second section will discuss the storage of verbal stimuli.

Nonverbal Stimuli

The four techniques to be discussed here are masking, divided attention, auditory persistence, and partial recognition.

Masking techniques

The rationale here is that if a short auditory stimulus produces a pre-perceptual auditory image, then a second auditory stimulus presented quickly afterwards should interfere with the image, and hence interfere with perception. Using brief visual displays Averbach and Coriell (1961) and Sperling (1963) found that presentation of a masking stimulus (a display of randomly arranged dots, occasionally referred to as "visual noise") immediately after presentation of the test display prevented use of an iconic image. Auditory masking experiments have looked at the effects of a masking stimulus upon detection thresholds and upon recognition.

One of the problems with the masking technique is well illustrated by an experiment reported by Elliot (1967) which concerned the influence of a backwards masking stimulus (i.e. a masking stimulus presented after the test stimulus) upon detection thresholds. The task was for listeners to say when they could hear a 10 msec tone which was followed by a 100 msec masking tone presented at an intensity of 70 dB. The masking tone was, subjectively, quite loud: conversation has an intensity of around 60 dB, a pneumatic drill an intensity of 80 dB. The interval between the two tones was one independent variable, the intensity of the test tone being the other. Elliot found that the effect of the masking noise upon detection thresholds was greatest with the smallest ISI (inter-stimulus interval, in this case an inter-tone interval) and decreased with increasing intervals with little masking effect with a silent interval of 100 msec. This might be taken to indicate the existence of an auditory image of the test tone which is available for up to 100 msec after stimulus presentation, but which may be disrupted by the presentation of an irrelevant tone during the life of the image. There is a flaw in this argument, however, as Massaro (1972a) has pointed out. If the loud masking tone had been perceived more quickly than the quiet test tone then the same result would be predicted and the notion of an auditory image would be unnecessary. It is quite possible, due to the inertia present in the auditory nervous system, that the quiet tone reached the processor at the same instant as did the loud tone. This being the case then the signal-to-noise (S/N) ratio of the detection tone would be lowered considerably. The shorter the ISI the greater would be the overlap between the quiet and loud tones. That loud stimuli are responded to more quickly than are quiet stimuli has been established by McGill (1961). This is not direct evidence of quicker perception, of course, for the difference could be due to initiation of responses after equally fast perception, but it does indicate the plausibility of the objection. McGill presented a 1 KHz tone in a simple response task, and found that whereas a 30 dB tone gained a reaction time of 216 msec, a 100 dB tone had a reaction time of 120 msec. So, although we cannot be certain that this intensity-reaction relationship is due to perception time differences, we cannot use intensity as an independent variable until we are certain that the relationship is not due to perception.

A second masking technique, which does support the notion of a preperceptual image, is that of recognition masking. In this paradigm the listener is asked to say which of a known set of tones has been presented, the recognition tone being followed by a masking tone. Massaro (1970a) presented one of two possible tones, each having a duration of 20msec. Their frequencies were 770 Hz, designated to the subjects as "low", and 870 Hz, designated as "high". At some interval after the test tone had terminated a 500 msec masking tone of 820 Hz frequency was presented. Test tones and masking tones had the same intensity. The listener's task was to press one of two response keys according to which tone had been presented. The silent interval between the two tones on each trial was varied between 0 and 500 msec. A subsequent experiment (Massaro, 1971) indicates that varying the duration of the masking tone between 50 and 400 msec makes little difference to the effect to be described. The recognition data for the three subjects tested are presented in Fig. 1.7. As the set of items from which the subjects selected the response (the response set) was only two in number, the probability of a guess being correct is 50%, thus we are only concerned with performance above this 50% cutoff. When the masking tone was presented with a short ISI it had a more disruptive effect upon the recognition process than when a longer ISI was used. The disruptive effect is related to the proximity of the masking stimulus up to an ISI of about 250 msec. Thereafter the presence of the masking stimulus makes little difference to the recognition response. Perhaps a silent interval of 250 msec is all that is required

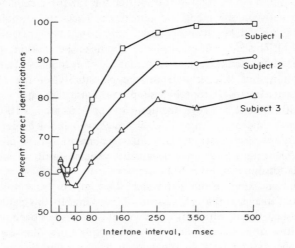

Fig. 1.7. Percentage of correct identifications of the test tone for three subjects as a function of the duration of the silent interval. (From Massaro, 1970a)

for extraction of information from the stimulus, or alternatively the image has decayed within this period and no further information can be extracted. Whichever limitation is appropriate, this is strong evidence for the existence of a preperceptual image: why else should a silence following presentation be necessary for the subject to give the correct recognition response? Alternative explanations may hinge on the possibility of the masking tone in some way influencing the post-perceptual categorization process (Treisman and Rostron, 1972), but Massaro himself considers that his subjects required at least 250 msec of silence in addition to the 20 msec of the tone to aid the recognition process, but that the image had probably decayed within this period, and so processing will have been terminated. A simple interference-of-processing explanation as Treisman and Rostron suggests is not adequate here, for Moore and Massaro (1973) have reported that the masking tone is effective, however much attention the listener is giving to the test tone. It has also been shown that a masking tone is effective, however much attention the listener is giving to the test tone. It has also been shown that a masking light stimulus, which might be thought to interfere with processing, had no effect upon perception of the tone at any interstimulus interval (Massaro and Kahn, 1973).

Divided attention technique

If a listener's attention is directed away from the presentation of auditory material by having him attend to another task can the auditory stimulus be recognized after presentation? Whereas Massaro's method leads to the suggestion of a preperceptual image which persists for up to a quarter of a second, use of the divided attention method has led to the suggestion of an image with a life in the order of 10 seconds. Eriksen and Johnson (1964) first found the individual thresholds for a number of subjects for the detection of 1 KHz tones, when the subjects were listening specifically for them. In the subsequent experiment tones were always presented at an intensity above the threshold for each subject, but attention was directed away from the listening task by the subject reading a novel which interested him. During the 2-hour period in which the subject sat reading a novel single tones were presented at unpredictable intervals. Some time after presentation of the tone the reading lamp was switched off at an interval between 0 to 10·5 seconds after the occurrence of the tone. A number of catch trials were also included, on which the lamp was switched off, but no tone was presented. These trials gave a false alarm rate, against which reports from the non-catch trials may be compared for validity. The results from this experiment are presented in Fig. 1.8. These data suggest that even with delays of 10 seconds between the presentation and test of a tone the detectability is well above the false alarm rate. A possible objection to this interpretation (see Massaro, 1972a) is that the experiment does not distinguish between two feasible strategies. On presentation of the visual cue the subjects may have turned their attention to the auditory modality in search of an auditory image, delay thus serving to allow decay of sensory, precategorical memory. Alternatively, subjects may have heard the tone on presentation and categorized the detection event at the time, delay in this case serving to reduce the memory strength of the categorization. The problem may otherwise be stated as that of whether or not attention paid to the novel precluded encoding of the tone on presenta-

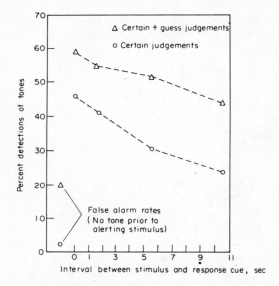

Fig. 2.8. The decay of echoic memory by two criteria.
(From Eriksen and Johnson, 1964)

tion. Fortunately, this question is answered for us by a second experiment reported in Eriksen and Johnson's paper. In this experiment, which was essentially similar to the first, detection rates were compared from trials with and without the visual alerting stimulus. Subjects were instructed to respond at any time if they thought that they had heard a tone. This spontaneous detection rate was only 10·7%, but if the light was switched off simultaneously the detection rate was 50·8%, indicating the necessity of some cue to switch the subjects' attention from the visual modality to the auditory. If our alternative explanation had been correct, and in the first experiment subjects had been noticing the tone on presentation but waiting for the lamp to go out before reporting that they had heard it, then we should have expected a much higher spontaneous detection rate than 10·7%. Whereas this suggests that the reading task was sufficient to prevent attention being allocated to the detection task, one of the conditions of the original experiments indicates that the preperceptual memory described by Massaro (1970b, 1972a) was not being tapped. The presence of a variable pitched signal (500Hz to 5000Hz and back to 500Hz in a 3-second interval) had no effect on the mean number of detection responses, even though this signal sometimes occurred after presentation of the detection tone and before presentation of the alerting stimulus. Massaro's backward masking experiments suggest that the occurrence of a tone, after occurrence but before analysis of a detection tone, should disrupt the contents of the preperceptual store, and decrease the probability of detection. Eriksen and Johnson's result of auditory memory after 10 seconds is certainly surprising in view of other estimates of the duration of preperceptual memory. Massaro estimates 250 msec, and this is the order of magnitude of the estimates of other workers. Guttman and Julesz (1963), for example, presented their subjects with multi-frequency ("white") noise which was made up of repeating cycles. The longest cycle which subjects could detect easily was about 1 second in duration, a period which Guttman and Julesz equated with the life of auditory memory. Other estimates of the persistence of auditory inputs, including those mentioned in the remainder of this section, do not vary significantly from these figures. Eriksen and Johnson's estimate does, however, and so their experiments merit a very cautious interpretation.

Auditory persistence technique

Does an auditory stimulus appear, subjectively, to last longer than its physical presentation? Efron (1970) asked subjects to match the offset of a noise burst with the onset of a second stimulus, a light. A representation of this situation is contained in Fig. 1.9. A series of noise-light stimulus pairings are presented, each time the subject responding as to whether offset of the noise coincided with the onset of the light. With an ideal perceptual system observers should have reported simultaneity when *b* corresponded in time with *c*. With relatively long durations of noise (*a - b* greater than 130 msec) subjects had little difficulty, and reports of the simultaneity of *b* and *c* tended to approach their physical reality. However, when the noise had a shorter duration (*a - b* less than 130 msec) its perceived duration increased accordingly, such that the interval between *a* and *c* was constant at 130 msec. So, if the noise had a duration of 80 msec the subject would report simultaneity when the onset of the light occurred

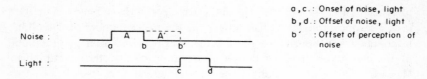

Fig. 1.9. Auditory persistence measured by the subjective offset/onset method.

50 msec after offset of the noise (i.e. $a - b$ = 80 msec, $b - c$ = 50 msec for perceptual simultaneity to occur). Two points emerge from Efron's work. The first is that the figure of 130 msec is the minimum duration of an auditory perception. Stevens and Davis (1938) indicate that we need about 10 msec of a 1KHz tone before reporting the sensation, but Efron indicates that the time of a brief noise exceeds its presentation time, and that we need at least 130 msec for perception. The second point is that Efron's subjects cannot have been able to distinguish between the presentation of the tone and its afterimage. In Fig. 1.9, subjects could not say when A finished and A' starts. To the listener the event A' has the same properties as the event A. This conclusion supports the notion of preperceptual images for brief stimuli at least. Massaro (1970), it will be recalled, used a test tone duration of 20 msec to establish the necessity of a silent interval after presentation which, we may assume, was used by the listener for perception of the tonal image. In a later experiment Massaro (1972b) varied the duration of the test tone from 20 to 440 msec. Even with long masking tone durations and short intertone intervals, the perception of the longest test tones was not significantly disrupted by the presence of masking tones.

Robinson (1973) has reported that the phenomenal experience of a persisting auditory image cannot be corroborated by response time data. If the experience of a brief tone exceeds the duration of that tone then we might expect subjects to give longer response latencies to the offset of a brief tone (less than 130 msec) than to the offset of a longer tone (greater than 130 msec). In this situation, however, perceptual experience does not appear to govern performance. Robinson's subjects were required to press a key as soon as possible after the offset of a noise burst which lasted between 5 and 200 msec. Had perception time corresponded to response time then responses to brief stimuli would have been longer than responses to the longer stimuli, because with stimulus durations of less than 130 msec subjects would have been responding to the offset of the image (time b' in Fig. 1.9) rather than offset of the stimulus. This was not the case, and response times were relatively stable when the duration of the noise burst was varied. This result does not negate the postulate of a preperceptual image of a brief auditory stimulus, but it does make interpretation less straightforward. The postulated lack of correspondence between perception of offset and reaction to offset could be due to any number of intervening processes, such as a strategical conservatism in responding to the longer stimuli. On half of the trials Robinson presented a 1 second tone, intended to prevent subjects from responding to stimulus onset rather than offset. Now, if subjects were more cautious with the longer test trials than with the shorter tones then any delay in response enforced by a tonal image would be cancelled by conservatism with longer tones. Robinson discusses a number of reports in the literature which have found that performance to stimulus offset does not correspond with perception of offset.

Partial recognition technique

This is essentially similar to the method used by Sperling to establish the existence of iconic memory. Treisman and Rostron (1972) presented three tones simultaneously over separate loudspeakers. Immediately afterwards another three tones were presented. The duration of each tone was 100 msec, and so within a period of 200 msec a total of six tones was presented. After a delay ranging from 0 to 1·6 seconds after offset of the second set of tones a probe tone was presented, and this tone may or may not have been present in either or both of the sets of three tones. The test tones were selected from a group of six, and were easily discriminable, varying from 100 to 6000 Hz. Any of the ensemble could be present in both of the stimulus sets of three, but no tone could be presented at the same time over different speakers. On presentation of the probe the subject was required to make two independent responses: was the probe present in the first stimulus set, and was it present in the second set. Fig. 1.10 presents the results of the experiment in terms of d', which is a psychophysical measure of detectability (see Swets, Tanner and Birdsall (1961) for a discussion of this measure, and Banks (1970 for a discussion of its use in the determination of memory strength),

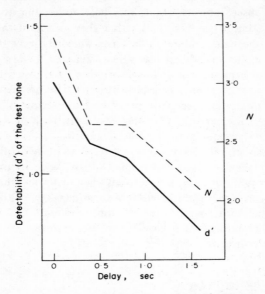

Fig. 1.10. The continuous line gives the mean value of d' for the two subjects at the four delay intervals and the dashed line gives N, the number of items in store. (From Treisman and Rostron, 1972.)

and in terms of the number of items inferred to be in the preperceptual auditory store at the time of testing. When four tones are presented simultaneously and the subject required to give a judgement on each, then an estimate of 2·62 is obtained for the span of apprehension. In comparison with an inferred number of items in store of 3·1 using the partial report technique this experiment appears to confirm the existence of a preperceptual store. However, this method does not rule out the possibility of contamination through storage of the tones in short-term memory. The tones used by Treisman and Rostron were highly discriminable, and it would be quite possible for subjects to encode them categorically, labelling them on presentation and storing these labels until presentation of the probe tone. If the comparison was one of matching a categorized probe with a set of categorized items then preperceptual storage cannot be said to have been tested.

Having found empirical evidence in favour of the existence of acoustical storage of nonverbal material (tones and noise bursts) prior to categorization, using the backwards recognition masking and auditory persistence methods, it is now not unreasonable to ask whether this form of storage exists for verbal material, and if it does, then what are its characteristics and how is it employed? The two methods which have sought answers to these questions, and which will be discussed here are those using the stimulus suffix and partial report.

Immediate Storage of Verbal Stimuli

To describe the effect of the stimulus suffix it is first necessary to describe the serial position effect in the recall of lists of words. When we present a list, the length of which exceeds the subject's memory span, the items which the subject fails to recall tend to be from certain positions of the original list. The final items typically are recalled slightly more successfully than the central items, and this is referred to as the recency effect, and it is this effect which concerns the operation of the stimulus suffix. The superior recall of early items in the list over recall of central and late items is, incidentally, referred to as the primacy effect, and we shall give full consideration of the cause of this effect in a later chapter.

Experiments using the stimulus suffix present a list of words to the subject, and added to the end of this list is an irrelevant word, a suffix, which need not be recalled, but which has a considerable depressing effect upon the recall of words in the recency part of the list, i.e. the words immediately preceding the suffix. Modality of presentation is an important variable (Morton and Holloway, 1970) and all of the experiments to be described here use auditory stimuli. The effect of the suffix item was first demonstrated by Dallett (1965) who found that recall of a series of seven digits was the same whether an eighth digit ("zero") was relevant and had to be reported by the subject, or was irrelevant and not reported. Reporting the eighth item had little effect upon report of the seven test items, and subsequent work indicates that it is the mere presence of the redundant "zero" at the end of the list which is critical here. For instance, Crowder (1967) checked upon the importance of the spatial location of the redundant item by presenting it, as Dallett did, immediately after the list of digits, or requiring the subject to start recall of the list after generating a "zero" for himself. In one condition the list of eight digits is heard and is followed by a suffix being spoken, vocal recall following immediately, and in the other condition a "zero" is spoken by the subject immediately after list presentation. These conditions were compared against recall of control lists of eight or nine digits without a suffix being presented or a prefix being generated. The errors made in recalling these four list types are indicated in Fig. 1.11. In the suffix condition (denoted 80:8, meaning eight digits + zero, recall eight digits) the final three serial positions collect many more

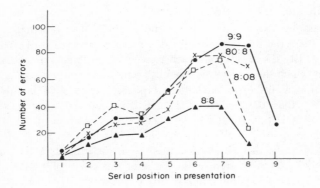

Fig. 1.11. The relation between serial position and error frequency with vocal presentation for eight- and nine-digit controls (8:8 and 9:9), a stimulus suffix condition (80:8) and a response prefix condition (8:08). (From Crowder, 1967.)

errors than in the eight-digit control condition (8:8) In the prefix condition (8:08) the effect upon the final digit is minimal in comparison with the effect of the suffix, although earlier serial positions than the last are affected to a considerable extent. However, the effect of a redundant suffix item may be said to increase the number of errors of recall with increasing serial position, with the final recall item being most affected.

Crowder and Morton (1969) have presented an influential paper describing the effect of the suffix as a backwards-masking stimulus in terms of what they call Precategorical Acoustic Storage. This storage may be the same as Neisser's (1967) echoic memory and Massaro's (l970a) preperceptual storage, which all appear to have a similar function, that is, to retain the stimulus prior to analysis so that the perceptual system does not have to be directed to a stimulus at the time of presentation. Crowder and Morton consider that the suffix item depresses recall of the final item because of a backwards masking effect in a way comparable to the masking tone in Massaro's experiments affecting recognition of an immediately preceding test tone. Without the suffix the final "recall" item can remain in auditory storage and may be available for analysis for a longer period than when it is followed by another auditory stimulus. The suffix is said to displace items from the very limited capacity echoic store, and cancels the extra readout time usually available for the final word in the presentation. Aaronson (1967, 1968) and Massaro (l970b) have argued convincingly that recall depends upon the time available for analysis, improved recall being a consequence of increased time for perception. So, if centrally positioned items are analyzed for less time than is the final item, by virtue of the final item not being displaced by any items following it into echoic memory, then we would expect the final item to have improved recall over the central items. This is just what happens, except when an auditory suffix is presented which acts to equalize the perception durations of central and final items. Fig. 1.12 gives the relationship of the precategorical acoustic store (PAS) to the categorical processing of information. At the initial stage of "Acoustic analysis and PAS" discriminative sensory features are extracted from the stimulus. As sensory information is processed out of PAS (or the visual store) it interacts with contextual information relevant to the stimulus and retained from previous stimuli. Both types of information are important to word recognition. Increasing the amount of contextual information about a stimulus can reduce the amount of sensory information necessary for recognition. The outcome of the interaction, which is said to occur in the "logogen" system, is a recognition decision, whereby the stimulus is categorized. Thus, the processes acting upon sensory information prior to the logogen system are described as "precategorical".

If readout time is the crucial factor influenced by the suffix, then delaying the presentation of the suffix should have a diminished effect upon masking of the final item, because this would leave a longer duration for processing the final item into categorical memory. This was the pre-

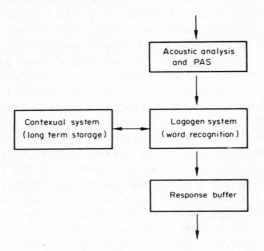

Fig. 1.12. A system for the storage and recognition of auditory information as proposed by Crowder and Morton (1969).

diction tested and verified by Crowder in 1969, and his results are given in Fig. 1.13, compared against a control condition in which no suffix was presented. With a suffix onset delay of 2 seconds the recall rate for the final item is at almost the same value as with no suffix. The suffix delay of 0·5 seconds is described as "immediate" here, although there would be a period of silence immediately following the final memory item. The delay figures refer to the times between onset of the final item and onset of the suffix. However, most of the relevant information appears to have been transferred out to PAS within 2 seconds, although an alternative view would be that the sensory trace had faded by this time, and further information could not be extracted, suffix or no suffix.

Two problems with this interpretation of the suffix effect might be mentioned at this point. First, the decay function involved does not correspond with the 250 msec decay of Massaro's auditory image. This might just be another difference between the storage and analysis of speech and non-speech, or it may indicate that preperceptual storage and precategorical storage are quite distinct functions. Secondly, if the suffix was simply an auditory masking stimulus or a displacing item,

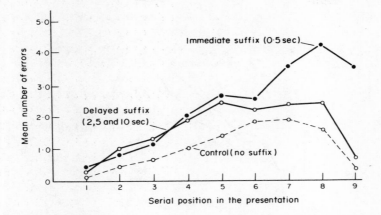

Fig. 1.13. The effect of delaying a suffix on an auditorily presented stimulus list. (From Crowder, 1969.)

then its effect should be restricted to the items in the echoic store, the final one or two items in the list. Figs. 1.11 and 1.13 indicate that this is not the case. The effect of the suffix is greatest at the final serial position, but is also evident in the earlier list positions, suggesting that the suffix operates in a more profound way upon the storage of the list than simply disrupting a limited capacity acoustic store.

The predominantly nonlinguistic effect of the suffix has been demonstrated by Crowder and Raeburn (1970), in an experiment using three types of list. One group of subjects, acting as controls, recalled lists of nine digits, a second group were presented with lists of nine digits plus a suffix ("zero") as a redundant final item, and a third group recalled lists of nine digits to which a nonlinguistic speech sound had been added as a suffix. This speech sound was the "zero" used in the second condition removed from the tape and spliced back upside down. This ensured that the suffix had all the qualities of speech, but none of the qualities of language; it was a meaningless noise. The results of this experiment are shown in Fig. 1.14, where recall of the normal suffix lists is seen to differ considerably from recall of the control lists, and recall of the reversed speech suffix is statistically indistinguishable from the

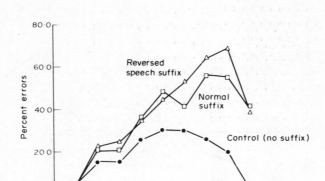

Fig. 1.14. Error percentages as a function of serial position for lists when the suffix was a normally spoken "zero", and when the "zero" was played backwards over the tape recorder. (From Crowder and Raeburn, 1970.)

normal suffix. Thus, the linguistic content of the suffix is irrelevant to its effect; the single quality of being a speech sound appears to be sufficient to displace the PAS traces of the recall items in the final serial positions. There are two of the major lines of research which have been used to describe the effects of the suffix stimulus — the establishment of the nonlinguistic and of the acoustic nature of the effect.

That the effect of the suffix is independent of its meaning is also shown a number of times in a huge experimental paper by Morton, Crowder and Prussin (1971). For example, in one of their experiments subjects were required to recall lists of six common nouns which were either followed or not followed by a suffix. The lists were drawn from one or two categories of nine items, animals ("bull", "cow", "dog", etc.) and utensils ("bowl", "cup", "dish", etc.), and when a suffix was presented either it belonged to the same semantic category as the list, or it belonged to the other category. Whereas the semantic related-ness of the suffix to the list of items to be recalled made little difference to the extent of the effect, both categories of suffix had a considerable effect upon recall of the final items. This evidence is consistent with the view that the suffix affects precategorical storage. If the semantic qualities of the suffix had been used then we might have expected a greater effect of disruption with a related suffix than with an unrelated suffix. However, this experiment was designed in such a way that subjects need not process the semantic attributes of the stimuli — recall items or suffix items. Each word in each list presented to the subject for recall started with a different letter. During the experiment the complete stimulus population was available to the subject and the subject responded by writing the initial letter of the appropriate word. The problem is that to perform adequately the subject need not process the whole of each word as it was presented. A valid strategy for a subject would be to remember six initial letters, and at the end of the presentation decode these letters into words using the complete set of stimuli which Morton *et al.* provided for them. Since every word started with a different letter there was no chance of confusion. The only snag here is for the subject to decide which category of words had been presented, given that he remembers "B, C, D" etc., should this be decoded as "bull, cow, dog" or as "bowl, cup, dish"? As presentation of the lists to the subjects was in blocks, that is 20 lists composed of words from one category, a permissible strategy would be to listen to a single word from the first list in each block, encode the category of that word and only decode letters from that block of lists into that category. If the subject does not have to encode the stimuli semantically, then why should any theory predict an effect sensitive to semantic differences?

The foregoing criticism is not means as a refutation of the precategorical nature of the suffix effect for it seems unlikely that any subject would be so devious without knowing the purpose of the experiment and having intentions to prove PAS theory incorrect! However, it is a valid objection, it leaves room for doubt, and it also indicates the care which is necessary in designing psychology experiments. A more pertinent objection would be on the grounds that semantic processing does not appear to be essential for short term storage (more of this in the next chapter), so again, why expect an effect if the subject does not have to process the information semantically in order to perform adequately?

A further set of experiments reported by Morton *et al.* aimed to establish the purely acoustic nature of the suffix effect. For example, it was found that speech noise itself is necessary to disrupt recall of the final items, and that synthetically produced noise has the same effect as no suffix at all. In that experiment the suffix took the form of a "zero" spoken after the final item either at the same loudness as the list or louder, or was a burst of "white" noise with the same onset time and same duration as the "zero". The noise was also presented at either the same subjective intensity as the speech of the list, or was louder. Whereas a suffix of equal or greater loudness to the list had a disruptive effect if it was spoken, the suffix had no effect if it was nonspeech noise. It is a point of interest here that a loud speech suffix was less disruptive than a soft speech suffix. This suggests an additional feature of the suffix effect which is that it may to some extent be under the strategical control of the subject. A loud suffix is differentiated from the rest of the presentation by the additional quality of its loudness, and this quality may be sufficient cue for the subject to be able to ignore the suffix, and hence it would have a less disrupting effect. We have seen from the work on the selection of information from briefly presented visual displays that subjects were able, in the partial report situation, to select information on the basis of physical cues, but not on the basis of semantic cues (Sperling, 1963; Clark, 1969; Turvey and Kravetz, 1970). This is simply because this information is stored in a precategorical store, that is, the semantic features of the stimuli had not been realized at the time of selection. Now, if physical but not semantic cues may be used in the selection and rejection of which precategorical stimuli will be attended in the case of vision, might we expect physical but not semantic features be used in the selection and rejection of precategorical auditory stimuli? This is a point which emerges from a number of the suffix experiments. When a physical cue differentiates the suffix from the list to be recalled then the effect of the suffix is lessened.

Concerned with the importance of voice similarities of the suffix to the list Morton *et al.* have presented the suffix read out by a number of different speakers. In one condition the suffix was spoken by the same female who read out the seven digits for recall, in the second condition a different female read out the suffix, and in the third condition a male speaker read the suffix. The relative effects of these suffixes suggest the general conclusion that the effect is proportional to the extent of physical similarity between suffix and list. A suffix spoken by a totally different voice to the list has the least effect upon recall, and a suffix spoken in the same voice has the greatest effect. Again, however, this result may be due to the acoustic trace of a suffix having a larger effect upon the acoustic traces of the final recall items when those traces coincide, or it may be due to the physical differentiation between relevant and irrelevant items being more difficult when the suffix is spoken by the same voice as the list. The masking voice explanation is supported by an experiment concerned with selective attention, and reported by Underwood and Moray (1971). In this experiment subjects listened for occasional digits in lists of letters. The digits were spoken either by a male or a female. When simply listening to the lists the sex of the listener made little difference to the number and type of digits detected: for instance, female subjects did not detect more digits spoken by one sex of speaker or the other. When shadowing, the sex of the listener did make a difference. Shadowing is the task of repeating aloud each stimulus as soon as possible after it has been presented, thus allowing the voice of the subject to mask further stimuli as they are presented. When males were shadowing they detected fewer male voice digits and more female voice digits than did females. This result could be due to the shadowing voices of male subjects disturbing the precategorical acoustic traces of male voice digits more than those of female voice digits, and conversely of course for female subjects.

In a further series of experiments Morton *et al.* attempted to define the location of the precategorical acoustic store: whether it is a feature of the sensory receptors, or a more central effect operating on information after the combination of inputs, but this is not the feature of the experiments which is of interest to the point being made here. The four conditions compared were: control (no suffix); ipsilateral (suffix to same ear as a monaural presentation of the list); contralateral (suffix to opposite ear as the list); binaural (suffix to both ears but list to one ear). The greatest disruption was caused by an ipsilateral suffix but the contralateral and binaural suffixes also had an influence in comparison with the no-suffix condition. If we have PAS functions for each of the ears as well as a third PAS function common to both ears (i.e. two specific stores and a binaural store), then the monaural list would be represented in two of these three stores leaving the store specific to the contralateral ear empty. The ipsilateral suffix would thereby mask those parts of the list remaining in both stores at the time of presentation of the suffix, and have the greatest possible effect upon recall of the final items. A contralateral suffix would mask only the acoustic information in the common store, leaving the ear-specific store unmasked. Some acoustic information could then be used when a contralateral suffix is present, but not as much as when no suffix is present, thus accounting for the differences between the ipsi-, contralateral, and no-suffix conditions. The problem with this theory is that a binaural suffix should mask both the ear-specific store and the common store, having the same effect as an ipsilateral suffix, but it has a smaller effect. Morton *et al.* therefore reject this model and offer in its place the explanation that PAS operates after the combination of information from the ears, and that it is a post-attentional effect. In the ipsilateral suffix condition the redundant element is not differentiated by a physical cue from the rest of the list whereas in the contralateral and binaural suffix conditions physical information is available to the subject to indicate the irrelevant nature of the stimulus — the suffix is discriminated quite easily without reference to its semantic content.

Morton and Chambers (1972) also report a suffix experiment in which the discrimination and attention hypothesis is supported. They found that a suffix produced artificially by a speech synthesizer, when added to a list of digits produced by a human speaker, had little disruptive effect. This suffix was clearly discriminable on a physical dimension.

A number of objections have been raised concerning the view of Crowder, Morton and their colleagues that the effect of the suffix upon recall of the final items in the list is due to precategorical operations. It should be noted, however, that "precategorical" is not intended as a synonym for "preperceptual", and this distinction is made by Crowder and Morton (1969) when they say that information in the precategorical store "may well not be completely unprocessed information", and "could be processed and coded to the level of feature analysis". Categorization, in their sense, is said to occur when the stimulus is processed linguistically and is recognized as a word. The distinctions between preperceptual and precategorical storage are not clear empirically, but it is interesting to note that whereas the ear of presentation of a suffix does make a difference to the extent of the effect upon response to an immediately preceding monaural stimulus (Morton *et al.* 1971), the masking tone used by Massaro (1970a) was equally effective regardless of the ear of presentation. One interpretation here is that strategical shifts of attention do not prevent disruption of the contents of the preperceptual store (hence the suffix result).

The advantage of the final items in an auditory serial presentation is not due to extended preperceptual storage in the absence of categorical storage, but to the availability of linguistic information *and* prelinguistic (or precategorical) information. Crowder and Morton were able to reduce the extent of the recency effect by presenting a speech suffix because the suffix reduced the amount of physical information available about the final items. It had no effect upon categorical information relevant to these items, information actively extracted at the time of presentation. The combination of information from categorical and precategorical stores is indicated to be responsible for the recency effect by an experiment reported by Watkins and Watkins (1973). The recency effect is not nearly so pronounced with visual presentations, indeed, the recall curve looks remarkably similar to the curve of recall of an auditory list plus suffix. It is this "modality effect" which Crowder and Morton (1969) used to support their argument for the use of precategorical acoustic storage in the extraction of further information about the final items of the presentation. Precategorical visual storage is assumed to decay too swiftly to be of use in recall. Now, if precategorical information is extracted from a limited capacity and rapidly decaying auditory store, and used in the formulation of a response, then the size of the modality effect should be dependent upon the acoustic size of the items in the list. Watkins and Watkins argued that if PAS is filled by one multisyllabic word then the effect should be restricted to enhanced recall of that one word with an auditory presentation. On the other hand, if PAS can hold four short words then the modality effect should be more extensive. They tested this prediction by having subjects recall lists of one-syllable and four-syllable words which were presented either visually or aurally. Whereas the final few items were recalled more successfully when presented aurally rather than visually, this advantage held for about the same number of items in the list regardless of the length of those items. The auditory advantage spans about three items in both the case of one-syllable and four-syllable words. Clearly, it is the word that is the unit of retention, and not the auditory space taken up by a fixed number of syllables. This confirms that categorization has taken place, and that "raw" auditory information alone is not responsible for the modality effect.

The conclusion that categorization and auditory storage are not mutually exclusive may also be extended to an experiment reported by Darwin, Turvey and Crowder (1972), which attempted to replicate the Sperling partial report result for the case of auditory stimuli. Subjects heard three lists of words (letters and digits) simultaneously presented to different spatial locations (right ear, left ear, middle of the head) within 1 second, and after a variable delay were cued to recall part of this presentation on the basis of spatial location or word category. Recall under partial report conditions was compared to attempted recall of the whole of the list, and thus the situation is very similar to the Sperling design. Subjects are presented with nine items within 1 second, and these items are differentiated by spatial and semantic cues. Some time after the presentation is required for recall. The crucial difference between this and the Sperling design is caused by the temporal nature of speech: with visual displays the presentation time can be very brief, so brief as to exclude the possibility of the subject analyzing the information during presentation, but with an auditory display the presentation time cannot be so brief as to exclude this possibility. Although Darwin *et al.* presented a large number of stimuli during the 1-second period we cannot be sure that no analyses were performed during presentation. However, an advantage for recall was found with the partial as opposed to whole report procedure, and the extent of this advantage can be seen as a function of the delay of the report cue in Fig. 1.15a. This is the advantage of partial report cues relating to spatial location, and is essentially the same result as reported for the case of vision by Sperling (1960, 1963), with the exception that whereas Sperling found that the advantage was lost if the report cue was delayed by ½ second, Darwin *et al.* found no significant difference from the whole report condition when the report cue was delayed by 4 seconds. So if preperceptual storage is being tapped here then we may conclude that for the case of aurally presented stimuli items in this store have a life of about 2 seconds. The problem now is to decide whether precategorical storage is responsible for the advantage, or whether the words were analyzed on presentation. That the nine words were held in precategorical storage until the report cue was presented is a conclusion suggested by the absence of an advantage in the partial report condition when selection was required on the basis of semantic categories.

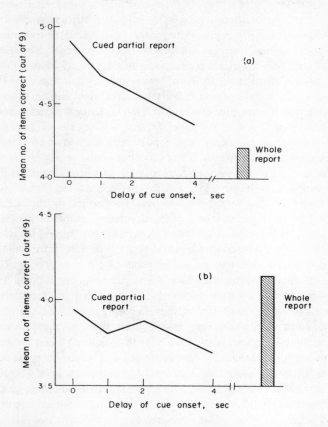

Fig. 1.15. a-b. Recall of items from three-channel auditory presentations with partial and whole report procedures. Partial report was cued by (a) spatial location, or (b) category membership. (From Darwin, Turvey and Crowder, 1972.)

When selection was required on the basis of spatial location the report cue allows listeners to recall more of the particular set of items which are cued than they can if they are required to recall all of the items presented. Asking for recall of only part of the presentation allows subjects to process a limited number of items out of an auditory store, the contents of which would have decayed rapidly and thus preventing the processing out of more than a limited number. With partial report this limited number is not exceeded, with whole report it is. However, the advantage does not hold if we ask for the digits *or* the letters (see Fig. 1.15b). As the items are in *precategorical* storage "digitness" and "letterness" have not been analysed, and only after processing out of this store may items be reported on the basis of these characteristics. This result was also found for the case of visual displays by Sperling (1960): we can select information on the basis of physical cues but not on the basis of semantic cues, a recurring theme.

The analysis of the experiment reported by Darwin *et al.* is not quite this straightforward, however. Their conclusion that location may be used for selection, but that semantic properties may not, is questioned by the comparison of Figs. 1.15a and b. In the first experiment (data in Fig. 1.15a) subjects are required to give the names of the items from a particular location, so they need to retain categorical and location information (or at least information by which identity and location may be derived). In the second experiment (data in Fig. 1.15b) they were cued to recall on the basis of category but also had to give the location of the information, and therefore the information required in the two experiments is the same. So in a sense the subjects must retain the same information in both cases, but in the category-cued situation (Fig. 1.15b) subjects recall proportionately fewer items than in the location-cued situation. When location is cued we infer that between 5 and 5½ items are available with 2 seconds of presentation, but when category is cued between 3½ and 4 items are available. A possible cause of this result is that when location is cued only 3 items are required, but when category is cued a mean of 4½ items are required − the two situations have different demand characteristics. This remains as a problem and clouds the interpretation.

Before we engage in further consideration of the representation of speech in memory, in precategorical and categorical forms, it is worth making the point here that poets knew about acoustical storage and recency, if not in those terms, long before psychologists attempted to describe them. It is certainly true for traditional poetry (and modern songwriting) that the form of the poem is maintained not only by rhythm (the psychological discovery of which is discussed in Chapter 3) but also by rhyme - the last words of adjacent or alternating lines rhyme with each other. Psychologists would describe these words as being acoustically confusable, as they have acoustical features in common with each other. Now, why should these words be placed at the ends of lines if poets did not know about the recency effect and its reputed cause, precategorical acoustic storage? Words at the end of lines are followed by a pause and are allowed to persist in echoic memory, their sounds are allowed to become dominant features of the poem, and the similarity between sounds of final words is recognized by the listener as rhyme. Rhyming words in the centres of lines are far less effective because of a backwards masking effect — their echoic representations are disrupted by the words which follow rapidly. The strong rhyming effect of final words is also evidence of precategorical *and* categorical storage: even when final words are identified and their meanings extracted their acoustic characteristics may still reverberate.

Is PAS a Tape-recorder?

The question to be discussed here is whether information held in the acoustic store is represented perfectly, as in a tape-recording, or whether the input is processed in some way and only certain features of speech then represented. The differences which we have encountered already are sufficient to suggest that echoic or precategorical memory does not store a direct representation of the stimulus, but that it is a second stage of processing. The model offered here suggests that information in the preperceptual memory described by Massaro (1972a) may or may not be processed into the precategorical memory described by Crowder and Morton (1969). Whereas "raw" sensory information may be thought to be stored in preperceptual memory in a totally unprocessed manner not all of this information is held in precategorical memory. We shall conclude by suggesting that precategorical memory does not retain all of the acoustic features with which it is presented, but that far from being a selection processor, it loses information through inefficient storage. Certain features of speech are not *selected*, it is that others are not *retained*. To appreciate which features of speech should be present for categorization to be possible we first need to consider the problem of speech perception from a different point of view.

The Right Ear Advantage and the perception of speech

Kimura (1961) reported that when dichotic lists of words are presented to subjects the majority tend to be able to recall more words which were presented to their right ears than to their left ears. This, basically is the Right Ear Advantage (REA). This finding has clinical implications and was initially used to determine the location of the speech centre (right or left cerebral cortex) in patients prior to cortical surgery. We know that the speech centre is generally located in the left cerebral hemisphere ("dominant" hemisphere) in right- and left-handed people, but between 10% and 20% of the population have the speech centre located in the right hemisphere (Milner, Branch and Rasmussen, 1964), and so a check is necessary before surgery. (Gerschwind, 1972, suggests that a much lower percentage of the population have right dominant hemispheres.) Prior to the use of Kimura's method sodium amytal was injected into the carotid artery on the left and right sides of the patient on different days. The sodium amytal, which is a depressant, is injected whilst the subject counts aloud, with his arms raised and his fingers moving. If the injection is to the non-dominant hemisphere then within a few seconds the subject stops counting and loses control of the arm on the opposite side to the injection. After a further few seconds the subject is able to resume counting and can complete tests of verbal comprehension, indicating the use of language functions. If the injection is to the dominant hemisphere he is unable to start counting again and is dysphasic for a few minutes.

Kimura's dichotic listening method is somewhat more desirable in that it was present in the stimulus series. In Shulman's experiment ten of speech. The subject is presented with a few simultaneous pairs of words, one to each ear, and immediately recalls as many as possible. When speech is located in the left hemisphere the subject recalls the items presented to the right ear more efficiently than he recalls those presented to the left ear. Kimura has also demonstrated a Left Ear Advantage for the recall of speech in patients known to have a dominant right hemisphere. The advantage for the right ear/left hemisphere is clarified by the supposition that contralateral connexions between ears and hemispheres are stronger than ipsilateral connexions (Rozenzweig, 1951).

Kimura suggests that the REA is a function of perception of speech rather than a function of differential storage, and that there is superior perception of speech and speech sounds arriving in the dominant hemisphere. Inglis (1965) disputed this interpretation, however, on the basis that the REA is due to a recall paradigm rather than a perceptual effect, and that the accurate recall of right ear material is simply due to that material being recalled first. The left ear material, being stored until the right ear material is reported, is then vulnerable to more forgetting than the right ear material, and so recall will not be so accurate. This model suggests that dominance biases the subject to report the right ear material first.

So here we have three possible models to account for the REA:

(i) Efficiency of Perception, whereby speech arriving in the dominant hemisphere is perceived more efficiently than speech arriving in the non-dominant hemisphere.

(ii) Differential Storage, whereby the storage processes for speech presented to the left ear are less efficient than the storage processes for speech presented to the right ear. Left ear material might be subject to more decay or interference than right ear material (see Chapter 2 for a more extensive discussion of forgetting).

(iii) Order-Effect Biases, whereby the superiority of recall of right ear material over left ear material is accounted for by a tendency on the part of the subject to report the right ear material first, allowing more forgetting of left ear material. The REA is therefore due to bias in the order of the report.

We can dispense with the order-effect model by testing the prediction made by the model that when order of report is taken into account the REA should disappear. By instructing the subject to report the left ear items first on half the trials and the right ear items first on the other half and pooling the recall data no advantage for either ear should be seen. Subjects should then show a REA when instructed to report right ear items first and a LEA when instructed to report left ear items first. Bryden (1963, 1965) has used this experimental design, and found that the REA still shows through. A second experiment also provides data with which we can reject the order-effect model. Broadbent and Gregory (1964a) presented a dichotic list followed by a recognition probe. The subject had to respond "yes" or "no" as to whether or not the probe word had been presented as part of the dichotic list. When the probe was part of the right ear list subjects were more successful at recognizing it than when it was part of the left ear list. There are no order of report biases permissible in this experimental design, but the REA still shows through.

The differential storage model considers that the REA is due to more efficient storage of speech presented to the right ear over that presented to the left ear. A prediction from this model is that the longer the material is stored the greater will be the REA. So, we can test the model by comparing the recall order of right ear items first, left ear items second, against the recall order of left ear items first, right ear items second. Borkowski, Spreen and Stutz (1965) made such a comparison, finding a REA (right ear items over left ear items) of 7% for the first reported channel, and a REA of 6% for the second reported channel. It makes no difference whether the right ear items are reported first or second, they have a consistent advantage over left ear items. There is a negligible difference in the REA over time, contrary to the prediction of the differential storage model.

Strong support for the perception hypothesis of the lateralization effect, which at the same time discounts both the order-effects hypothesis and the differential storage hypothesis, has been provided by Springer (1971). Subjects were presented with dichotic lists of consonant-vowel syllables and were instructed to listen for a target syllable which was specified at the beginning of each trial. The target syllable was presented equally often to the two ears, but subjects detected right ear targets more often than left ear targets, and when they did detect a target they were significantly faster in making a manual response to indicate right ear targets than in responding to left ear targets. Subjects could respond more often and quicker to target syllables presented to their right ears in a situation where the emphasis is not to store the detected stimulus but to respond to it. Furthermore, because Springer used a manual detection task we cannot attribute the REA to lateralization of verbal output, a feature not controlled for in the experiments described so far.

We are now in a position to support Kimura's (1961, 1967) perceptual processing hypothesis of the REA for response to speech. The REA does not hold for all auditory stimuli, however, and here we are approaching an explanation for the discrepancy between Massaro's data and those of Crowder and Morton. Kimura (1964) has found a left ear advantage (LEA) for the perception of dichotically presented melodies, and other LEAs have been found for the perception of sonar signals, clicks and vocal but (nonverbal) sounds such as laughing, crying, and sighing (Chaney and Webster, 1965; King and Kimura, 1972; Murphy and Venables, 1970). So, linguistic sounds are perceived more efficiently when presented to the right ear, and non-linguistic sounds have an advantage when presented to the left ear. The questions arising from this generalized conclusion involve the stage in the perception of speech at which hemispheric differences occur, and the manner in which the classifications of "language" and "non-language" are made. For instance, if the perception of speech is seen as a task of discriminating between distinctive features by a process of analysis-by-synthesis (Liberman, Cooper, Shankweiler, and Studdert-Kennedy, 1967), then one way of discovering all these psychologically distinctive features is to find out whether all speech sounds and parts of speech are exclusively handled more efficiently when presented to the right ear.

To discover which parts of speech are important for the perception of speech Shankweiler and Studdert-Kennedy (1967) looked for REA using synthetic consonant and vowel sounds. A REA for a part of speech would indicate processing of that segment by the dominant hemisphere, in which the language areas are located (Gerschwind, 1972). Shankweiler and Studdert-Kennedy presented dichotic pairs of speech sounds, and the subject was asked to identify each member of the pair on each presentation. Two tests were made, one in which consonant-vowel syllables were presented, the vowel component remaining constant on all trials, (it was /a/ as in "father"), and in the other test vowels were presented without consonants. So basically the subject must attempt to identify two consonants in the first experiment, and two vowels in the second experiment. Six possible consonant-vowel syllables were used in pairs in the first experiment, the vowel being combined with one of three voiced stop consonants /b,d,g/ or one of three unvoiced stop consonants /p,t,k/. No consonant was dichotically paired with itself, and idenfification was as quickly as possible after presentation. The REA effect was confirmed for the case of stop consonants by the experiment as subjects identified more of the right ear syllables (45% correct) than they did the left ear syllables (31% correct).

The second experiment presented dichotic pairs of steady state vowels, each vowel being 300msec in duration. A similar procedure to that employed in the first experiment was used, and the five vowels for pairing were /i,e, ae, a,u/ as in "beet, bet, bat, father and cool" respectively. This time left ear stimuli were identified on 41% of occasions and right ear vowels on 45% of occasions. The absence of a REA for steady state vowels might correspond to the central position which these stimuli hold in the continuum between speech and non-speech. Kimua (1964) reports a LEA for the perception of melody, and Darwin (1969) for the perception of oboe phrases, and it could be argued that as steady state vowels have similar qualities to these stimuli they may be analyzed by either hemisphere.

Haggard (1971) has extended the case for vowels to the semi-vowels or lateral consonants /w,r,l,j/ as in "what, rot, lot, yacht" respectively. These consonants have certain similarities with vowels in that they have a longer duration of articulation than the stop consonants, but showed a REA of only 5% in a dichotic listening situation similar to that used by Shankweiler and Studdert-Kennedy. This indicates that the similar properties of formant transition (i.e. slow frequency changes, but see Liberman *et al* for a complete description) of semi-vowels, and vowels are relevant to the REA, and hence to the processing of these stimuli by the speech areas. However, Haggard's REA effect for the semi-vowels was slightly larger than Shankweiler and Studdert-Kennedy's effect for steady state vowels. The former was a statistically significant difference whereas the latter was not, and so Haggard considers this identified the semi-vowels with the stop consonants. A subsequent report by Cutting (1973) also indicates that the midpoint of semi-vowels between steady state vowels and stop consonants is reflected in the relative magnitudes of the REAs for these stimuli.

Haggard (1971) and Darwin (1971) have both found REAs for vowels under certain conditions: Haggard when subjects listened to vowels with contextual uncertainty as to the pitch of the voice, and Darwin when subjects are uncertain as to the vocal tract size but certain as to pitch. Whether an ear difference appears or not depends upon the complexity of the perceptual discrimination involved. In general there is little to choose between the vowels. They transmit little information to the listener, and no hemisphere needs to be specialized for their processing.

The relationship between information content of an auditory stimulus and the extent of the REA associated with simultaneous dichotic presentation of two such stimuli is important for the model of speech perception offered by Liberman *et al* (1967). In this model the complexity of an auditory stimulus is described as "encodedness", the stop consonants being highly encoded, with the vowels at the other extreme of this continuum. Decoding of the acoustic signal is said to require processing by the speech centre which is located in the dominant hemisphere. Hence a more encoded stimulus will require more processing by the left hemisphere, and will show a greater REA. That the lateral consonants (sometimes called liquids) show an intermediate REA, and may be described by this group of workers as being moderately encoded, lends support to this model.

The Right Ear Advantage and Acoustic Memory

This line of investigation, showing an REA for encoded stimuli but not for less encoded stimuli, has some interesting implications for work on acoustic memory. A redundant "zero" suffix added to the end of a list of items reduces the extent of the recency effect for aurally presented words, as we have already, and this effect has been interpreted as evidence in favour of the notion of precategorical acoustic storage. The final items of a list generally have extra readout time from this acoustic store, but the suffix acts to mask the final items, or displace them from the store. Now, whereas non-verbal vocal sounds successfully acted as suffices, non-vocal sounds failed to produce the effect (Morton *et al*, 1971). Buzzers, tones, bursts of white noise, and even speech which was synthetically produced all failed to disrupt the recency effect, but a non-verbal "uh" was as successful as a "zero". From the data so far we may conclude that a necessary feature of a suffix, if it is to disrupt recency is that it is a human noise. This alone is not sufficient evidence to suggest different memory functions of speech and non-speech, because a different-voice suffix also has an effect upon recency which is markedly reduced. A series of experiments reported by Crowder (1971) does attempt to describe different memory functions for different sounds, however and in particular, this paper investigated differences between vowels and stop-consonants. In one experiment the subject was required to recall lists of seven synthetic consonant-vowel syllables drawn from the set /ba,da,ga/. The synthetic suffix was "go", and in a control condition a tone was presented as a control. The results from this experiment were that no recency effect was present and the suffix did not have any differential effect upon syllables in the final positions of the list. It should be noted that these stimuli differ only in their initial stop consonants. The data with which the experiment should be compared are from trials in which consonant-vowel syllables were also presented for recall, but in which the stop consonant was always the same /g/, and the vowels varied /æ, ɔ,ʌ/ to produce the set of sounds as in "gap, got, gut" respectively. The suffix was either the syllable /ba/, which resembles 'bah', or was a tone. The recall data from this experiment indicated that the recency and suffix effects appear to have been restored. An incidental point is that our conclusion that human noise is necessary for a suffix effect to appear is now invalidated. A synthetic suffix can affect recency if recency itself is produced with synthetic stimuli, and provided that the vowels of the recall items carry information.

These two experiments permit us to reject the hypothesis that acoustic memory records all speech information – the perfect tape-recording model – and suggest that only vowels are held in PAS. This could be due to different perceptual functions, with consonants being decoded in different ways to vowels as Liberman *et al* suggest, or to storage functions, with consonants having a shorter life in PAS. Cole (1973) also provides evidence that vowels and consonants are retained in acoustic memory differently. Vowels were preserved more accurately than consonants with an auditory presentation, but this difference was not maintained with a visual presentation. Consideration of the evidence of the REA studies and of acoustic storage of consonants and vowels led Crowder (1971) to suggest that "the really tempting hypothesis is that PAS is a property of the nondominant (right) hemisphere". A check on the consonant-vowel distinction is possible by looking at the REA and acoustical storage of the intermediate sounds. Stop consonants and steady state vowels fit the Crowder hypothesis, but where do the semi-vowels (e.g.,/w,r/), fricatives (e.g.,/s,z/), and dipthongs (e.g.,/ei,ou/) stand? If a sound shows a REA then it should not be represented in PAS according to the simple version of this hypothesis. Darwin (1971) has shown a considerable REA for the fricatives (/f, s,ʃ, v, z,ʒ/ as in "fill, sill, shall, vine, zip, azure" respectively), which are similar to vowels in that they contain steady state features. Because they have a REA then we might expect them to have no representation in PAS, being processed in the dominant hemisphere. Crowder (1973) found that the opposite was true. Lists composed of the consonant-vowel syllables /ve, ze, e/ showed recency in recall when suffixed by a tone, but not when suffixed by "zero". In this sense the fricatives were behaving as if they were vowels, and we must reject the simple "vowel-consonant: PAS — not PAS" distinction to account for the results. Crowder goes on to consider that PAS preserves steady state sounds rather than transient sounds, a position supported by the data on acoustical storage. If transient sounds are not stored precategorically then they must be decoded into categorical memory on presentation, but this leads to a counter-intuitive position on the function of PAS. The steady state sounds have less need for acoustic storage than transient sounds because of this distinguishing feature. If the processor misses one segment of a transient sound then unless it can look again at the input then an inaccurate categorization may result. With the steady state sounds the need to look again is less essential. If one segment is lost the next segment may be used because it contains the same information. This is the point over which Crowder offers reconciliation with Massaro's position. The time course of Massaro's preperceptual store is of the same order of magnitude as that required to store the distinguishing features of the stop consonants. Lisker and Abramson (1964) showed that the only necessary feature for a listener to distinguish between the synthetic sounds /ba, pa/ was the onset time of the voicing component, the low frequency laryngeal pulsing. Whereas /ba/ has a voice onset time (measured from onset on the first sound) of 10 msec, /pa/ has a voice onset of 100 msec. If the cues which distinguish these sounds differ in timing by less than 100 msec then storage for a few hundred msec is all that is necessary to permit analysis after presentation.

The short-life preperceptual store could have this function, but if it does, then why do we also have the capacity for precategorical storage? We can move towards a solution to this problem by looking at an alternative approach to the data.

The data discussed above have considerable implications for the Liberman *et al.* (1967) theory of encodedness — consonants being very encoded and vowels being less encoded and therefore perceived continuously whereas consonants are perceived categorically. The stop consonants are said to be perceived categorically in that listeners appeared to be unable to hear differences in the synthetic stimuli unless the different stimuli could be given categorical names (Liberman, Harris, Hoffman and Griffith, 1957), whereas listeners were able to discriminate more differences between steady state vowels (Fry, Abramson, Eimas and Liberman, 1962) and are said to be perceived in a continuous mode. The whole question between the perception of consonants and vowels has been thrown open by a number of experiments which show that if the length of the vowels is shortened, then they are perceived categorically (Fujisaki and Kawashima, 1968; Pisoni, 1973). This result may suggest that different perceptual results, including the REA effect, are not due so much to differences in the categorization process alone, but that they are due to differences in the acoustic storage of the cues, distinguishing the two classes of speech sounds, and which form the basis of the classification. The appealing simplicity of this argument is that because the vowel cues have a longer duration than stop consonant cues the former are preserved in auditory memory better than are consonant cues. This argument is leading us to a reinstatement of the tape-recorder model in which all stimuli are held in PAS, but only in a rough form without the finer features which are critical to the discrimination between consonants. The alternative view is that storage in acoustic memory is a function of encodedness, that more encoded stimuli are not stored in acoustic memory because their acoustic cues have been lost during a special process which "strips away all auditory information and presents to immediate perception a categorical linguistic event" (Liberman, Mattingly and Turvey, 1972). This process is located in the dominant hemisphere, and is responsible for the REA effect. By the encodedness model a steady state speech input, whether nominally a consonant or a vowel, is not perceived as a categorical event, its acoustic features are not immediately perceived by the special processor and it is allowed to reside in acoustical memory. A transient input, on the other hand, is immediately perceived as a categorical stimulus and this act of categorization uses and dispenses with the acoustic cues that would have otherwise have been retained in PAS. For Liberman *et al.* there can be no precategorical *and* categorical storage of an encoded input, storage is dependant upon the processor. The alternative is that acoustical storage is independent of encodedness, but that because of the nature of transient sounds they are not stored in PAS because only an inaccurate copy is made. The less transient and more steady-state a sound becomes (or less encoded as Liberman *et al.* would describe it) the greater is the accuracy of acoustic storage.

The encodedness model has been questioned recently in a paper by Darwin and Baddeley (1974) which reports a number of experiments concerning recall of sequences. First, they showed a recency effect (indicating acoustic storage) for *discriminable* consonant-vowel syllables ("sha, ma, ga" and "ash, am, ag"). Crowder (1971) failed to obtain this effect with syllables constructed of stop consonants and vowels ("ba, da, ga"), confirming that distinctions between storage stages are not a simple matter of the distinctions between consonants and vowels. If the consonants are sufficiently discriminable then they too will be stored in acoustic memory for long enough to be useful after presentation. The property of encodedness of consonants is evidently insufficient to prevent their storage in PAS. Darwin and Baddeley also show that with recall of sets of consonant-vowel syllables composed of /b/ plus acoustically similar vowels /I, e, æ/ to give the sounds as in "bit, bet, bat" respectively, no recency effects are present. A comparable experiment with dissimilar vowels did find a recency effect. Storage in PAS depends not upon the part of speech which is presented, but upon the variability of the set of items used. If the items are acoustically similar then acoustic memory will be poor; storage is not dependent upon the categorization of parts of speech but upon the acoustic similarity of the items in the vocabulary used. These experiments do not support the suggestion that transient sounds are preserved in PAS less well than are steady-state sounds, and we are brought back to the tape-recorder model. If the recording holds not a perfect but a crude representation then a set of items with similar features would become indistinguishable, leading us to believe that no acoustic storage was present, and no functional storage would be present. When the set of items are clearly discriminable, no matter how transient, then even with a certain amount of degradation and loss of transient features, they may still be discriminable from each other.

From this discussion it is concluded that PAS does serve as a tape-recorder, albeit an inefficient one, and that all parts of speech are available for analysis after presentation. PAS is therefore a facility which may be available before and after categorization, it is not erased by the categorization process. Dichotic listening experiments indicate that transient (more "encoded") parts of speech are processed better when presented to the dominant hemisphere, where, it has been argued, they have immediate access to the special processor (Liberman *et al.* 1972). The tape-recorder model as described by Darwin and Baddeley is also able to account for the REA data without recourse to distinctions between categorical and continuous perception. This model holds that only discriminable speech sounds will be processed successfully when presented to the left ear, and makes no assumptions about special processing of consonants or vowels. When transient stop consonants are presented to both ears, as in the Shankweiler and Studdert-Kennedy (1967) experiment, the right ear consonant is immediately processed by the speech centre in the left hemisphere, but processing of the left ear consonant is delayed or even inhibited (Studdert-Kennedy, Shankweiler and Pisoni, 1972) by the prior processing of the right ear consonant. Whilst the left ear stimulus is being stored in PAS, awaiting processing, its representation is degraded, and the small distinctive feature which characterized the stimulus may be lost. Hence a REA for consonants. When steady state vowels are presented dichotically they are processed and stored in the same way as consonants, right ear vowels being processed first and left ear vowels being stored for a short time. However, whereas consonants lose their distinctive features whilst in PAS the tendency for steady state stimuli to become unrecognizable is less so, even though they do become degraded. The reduction of the amount of information in PAS stands for all stimuli, however well "encoded". The critical factor is the distinctiveness of the set of items being stored. The model is given considerable support by data reported by Weiss and House (1973), who found a REA for vowels in a dichotic listening task with unfavourable listening conditions (a S/N ratio of -12 dB). In this situation distinctive features between the vowels are degraded during input and so the adverse effects of storage in acoustic memory are increased, the distinctive features of left ear vowels being lost. This is a crucial experiment, for Liberman's encoding model would not consider that because a vowel is degraded it becomes more encoded, perceived categorically, and therefore entitled to a REA.

The main points of this chapter have been to stress the importance of the variability of strategies of processing information contained in the visual image, to establish the necessity of acoustic storage, and to indicate how sensory information is passed into categorical memory. As we pass on to look at the storage of information in permanent memory the reader should also specifically bear in mind our conclusion that by the time a stimulus is processed out of sensory memory it is multi-addressable — the same stimulus may be retrieved on the basis of acoustic, visual, or categorical cues. It is this multiple retrieval system which is one of the more prominent features of human memory.

CHAPTER 2

CATEGORICAL MEMORY

As mentioned previously, psychologists have tended to dichotomize our information storage system, and there is by now a considerable body of physiological and clinical evidence in support of the view that humans have (at least) two categorical memory systems. For example, retrograde amnesia is shown to be time dependent when caused by electroconvulsive shock, convulsive or depressant drugs, spreading cortical depression, hypoxia, or hypothermia. (Reviews have been provided by Deutsch (1969, 1973) and by Pribram and Broadbent (1970).) The degree of impairment of memory decreases as the time between training and treatment is increased, and with a certain delay of treatment no further impairment is observable. These treatments are thus said to affect the consolidation processes, the transfer of information from short-term memory to long-term memory. Although there are many problems in the interpretation of these results the consolidation model has gained general acceptance (see Weiskrantz 1966; Cherkin, 1969; McGaugh and Dawson, 1971). One of the major problems here is that estimates of the time needed for transfer to long-term memory vary between 10 seconds and 24 hours. Other inconsistencies from the animal literature have been discussed by Norman (1973). However, the validity of the distinction between short-term and long-term memory which is based upon physiological evidence is not questioned here, but the admissibility of this evidence is questioned. If a behavioural distinction exists between these two storage systems then the distinction should be manifest in behaviour which is not constrained by electrical shocks, convulsive drugs and other treatments. If humans have uses for short-term storage and long-term storage of information then psychologists should be able to observe these operations without recourse to artificial interference which undoubtedly does more to the organism than merely disrupt consolidation of the memory trace. Psychological evidence should be consistent with physiological evidence of course, and by assessing constraints of behaviour imposed by physiological mechanisms insight into psychological processes may be gained. If psychology is a distinct discipline then it should be able to observe and explain behaviour by its own methods. So far as the present discussion is concerned these methods do not include direct physiological interference with the organism. Whereas we do not go so far as Skinner (1972) in his view that "physiological research is regarded as simply a more scientific version of introspection", we do consider that physiologists can give us limited assistance in the description of human memory. An underlying assumption in this rejection of physiological evidence is that Joynson's (1970) dilemma is quite inappropriate, and that the theoretical basis for the explanation of within-subject factors in behaviour will not be restricted to a physiological description. A psychological description of behaviour is supportable and independent of other descriptions.

Immediate Memory and Categorical Memory

Descriptions of short-term and long-term components of human memory have been refined considerably over the past 20 years, and we shall follow Baddeley and Patterson (1971) in the use of one particular refinement. Assuming, for the present purposes of description, that humans do have two components of categorical memory then we shall use the terms "short term memory" and "long-term memory" to describe experimental procedures, and the terms "primary memory" and "secondary memory" to describe the systems and operations used by the human subject in experimental situations. Short-term memory (in the sense used so far here) and primary memory may not be necessarily identical. Other differences than those of time in store may exist between items in primary and secondary memory. A major problem of the investigation of these differences is that a short term memory task may involve both primary and secondary memory components, and so we can only *infer* which memory systems have been operative in any experiment.

The descriptive term "primary memory" was first used by William James (1890), and has been recently revived in an influential paper by Waugh and Norman (1965). James's distinction between the two systems was related to his views on the nature of consciousness. Information in primary memory was considered to be that matter currently in consciousness, that which belongs to the psychological present. Secondary memory items are said to have been absent from consciousness at some point, that they belong to the psychological past. This description is adequate qualitatively, but says little about the processing of information into and between the two systems, about coding operations used to store information, or about the   storage limitations of the systems. Waugh and Norman merged the primary memory/secondary memory distinction with a theory of memory of recent events put forward by Hebb (1949), and developed by Brown (1954, 1958), Broadbent (1958), and by Peterson and Peterson (1959). This theory argues that memory traces of permanently remembered   events differ from traces of recently perceived items by the nature of the cause of forgetting of associations between items. Whereas items in the vast secondary memory system are forgotten according to the principles of Interference Theory, recently acquired items stored in primary memory fade autonomously in time unless some active effort is made on the part of the person to retain those items. Details of the distinction between interference and decay theories will be discussed at a later point in this chapter (pp.78ff.), but the basic difference is as follows. If a number of items are not recalled at a particular time because of the action of other items then forgetting is said to be due to interference, but if a number of items are not attended to then decay theory says that their memory trace strengths will decrease and these items will become irretrievable under any circumstances. Waugh and Norman consider that items in primary memory are vulnerable to forgetting through decay unless maintained in that system by the process of rehearsal (subvocal, or otherwise). If items are rehearsed then they are more likely to be transferred into the more permanent secondary memory system. It should be noted that presence in one memory system does not exclude simultaneous presence in the other memory system, and that entry of a visually presented item to primary memory follows storage in the immediate or sensory memory described by Sperling (1960, 1963, 1967). These two points should be borne in mind when considering the simplified version of this model of memory as represented in Fig. 2.1. Sensory storage is not accounted for here, but Waugh and Norman consider that primary memory does not store "raw" sensory information, so they are assuming that at least initial processing has been applied to the stimulus. An input consisting of speech may be retained

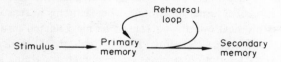

Fig. 2.1. The primary and secondary memory system envisaged by Waugh and Norman (1965).

in this store on the basis of the words which constitute the total input. This would amount to categorical storage, efficient categorization only being possible with familiar languages. A further stage of processing which may or may not be applied to information stored in primary memory is that of extraction of semantic features. Words can be remembered, without reference to their meaning, simply on the basis that they are words. Familiarity with a language may allow categorization of an input into units of words, without full reference to the meanings of the words taken together. Given the simple sentence "the man bit the dog", then we could decode the input into five words each with specific meanings but without analyzing the underlying meaning of the sentence. Recognition of the (unusual) deep structure of the sentence entails observations of the relationships between each of the meaningful components. Storage in primary memory may or may not be dependent upon the analysis of deep structure. If we are to keep the description of memory which James offered, with the only difference between primary memory and secondary memory being whether or not the information is in consciousness. If primary memory corresponds to a "working" memory, as this would suggest, then there is no difference in the level of processing between information held in the two systems. Waugh and Norman draw no such difference derived from the levels of processing, but more recent theorists have pointed to such a distinction (e.g. Kintsch, 1970; Glanzer, 1972; Craik and Lockhart, 1972). Powerful evidence exists to differentiate between the immediate sensory memory system, and the categorical memory system, but differentiating between the primary and secondary memory components of categorical storage is more difficult, and may even be invalid (Melton, 1963; Kay, 1968; Tulving, 1970; Murdock, 1972).

Three features which distinguish categorical memory from sensory memory will be mentioned here. First and foremost the bases for storage differ in quality of information stored; whereas items in sensory memory are stored as physical events and cannot be manipulated on the basis of their semantic features (Sperling, 1960), items in categorical memory are, as the very description suggests, remembered according to semantic features. Categorical memory is the storage system said to be used to remember telephone numbers, addresses, shopping lists, names of people and objects, relationships between objects, etc., etc.

The second difference between sensory and primary memory is in dispute. Whereas entry to sensory memory is pre-attentive, all information presented to the subject being stored in this system (Neisser, 1967), it is not clear whether or not entry to primary memory is so passive. Waugh and Norman consider that entry to primary memory is made on a passive basis, all information presented being categorized. This is clearly not consistent with subjective experience. In the "Cocktail-party" situation (Cherry, 1953) with numerous sources of inputs we are incapable of categorically analyzing all that is spoken. With two or possibly three inputs a case could be made for parallel analysis, but an extreme example of ten or fifty inputs must lead to selective processing with active selection of those inputs which are to be categorized. The outlet from this position would be to argue that categorization occurs at a stage later than primary memory, that primary memory is a precategorical buffer store. However, this is not the case that Waugh and Norman put forward, primary memory being a "faithful record of events just perceived" and hence being a store of categorized, meaningful events. The alternative argument of selective entry to categorical memory, is made by Broadbent (1958), Sperling (1960), Atkinson and Shiffrin (1968), and many others. This view is that processing beyond the level of sensory storage is under the strategical control of the subject. For instance in the case of multiple spoken inputs the theory of processing put forward by Neisser (1967) involves an active component of analysis-by-synthesis: a message is understood by reproducing it to oneself. Perception is seen as an act of reconstruction. We are limited in the number of messages which we can reconstruct or synthesize, and so unselected messages are not categorized. Only those messages which are actively selected may be perceived, others are not, and therefore cannot be stored in primary memory, which in this sense is synonymous with Neisser's "active verbal memory". That entry to categorical memory is under the strategical control of the subject is suggested by an experiment reported by Glanzer and Meinzer (1967). The repetition of a word in a list has no effect upon storage in primary memory. Once a word is registered in primary memory a further presentation of the same word does not lead to storage of a second representation. Primary memory stores a set of different words rather than all words which are presented, and repeated words do not gain admittance. However, if the recency effect reflects readout from primary memory, and if entry to primary memory is under the strategical control of the subject, then it might be thought that an irrelevant suffix item placed on the end of the list should not cause as much disruption of recall of the final items as is evident. Entry of the suffix items to primary memory should be under the control of the subject, and not be permitted to have an effect.

The third distinction between sensory and categorical memory is less equivocal than the second, and involves the loss of information. For the case of vision, Sperling (1960, 1963) has shown that information not processed out of sensory memory within a few hundred milliseconds becomes irretrievable. Whether the auditory analogue of visual sensory memory is Massaro's (1972a) "preperceptual" store with a life of a few hundred milliseconds, or Crowder and Morton's (1969) 'precategorical' store with a life of 1 or 2 seconds, we are led to the conclusion that the effective life of an event which is not categorized is less than 2 seconds for the cases of vision and audition. Categorized events have a decay function which extends over a period of 15-20 seconds, as can be seen in Fig. 2.2. This curve represents the probability of recalling a single categorized event which is not attended to during the period immediately after presentation up until recall is required. On each trial Peterson and Peterson (1959) presented a single trigram to the subject, and this was the item which they had to recall. The trigram consisted of three consonants which were selected randomly by the experimenters, and was spoken. Immediately after presentation of the trigram the experimenter read out a three digit number (e.g. "329") and the subject was required to count backwards from this number in threees on half of the trials (i.e. "326, 323, 320 . . ."), and in fours on half of the trials (i.e. "325, 321, 217 . . ."). The purpose of the backwards counting task was

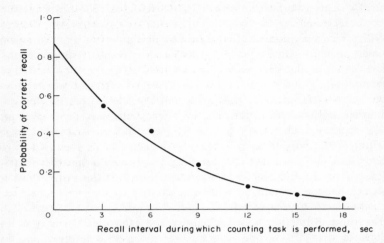

Fig. 2.2. Recall of a single consonant trigrams after intervals filled with a task which prevented rehearsals of the trigram. (From Peterson and Peterson, 1959.)

to prevent the subject from attending to the consonant trigram during the retention interval. Without the counting test no subject should have made any recall errors, because he would have been able to rehearse the trigram, and to keep it in primary memory. Rehearsal may act to increase the strength of the memory trace (see Massaro, 1970b), but Brown (1958) argued that rehearsal merely postpones the onset of decay of the trace. Some time after presentation of the trigram, and engagement in the distraction task a red light indicated to the subject that he should recall the consonant trigram, and this recall function is presented as Fig. 2.2.

The recall interval is the period between the experimenter speaking the third consonant of the trigram, and the onset of the red light which cues recall. So, whereas an item in sensory memory which is not attended to has an effective life of a few hundred milliseconds or thereabouts, after which the item is irretrievable through decay, an item in primary memory has a life in the order of several seconds when not attended.

So far as verbal information is concerned it is the precategorical-categorical distinction which is of major importance, and which has received the major proportion of attention by psychologists recently. If sensory features are not the basis of storage in primary memory, then what is the level of processing? In a review article Baddeley and Patterson (1971) argue that sensory characteristics are important at this stage, and that items are stored on the basis of their acoustic or phonemic features. This holds for both auditory and visual presentations, so the assumption is that the subject processes the stimuli into an acoustic or articulatory code. This is a notion similar to that of Sperling (1967, Model 3), primary memory now being analogous to the 'auditory information store'. If primary memory is a store of items coded acoustically and independently of other items (i.e. no effect of semantic context), as this argument suggests, then we are led to question its function. Is primary memory a term to ascribe those items currently in consciousness as James considers, a working memory, or is it simply an intermediate stage of processing presenting acoustically coded items to another processor? By eliminating interaction with the lexicon altogether the function of primary memory is resolved to that of coding process, whereby the visual or auditory image is transformed into a categorized item retained on the basis of the acoustic characteristics associated with the subvocal naming response. If this is the case then primary memory is a necessary component of working memory or short-term memory, but only serves to provide the units of information which are operated upon by some other system. The discussion here and in the chapters which ensue will argue that all items presented which are words will contact the lexicon, but that not all of these words will enter consciousness. Primary memory will be seen as being analogous to a phonemic store, with forgetting dependent upon the maintenance of attention to the phonemic representation. Not all words which exceed the sensory threshold are represented in this phonemic or articulatory code. Those which are may be remembered more easily than those which are not, but behaviour is not totally dependent upon phonemic encoding. The information in primary memory contributes to the matter currently in consciousness, and attention governs which items gain admittance to consciousness and which items are maintained there. Attention is almost always necessary for admission to consciousness and all words presented to us are accessible to consciousness where they may be related to each other and organized into a sequential response. Items remembered but not in consciousness have been described elsewhere as being stored in secondary memory, but the argument here is that they differ from those items in primary memory in quality only in the attribute of absence from consciousness. Secondary memory may be viewed as the lexicon, or word and event store, and where relationships between items are stored after their directed development in primary memory. Thus, storage in primary memory is analogous to a state of excitation of events in secondary memory. The entry of two or more words to the "primary memory system" will lead to an association between those words being established and stored in the "secondary memory system". If words are to be associated with each, assimilated into the individual's schema, and used in solving problems, then they must be attended to, and the process of attending to a word here is the same as admitting that word to primary memory in other descriptions.

Distinctions between Primary Memory and Secondary Memory

Storage capacity differences and the magic number three

A guide to the solution of the problem of the function of primary memory may be provided by attempts to estimate the storage capacity of such a system. Working memory clearly needs a reasonably large store, in the order of the estimate provided by Miller (1956) of about 7 items. A mean estimate of the number of digits in a short-term memory span is 7.70, whereas the estimate for letters is 6.35 (Cavanagh, 1972).

The independence of primary memory from such a short-term memory or working memory is demonstrated by very different estimates of the size of the store. Craik (1968) based his estimate of the span of primary memory on the assumption that the extent of the recency portion of the serial position curve reflects output from primary memory (Glanzer and Cunitz, 1966). In a free recall experiment when the subject may recall the list members in any order he chooses there is a tendency to first recall the few items which were presented last. These items are said to be present in primary memory at the time of recall. Evidence in favour of this view is provided by Glanzer and Cunitz (1966), who presented a list of fifteen words for recall. The subjects recalled the lists immediately, or after a 10-second counting task, or 30 seconds after the end of the list with the counting task interpolated between list and recall. The results are presented in Fig. 2.3. The usual recency effect is produced in the immediate recall conditions, but when recall is delayed

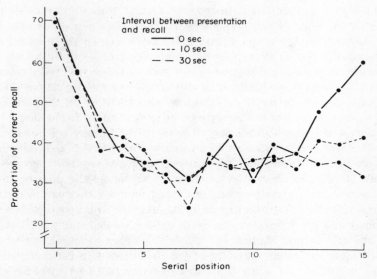

Fig. 2.3. The effect upon recency of delaying the recall of a list. (From Glanzer and Cunitz, 1966.)

recency is reduced or eliminated. The storage of items from primary memory is reduced by the interpolated activity, and this consequently leads to a reduction of the recency effect which is said to be due to retrieval of items from primary memory. This result has been extended by Craik (1970) who found the usual recency effect with each of ten lists when recalled immediately, but a *negative* recency effect when at the end of the experiment the subject had to recall as many items as possible from all ten lists. When each word from this final recall attempt was plotted in its original serial position of presentation it emerged that recall of items at the ends of lists (the "recency" items) were recalled less often than items in the centre of the list. This is strong evidence in favour of different mechanisms of storage and retrieval of recency items and non-recency items. An explanation in terms of the primary memory hypothesis argues that recency items are recalled first in immediate free recall and hence are more likely to be recalled accurately. They are the items still in consciousness, and because they need not to be transferred to more permanent storage in order to be recalled immediately they cannot be retrieved from permanent storage on the final recall attempt. Central and early items, on the other hand, are stored in secondary memory even for immediate recall, and so when it comes to retrieving them after some delay they can still be retrieved from this permanent store. The distinction between secondary and primary memory is therefore argued to manifest itself in the recency effect, but estimating the capacity of primary memory is not simply a matter of counting the number of items in the recency region of the recall curve. This is because final items may be processed and retrieved on the basis of information in primary memory *and* secondary memory. Craik (1968) described three methods of separating the primary and secondary memory components, one based on age differences in recall (primary memory capacity is said to be invariant with age), one based upon list length differences (the more items presented, the smaller will be the relative contribution of storage in primary memory), and one based upon the recall advantage of the final items of a list over items from the middle of a list (final items being recalled on the basis of primary and secondary memory cues, and middle items on the basis of secondary memory cues alone). The "recency method" is derived from a method used by Waugh and Norman (1965), in which the secondary memory component of recall of the central items is first estimated by obtaining the probability of recall of these items. This estimate is then assumed to be the secondary memory component for recency items also. (This is clearly not the case, or Craik (1970) would not have found a negative recency on final recall, but no recency in either direction — recall of central and final items all being made on the basis of secondary memory cues.) Given the supposed secondary memory component $S(i)$ of recall of any one item i, which is said to be the same for all items, and the probability of recall $R(i)$ of any item, then the primary memory component $P(i)$ for any item may be calculated by substituting in the following equation:

$$P(i) = \frac{(R(i) - S(i)}{(1 - S(i))}$$

In this way the primary memory component for each of the last seven items in the list is calculated, and then totalled to give the total span of primary memory. This method gave Craik (1968) mean estimates of between 1·9 and 3·3 items as the span of primary memory for young adults. Murdock (1972), using the same method, put this estimate at between 2·7 and 3·3 items.

Another, simpler, method of estimating the primary memory span was described by Baddeley (1970). This method used the differences between immediate and delayed recall. Whereas immediate recall is dependent upon retrieval from primary and secondary memory, recall after a 30-second interval is dependent upon retrieval from secondary memory alone. This method leads to an estimate of the primary memory span of between 2·1 and 3·2 items. A problem with this method is that it assumes that the secondary memory component is constant whether recall is immediate or after 30 seconds, that there is no forgetting of items in secondary memory over this period. Whereas it is undoubtedly true that most forgetting would be of information in primary memory, it is also quite likely that there would be some forgetting of information in secondary memory.

In spite of methodological problems associated with these estimates they provide a remarkably consistent value for the primary memory span — about 2 or 3 items. This is clearly different from Sperling's (1960) estimate of the storage capacity of visual sensory memory and from our knowledge of the storage capacity of secondary memory. Estimates of the number of items stored in secondary memory vary wildly, with Craik and Lockhart (1972) concluding that there is "no known limit" to the number of items which may be stored in this system.

The discrepancy between estimates of primary memory span and estimates of the short-term memory span are said to arise through secondary memory contamination in the short-term memory situation.

In the previous chapter (which claimed to deal with sensory memory) a number of experiments were described which attributed the recency effect as being due to retrieval of the final items from precategorical memory (e.g. Crowder and Morton, 1969; Morton, Crowder and Prussin, 1971). However, some of the estimates of primary memory described in this chapter (which claims to deal with categorical memory) also depend upon the recency effect, which is attributed to retrieval of the final items from categorical memory (e.g. Waugh and Norman, 1965; Craik, 1968). This contradiction is partly resolved by the demonstration of Watkins and Watkins (1973) that recency is a post-categorical effect. The extent of recency is independent of word length, contrary to what one would expect if recency reflected retrieval from a store sensitive only to acoustical features. Craik (1968) also found that the primary memory span, as measured by Waugh and Norman's recency method, was remarkably independent of word length. The intermediate nature of this memory system is pin-pointed in references by Murdock (1968, 1972) and by Waugh and Norman (1965) to primary memory as the "echo box".

Categorization

Is primary memory a categorical store or isn't it, and what exactly do we mean by "categorical"? It is not unlikely that a single item may be retrievable on the basis of two or more cues, and indeed it is this multiplicity of retrieval cues of recently presented items which Tulving (1968, 1970) sees as the only defensible distinction between "primary memory" and "secondary memory". An item in primary memory may be stored on the basis of its acoustic characteristics and at the same time have made contact with the lexicon and be categorized as a word. It is by this view of storage and processing into storage that the suffix experiments (suggesting precategorical storage is responsible for the recency effect) and the word-length experiments (suggesting that post categorical storage is responsible) and compatible. The "echo box", consciousness, and primary memory can all refer to the same level of processing but they are not synonymous all of the time. An item may be retrievable using its acoustic properties and its categorized properties, with both retrieval systems being used whilst the item is in consciousness. But an item in consciousness may have been analyzed beyond its basic categorical properties. When the word is fully processed at the semantic level of analysis it is argued to be stored in secondary memory. At this level the verbal associates of the word are available to the subject, the word is within the subject's schema (Bartlett, 1932), and this is described by Tulving and Madigan (1970) as "elaboration coding".

That a word may be processed and stored at the lexical or unelaborated level of analysis has been shown by several experiments. Using a simplified recency method of establishing retrieval from primary memory

Tulving and Patterson (1968) found that the semantic relatedness of words in primary memory does not increase the span. Four highly related words (e.g. "north, south, east, west") are treated as four units in primary memory, but as one unit in secondary memory. The number of words recalled from primary memory is independent of any semantic relationship between them but presenting related rather than unrelated words increases the number recalled from secondary memory. The unit stored is the word, but a word distinct from any other stored. Similarly, Raymond (1969) found that the frequency of words in the language was independent of the number stored in primary memory. More common words are recalled from secondary memory better than infrequent words, indicating a contextual effect in retrieval, but no such effect is evident for words stored in primary memory. A further difference between recall of primary memory and secondary memory words was found with trilingual subjects by Tulving and Colotla (1970). They tested subjects who were proficient in English, French and Spanish on a free recall task with lists of 12, 18 and 24 words. The lists were composed of words from one, two or three of the languages spoken by the subject, but primary memory recall was independent of this factor. The number of words recalled from primary memory (using the Waugh and Norman method) were 2·98 for unilingual lists, 2·98 for bilingual lists, and 2·95 for trilingual lists. It appears that the span of primary memory is fixed and cannot be increased by different codes for the words presented. Secondary memory recall did vary with the number of languages used, unilingual lists allowing higher recall than the multilingual lists. Tulving and Colotla concluded that the secondary memory difference in recall of unilingual and multilingual lists was due to a mnemonic organization difficulties with the mixed lists imposed by a person's languages existing in relative isolation for each other.

These results and others have been cited frequently as convincing evidence of the separate existence of the primary and secondary memory systems, if not always with these particular labels (e.g. Atkinson and Shiffrin, 1968; Baddeley, 1972; Broadbent, 1970; Craik, 1968, 1971; Glanzer and Cunitz, 1966; Kintsch, 1970; Norman, 1968, 1969a; Waugh and Norman, 1965; Wickelgren, 1970). This is the view supported by a large number of workers in the field of human memory, and indeed some of them would go further than a single primary-secondary division of categorical memory and argue for intermediate storage processes (see

Broadbent, 1970, and Wickelgren, 1970). The view that categorical memory is divisible on the basis of the nature of information stored at different states may be described as the conventional, dualist view. This view, it should be noted, does not necessarily hold that physically separate memory systems are employed, as a popular misconception has it and as the usual notation of describing systems may imply. The memory flow-chart type of description (for example, as used by Waugh and Norman — see Fig. 2.1. p. 55) does not necessarily indicate that the designer of the system suggests that primary memory and secondary memory are distinct physiological structures and that transfer from primary to secondary memory means removing an item from one box and placing it in another box. The conventional, two-system view does hold that an item may be stored on the basis of a number of features. If an item is being remembered because of its lexical content then it is said to be held in primary memory, a temporary holding system which is a part of our total categorical memory facility. On the other hand, if the item is remembered because of its associations and wider meaning for the individual then it is said to be held in secondary memory, which is a permanent holding system which is also a part of categorical memory. The dispute between the two-system theorists and the one-system theorists is over whether or not the change from primary memory storage to secondary memory storage is a continuous or an incremental process. If retrieval of the single memory on different occasions may proceed with the use of different attributes of that memory then there is no dispute here. On some occasions sensory attributes may be useful for retrieval, and on other occasions semantic attributes may be useful, but whether we need therefore to postulate different storage systems to account for the multiplicity of attributes is a debatable issue.

The unitary trace hypothesis has been stated very credibly by Melton (1963). This view is that we have one memory system and that the effects generally cited in favour of the dualist view appear because of the temporal characteristics of the item in store. Thus, a recently presented item, which is attended to and which might be argued to be stored in primary memory, is said to be vulnerable to the same influences as an item which might be argued to be held in secondary memory. All items are said to be affected in similar ways but items which are well encoded or consolidated are less affected by causes of forgetting than are less well consolidated items. The point has been taken up by Kay (1968), who indicates the logical error made in attributing a change in behaviour to separate mechanisms. Because a recently presented item is influenced by certain factors, and an old item does not appear to be influenced by these same factors, we are not justified in concluding that different mechanisms are at work or that different systems have been used. The example used by Kay may be instructive here. If a coin is dropped into water and immediately pulled out, then it shows no observable change apart from being wet. However, if the coin is left in the water for a year then distinct chemical changes are observable. This does not mean that different mechanisms are operating on the coin at different times, but that the measure used in the early observation of change is too crude to detect any difference. This is why we must take care in attributing any quantitative differences in behaviour to qualitative differences in the underlying structure of the system respon-sible for the behaviour. If recently presented items ("in primary memory") are stored on the basis of lexical features and older items ("in secondary memory") on the basis of elaborated semantic features then the differ-ence need not imply separate memories, but one memory which is em-bellished over time. Perhaps our measure of storage (i.e. the verbal res-ponse) is too crude to detect any elaborate coding for recent items. The continuation of the discussion of the issue of whether we can distinguish between the two hypothetical memory stores will first proceed through consideration of forgetting and coding phenomena.

Phonemic and semantic coding

Evidence relating to the distinction between primary memory and secondary memory has been sought by investigation of the nature of the coding of information stored in these two memory systems. Infor-mation held in primary memory has been argued to be stored on the basis of physical characteristics, and more specifically acoustic or phono-logical features, but information in secondary memory is argued to be stored on the basis of semantic features (e.g. Baddeley and Dale, 1966; Adams, 1967; Norman, 1968; Craik, 1971).

The case for acoustic coding of meaningful stimuli, whether presented aurally or visually, is by now well established. It is more debatable whether or not acoustic coding is exclusive to the contents of primary memory, and whether or not acoustic coding excludes all semantic processing. The most dogmatic "box" approach to the description of human memory might consider that primary memory stores items which are coded acoustically and without reference to their meaning, and that when these items are processed semantically they are passed into secondary memory. This view has fallen increasingly from favour with demonstrations of the existence of semantic coding in short-term memory experiments, and the existence of acoustic coding in long-term memory experiments. Supporting evidence for the process of coding into the auditory modality has come from a large number of sources.

One of the principal findings which has led us to conclude that information is recoded acoustically by the observer was reported by Conrad (1964), and his result has come to be known as the acoustic confusion effect. Conrad presented short lists of letter-names to his subjects, and asked for immediate recall. An important feature of the experimental design is that presentation was visual, using a film strip, and that recall was visual, the letters being written by the subjects. The rate of presentation was one item over ¼ seconds, and so the letters were well perceived provided that the subject was looking in the right direction and attending to the task in hand. The list of six letters presented on each trial was drawn from the set "B, C, P, T, V, F, M, N, S, X". The feature of interest in Conrad's result is that whenever a subject made a single substitution error in recall it was more likely that the erroneously recalled item would sound similar to the correct item than it would sound similar to the other set of items. Note that when the ten stimulus letters are spoken half of them commence with the vowel sound /e/ and the other half terminate with the vowel sound /i/, as in "bet" and "beet" respectively. A subject would be more likely to recall "T" when the stimulus was "B" than when the stimulus was "F". Considerable confusion was present in the subjects' responses *within* each of the two acoustically similar groupings, but there was little confusion *between* the groups. Two stimuli commencing with /e/ were quite likely to be confused with each other in recall, but a stimulus commencing with /e/ was less likely to be confused with a stimulus terminating with /i/. The presentation of stimuli was visual, and recall was visual, and yet acoustic confusion errors showed up in recall. Wickelgren (1965) excluded the possibility that this effect was due to misperception by having the subjects copy the lists of letters as they were presented. When perceptual confusions were eliminated from the results the auditory confusion effect still remained.

A second line of evidence which may be cited in favour of the argument that subjects code stimuli acoustically even when the visual coding is sufficient, or even essential, is presented by Corcoran (1966). Corcoran's subjects searched through prose passages crossing out all occurrences of the letter "e" as they did so. They missed more "e's" which were silent in speech than those which are pronounced, that is, a subject would be more likely the miss the "e" in "mile" than he would the "e" in "meal". The task did not require the subject to vocalize at any point, and yet errors occurred as a function of whether or not the target letter is vocalized in speech.

Rubinstein, Lewis and Rubinstein (1971) presented subjects with strings of letters visually, the task being to decide whether the letter-string was a word or a non-word. For instance "MAID" would be presented on a screen and the subject required (ideally) to respond "yes" as soon as possible, or "BRAKV" or "BLEAN" might be presented and the subject would (ideally) respond "no" as soon as possible. The phonemic properties of the letter-strings influenced the responses to them even though, again, the stimuli were presented visually and at no time was vocalization required. For instance, negative responses were fastest for non-word letter-strings which were unpronounceable, e.g. "BRAKV". That is, it took the least time for the subject to respond that the string was a non-word when it was also unpronounceable. Pronounceable non-words (e.g. "BLEAN") took longer for the subject to reject, and pronounceable non-words which were phonemically identical to words were rejected slowest (e.g. "BRUME", being a homophone of "BROOM"). This latter between homphones and non-homophones, again suggests that acoustic coding is relevant in tasks with no acoustic presentation of the stimulus. In constructing a phonological representation of a homophone a confusion might be said to arise over whether or not the stimulus does correspond to the item permanently stored in lexical memory. The confusion is only resolved by reference to the spelling pattern in the original visual stimulus, and this process takes more time.

These experiments lend support to the phonemic-encoding hypothesis of the processing of verbal material, which considers that a stimulus, visual or auditory, is converted into a phonological representation and that it is this representation which makes contact with lexical or categorical memory before the word-recognition process is complete. It is the maintenance of the phonological or acoustic representation which is said to correspond to storage of the stimulus in primary memory. The phonemic or phonological representation of a stimulus, which corresponds to Hintzman's (1967) articulatory representation, makes a clear distinction between the stimulus and its perception. An acoustic representation implies auditory storage of an auditory stimulus with little processing by the listener. A phonemic representation implies auditory storage of any stimulus on the basis of learnt rules of the meaning of objects. It does not necessarily imply that naming involves comprehension. Elaboration of the stimulus by the evoking of associations, images, etc. is said to correspond to storage of the stimulus in secondary memory.

We cannot argue that all meaningful stimuli are processed into memory or make contact with memory via phonological encoding. Shaffer and Shiffrin (1972) and Cohen (1973) found considerably accurate memory for complex pictures even when verbal and visual rehearsal was absent. Large numbers of complex pictures can be recognized with remarkable accuracy after hours or days (Nickerson, 1965; Shepard, 1967; Standing, 1973), and are clearly not being retained on the basis of verbal encoding. Exposure durations of the order of a few seconds do not allow formation of a verbal inventory of all of the features of the pictures, but the recognition process is not easily fooled by similar pictures to those originally presented (Allport, 1973). Baron (1973) has provided evidence which suggests that phonemic encoding is not always used when recognizing written language. His subjects were required to classify phrases as meaningful or not meaningful. For example, "HE SEAS POORLY" should gain a negative response and "HE SEES POORLY" a positive response. In this example of a negative phrase a phonological encoding would lead to a response delay whilst the spelling is checked, in comparison with a phrase which is not homophonical (e.g. "COME OVER ARE"). However, homophonic and non-homophonic phrases, to which negative responses were appropriate, did not produce different response latencies. Because "HE SEAS POORLY" sounds correct it should have led to an increased latency on the phonemic encoding hypothesis, but it did not, and Baron concludes that meaning may be derived directly from visually presented text. If this is the case, then either processing through primary memory is not always dependent upon acoustic coding, or that in certain tasks processing through an acoustically based primary memory is unnecessary.

Having established that acoustic recoding of meaningful stimuli is sometimes used by human subjects, let us now continue the discussion of whether or not acoustic coding may be associated with storage in primary memory, and semantic coding with storage in secondary memory. The effects of acoustic and semantic similarity of verbal stimuli upon recall has been investigated in a series of experiments reported by Baddeley (1966a, b). Baddeley (1966a) compared the effect of acoustic against semantic similarity upon recall of common words over short intervals. If a list was composed on random words which were acoustically similar then recall was lower than for equally long lists composed of words which were acoustically distinct. Recall of random words with different phonological characteristics was at a rate of about 75%, but with acoustically similar words the recall rate was less than 10%. With semantically related words within the same list the recall rate was around 60%. So semantic similarity does produce a recall decrement in a short-term memory situation, but the decrement is not as great as that observed for lists composed of acoustically similar words. The appearance of a semantic similarity effect in immediate recall does not refute the notion of non-semantic encoding in primary memory, of course, and astute readers will have anticipated the dualist's explanation of this and similar results, an explanation which considers that secondary memory may have been contacted even in the short-term memory situation.

The variation of the acoustic and semantic similarity effects over time was investigated by Baddeley (1966b). As in the previous experiment Baddeley found that recall of acoustically similar lists was poorer than control lists (acoustically distinct) of words over short intervals, but there was little difference between these lists on retesting 15 minutes later (see Fig. 2.4). In this experiment the same list of ten words was presented and recall required on four trials, and Fig. 2.4a indicates that the extent of the acoustic similarity effect is relatively constant over these trials. After recalling the list after the fourth presentation the subject engages in a series of digit recall trials, intended to prevent retention of the word list in primary memory, and ensure that all retrieval was from secondary memory. For semantically similar lists a different learning

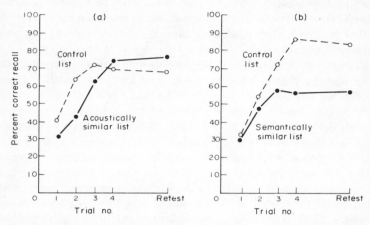

Fig. 2.4. Recall of lists which contain (a) acoustically similar words, and (b) semantically related words. (From Baddeley, 1966b.)

curve was produced, and this is presented in Fig. 2.4b. On the first few trials there is little difference between recall of the semantically dissimilar list and recall of the semantically similar list, but a disadvantage for similar material does become apparent on further trials, and is present on retesting.   Baddeley concluded that the acoustic similarity decrement indicated that acoustic coding was employed in short-term memory, and that the semantic similarity effect indicated the use of semantic coding in long-term memory.   This is undoubtedly valid, but the question still to be answered is whether the use of two types of coding confirms the distinct nature of two memory systems.

Kay's (1968) logical objection to the dualist position on the grounds that short-term differences may be immeasurable would seem less plausible if acoustic and semantic coding were demonstrated to be used exclusively by the primary and secondary memory systems respectively. However, this claim is not easily justified. Semantic coding has been found in short-term memory experiments, and acoustic coding in long-term memory. The problem is to decide whether the semantic coding in short-term memory experiments is due to a contribution from semantic memory, and similarly for acoustic coding and primary memory.

Although evidence of semantic processing in short-term memory experiments is available from a number of sources (e.g. Dale and Gregory, 1966; Loess, 1968; Wickens and Eckler, 1968; Bregman, 1968), we shall consider just one, very elegant, demonstration of the effect (Schulman, 1972). Shulman used a well-established technique in the study of human memory, that of probe recognition, whereby the subject is presented with a series of items, shortly followed by a probe or test item to which a response "yes" or "no" is required according to whether or not the probe was present in the stimulus series. In Shulman's experiment ten common words were presented serially on each trial. After the tenth word a cue was presented and indicated that the recognition response should be based on whether the probe was identical to any word in the list, or whether it was synonymous with any word in the list. The probe word was presented after the recognition cue. So, with two recognition cue conditions, and two possible responses with each condition we have four experimental conditions — subjects might be instructed to search for an identical word or a synonym of the probe, and might have to respond "yes" or "no" in either condition. This design is perfectly straightforward so far, but Shulman introduced a fifth condition to investigate any semantic encoding of the list members on presentation. In this condition subjects were instructed by the recognition cue to search for a word identical with any word in the list, but the probe was a synonym of one of the list members. The response in this condition should be "no" because the cue indicates that the probe relates to an identical word, but if the subject had encoded the list members semantically then false "yes" responses might appear. In the condition where subjects were cued to search for an identical word but were then presented with an unrelated word the mean proportion of false "yes" responses was 11% of all trials. This gives a base line for false recognitions when searching for an identical word. In the critical condition, with an "identical" cue and a synonymous probe the false recognition rate was 19% of all responses. This comparison demonstrates an increased tendency to make a false recognition as a consequence of the semantic similarity between the item in the list and the item to be scrutinized. Subjects were not cued to search for semantic similarity in any trial until the end of the presentation but this was nevertheless a task demand on a large number of trials and so they may have been encoding semantically during presentation of the list.

Semantic information may be stored and used in a short-term memory situation, we do not have to rely upon the acoustic or phonemic attributes of the stimulus.

The large number of results proclaiming no effect of semantic similarity in primary memory (e.g. Kintsch and Buschke, 1969, Craik and Levy, 1970; Baddeley and Levy, 1971) may only be considered as representing the absence of semantic coding in primary memory if they can also explain how semantic similarity effects show through in other experiments. To argue that coding in the two memory systems is flexible and that complete intercommunication between the two systems necessitates a common code serves only to eliminate a distinction between the two systems, and makes the dualist position even less defensible. A more valid objection to those results indicating the use of semantic coding in short-term memory relies upon some interaction between the items being remembered and information stored in secondary memory. Baddeley (1972) considers that the results of Shulman and others are due to the use of retrieval strategies which are dependent upon secondary memory. In the synonym recognition task subjects may have been recoding the probe into any number of its synonyms and searching the list for a word phonemically identical to the generated synonym. For example, given the "synonym" cue and the word "male" as the probe item, the subject may then generate the word "man" himself and search his memory of the list for any word which is phonemically identical to "man". It is difficult to see why the subject should engage in synonym generation activities when presented with the "identical" cue. Much more likely is that the subject has a semantically encoded list which is semantically confusable with the probe word when the probe is an inappropriate synonym.

In addition to semantic coding being demonstrated in short-term memory experiments, a number of results indicate that acoustic coding may be employed over long retention intervals. If secondary memory does not use a different form of coding from primary memory then the justification for the division of categorical memory is again weakened. Perhaps the most convincing demonstration of acoustic interference in secondary memory is also the simplest. This is the tip-of-the-tongue phenomenon (Brown and McNeill, 1966), and is an effect common to all of us from experience. When attempting to recall the name of a place

or a person, or a particularly apt adjective to describe something or someone, the process of recall gives us considerable insight into the organization of memory and the systems used to locate an item in storage. When
we know a meaning which we are attempting to express in a single word
it is often the case that we generate a number of alternatives. These
alternatives may all be semantically related to the word sought after,
but they may be rejected very rapidly unless they are also acoustically
related to the target word. Thus, when attempting to recall the name
of the town in which a particular friend lives the alternatives retrieved
may all be towns (i.e. semantically related) but a large number of them
may have certain features in common with the phonological representation of the correct town. For example, suppose that the correct town
is "Farnborough", then in addition to the names of towns in which other
friends live one might also retrieve the alternatives, "Farnham, Farns-
field, Flamborough". These retrieved words indicate that the search
process in secondary memory is not restricted to using semantic information. Phonological features are important, and a word may be accepted or rejected on the basis of the sound of any of the phonemes or the
number of syllables even though the word is being retrieved from a store
of semantic information. Brown and McNeill (1966) tested the validity
of this intuition by providing subjects with dictionary definitions of
uncommon words and asking them to respond with the word most appropriate to the definition. When the word could not be recalled successfully subjects would often know the first letter of the word of the number
of syllables it contained. Categorical memory contains information which
is retrievable on the basis of any number of attributes, recall after long
intervals does not rely entirely upon semantic cues.

As a special instance of acoustic coding being as useful as semantic
coding over a long interval, an experiment reported by Bruce and Crowley
(1970) in particular challenges the differentiation of categorical memory
on the basis of coding. Bruce and Crowley presented their subjects with
lists which were 32 words in length. After presentation of each list, at
the rate of one word every 2 seconds, the subject was engaged in a distraction task for 30 seconds before attempting to recall the words in the
list. The presence of the distraction task ensures that retrieval is from
secondary memory only. Two experimental and one control conditions
were used. In the experimental conditions four words in each list were

either acoustically similar (e.g. "gain, cane, reign, rein"), or semantically related (e.g. "bean, carrot, corn, potato"). All other words in experimental conditions, and in lists in the control condition were semantically related. The acoustic relationship between all words (other than the four critical words in the experimental condition) was determined randomly. The four critical words in the acoustic similarity and semantic similarity conditions were arranged in the list in one of three ways. They were either distributed evenly over the whole list (occupying list positions 5, 6, 7, and 8), or grouped together near the beginning of the list (positions 26, 27, 28, and 29), or grouped together near the end of the list (positions 5, 13, 21, and 29). The recall results from these three distributions for the three similarity conditions are presented in Fig. 2.5 a, b, c. When the four critical words were distributed over the whole 32 words in the list there was no advantage for recall of acoustically related words over lists composed of unrelated words, and there was a slight advantage for semantically related words. On the other hand, whenever the acoustically related or semantically related words were presented together they were recalled much more successfully than unrelated words presented in the same list positions in the control lists. Retrieval from secondary memory was facilitated by similarity between items whether the similarity was along a semantic dimension or an acoustic dimension. Acoustic coding can occur in secondary memory if the subject finds that addressing items along this dimension is useful. One limitation to the use of acoustic cues is that the items to be encoded on the basis of this characteristics must be presented together. This temporal contiguity may be interpreted as being essential because the relevant items must all be in primary memory together, if a dualist position is taken, or because acoustic features are quickly lost if they are deemed by the subject to be unimportant, if a single-trace position is taken. Whichever interpretation is made, the experiment does show that retrieval from secondary memory may be based upon the acoustic features of the words in store. Klein (1972) has similarly found that acoustic similarity and semantic similarity between items can each affect recall over long and short intervals. After hearing lists of words which were acoustically or semantically similar or were unrelated, subjects engaged in a distractor task for a variable interval. A single item was then presented as a probe to which the subject had to respond "yes" or "no" according to whether he recognized it as part

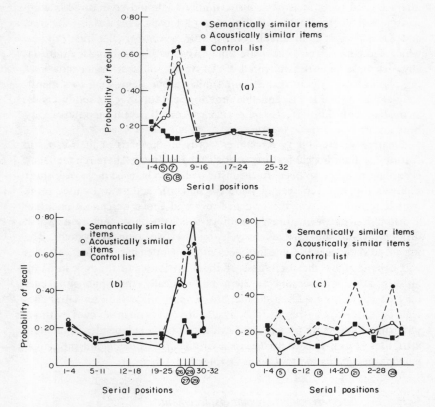

Fig. 2.5. Serial position curves for the recall of lists containing semantically related words, acoustically similar words and control lists, when the critical words were presented (a) early, (b) late or (c) distributed in the list. (From Bruce and Crowley, 1970.)

of the list. Over long and short intervals subjects made more recognition errors with acoustically similar lists than with semantically similar lists. If acoustic coding was used for storage in primary memory then we would expect greater confusion with acoustically similar material over short intervals. However, if semantic coding was used in secondary memory then greater semantic confusion should be evident over long intervals, and the effects of acoustic similarity should be resolved in comparison with their effects over the shorter intervals. This was not the case, and Klein's result is in direct conflict with a number of earlier studies, which show no effect of acoustic similarity over long intervals. Additionally, response latencies mirrored these trends. Subjects were slower at responding correctly to acoustically similar probe items than to semantically similar probe items, and this ordering held for all retention intervals. Acoustic confusion effects were evident for all retention intervals by both accuracy and speed measures.

Clearly, we are able to remember words on the basis of their acoustic features or their lexical features over all time intervals. There is a tendency according to some sources, for acoustic coding to be used more over short intervals (up to a few seconds) and for semantic coding to be used more over long intervals. On the evidence reviewed above we cannot maintain a distinction between primary memory and secondary memory in which different codes are used exclusively by the two memory systems. The use of acoustic cues in some instances and semantic cues in other instances will depend upon the usefulness of these attributes to the task in hand. Shortly after representing an item phonemically then phonemic cues may be the most readily available, but if appropriate then semantic cues will be used for retrieval. The availability of semantic cues without phonemic cues being present, and evidence of the independence of these attributes is available from the areas of dichotic listening and subliminal perception which are discussed in Chapter 5.

Forgetting: Interference, decay and displacement

Loss of information which is being stored by virtue of its acoustic or phonological features alone could be argued to be a result of decay or displacement of the memory trace, and loss of accessibility of semantically coded information might be due to interference between similar items. To demonstrate different causes of forgetting which can be argued to be specific to memory systems would be to offer strong evidence in favour of a multi-store view of memory, especially if these distinct causes of forgetting can be related to specific features of primary and secondary memory already discussed.

Primary memory, which is said to store a very limited amount of information on the basis of acoustic features, is also said to fail to retain information because of autonomous decay of the unattended memory trace and because of displacement. We have seen that primary memory has a limited capacity; it can only retain between two and four words at any time and the capacity is unaffected by semantic relationships between the words, and by speed of presentation. One of the more explicit descriptions of a memory system incorporating the notion of fixed capacity views primary memory as a buffer store (Atkinson and Shiffrin, 1968). If primary memory is synonymous with the rehearsal buffer with a fixed number of "slots" into which incoming items may be placed, then the moment that more items are presented than there are slots in memory items start to be lost by displacement. This model of memory is presented in Fig. 2.6. Each item which is passed out of the sensory register into the short-term store or primary memory stays there until displaced by an item which follows it. If the rehearsal buffer is full when an item is presented then one of the old items is displaced and no longer available. The longer an item is maintained in the rehearsal buffer the more information about it is transferred to secondary memory.

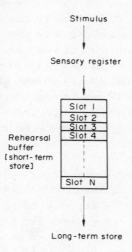

Fig. 2.6. The model of memory proposed by Atkinson and Shiffrin (1968). Primary memory here is a rehearsal buffer of limited capacity.

Items which are rehearsed frequently are more likely to be transferred than items which are not and retrieval is dependent upon presence in either of the two memory systems. If the item is present in the rehearsal buffer then retrieval can be relatively efficient, although a selective search for particular semantic attributes may be fruitless. If the item has been transferred to secondary memory then a semantically directed search would be necessary.

The displacement principle can account for the recency effect in the recall of serial presentations by considering the final few items not to have been displaced by any information which follows them. As these items spend more time in the rehearsal buffer than do centrally positioned items they have more information about them retained in secondary memory. This view of the recency effect is supported by the suffix experiments of Crowder and Morton and their colleagues. The suffix may be acting as a displacing item, reducing the number of list members being stored in primary memory. The fact that the next to last item of a non-suffix list does not have the same probability of recall as the last item in a suffix list (both of these items being the last but one auditory stimulus to be presented) does indicate that the suffix effect is not one of item-for-item displacement. When an additional item is presented to primary memory a single whole item may not be displaced, but some information from each of the items in store may be lost. For instance, if primary memory is storing a list of common words when an additional word is entered, then a feature may be lost which would otherwise distinguish "pat" from "bat" and other similar sounding words. The item would not be lost altogether but only part of the item would be retrievable as a result of a new item redirecting the subject's attention away from other items in store.

An alternative account of the recency effect, and of loss of information from primary memory, involves the notion of trace decay. As the final items in a list are not followed by further information which may attract the subject's attention they may be argued to have a longer decay onset latency than earlier items. The longer an item is being attended to the more delayed is the onset of the decay process (Brown, 1958), and hence the greater is the probability of the item being stored permanently. The process of decay may be equivalent to the adding of neuronal noise to the stored representation. Thus as the item decays when it is not being attended to noise is added and discriminating features are lost. The capacity of primary memory might then reflect the allocation of attention to items recently perceived. If item (i)1 is still available in an undecayed state when attention is directed toward item (i)2 then the capacity of primary memory is at least two items. However, if item (i)1 is not available because of decay when attention is directed to item (i)2 and then to item (i)3, and if items (i)2 and (i)3 are still available then the capacity of primary memory is two items only. Capacity would then be related to the rate of decay of unattended items. The simple version of this theory is unacceptable unless all words require similar amounts of attention for recirculation. Frequency of occurrence in language would have to make no difference to the attention required for maintenance because this factor does not influence the capacity of primary memory. That it would take no longer to maintain a four-syllable word than a one-syllable word seems an unlikely premise, but the additional redundant features of longer words may provide cues which would not all be lost by decay and which may serve retrieval and rehearsal. If only one feature of an item survives the decay process then retrieval may be possible, but if the item has only one distinctive feature and if this feature is lost through decay then retrieval will not be possible. Further, an experiment reported by Clifton and Tash (1973) indicates that searching one-syllable words held in memory is as fast as searching three-syllable words, indicating that the redundancy principle may be valid.

Trace decay has been seen as a feature which is specific to the temporary memory system (e.g. Broadbent, 1958), and the presence and absence of forgetting by decay may be seen as another distinction on which dual-storage theorists can base their argument. A major alternative in the account of forgetting has been Interference Theory, and at one time these two theories were considered to be in direct competition with each other, to be mutually exclusive. Current views allow for a compromise, with trace decay accounting for forgetting under some conditions and interference between items operating under other conditions. A dual-storage view holds that forgetting in primary memory is a result of decay or displacement of the trace, and that forgetting in secondary memory is a result of semantic interference between items. As with evidence from the acoustic and semantic confusion effects, disproof of the specific nature of causes of forgetting does not disprove the dual-storage theory but it does weaken the case if a feature which may distinguish between operations can be demonstrated to be untenable. Whereas the displacement principle would clearly be appropriate to any system which has a limited capacity both interference and decay principles can apply to a system of limited or unlimited capacity. The effects of interference and decay are not easily differentiated, but attempts to do so will now be considered separately.

The Interference Theory of forgetting considers that recall is impaired by the learning of other events (previous and subsequent) which make the memory trace less accessible. Information is not lost altogether, but the breakdown of associations between items causes information to be difficult or impossible to retrieve. Using a filing system analogy forgetting by interference is seen as the accurate storage of information (i.e. sheets of paper are preserved in the filing cabinet) but their addresses are lost or jumbled (i.e. the sheet may be in the wrong order or the index cards referring to the sheets may be lost or otherwise useless). Information is stored accurately but because the system has become overloaded we are unable to retrieve it efficiently. The basic principles of Interference Theory were first stated in detail by McGeoch (1932) in his article "Forgetting and the law of disuse", disuse being argued to have no effect upon storage and thus being in conflict with a lay account of forgetting. Disuse over a period of time cannot have any effect upon retention, but processes which are active during this period can do so, whether they are interference or decay processes. McGeoch was concerned mainly with the forgetting due to the learning of subsequent events. This is known as retroactive interference (sometimes referred to as retroactive inhibition). The principle of retroactive interference holds that the learning of an association between the two items or events A and B is maintained despite disuse, and that failure to retrieve B, given A, is due to the learning of other associations between A and C, or A and D. In a retention test we might expect that given A when the response B is required, the response C might be offered in error. In the laboratory the paradigm most often used to test Interference Theory is that of paired-associate learning. The subject is required to learn lists of pairs of words (e.g. "FISH-CHAIR, HAT-BOOK, . . ."), and in testing is presented with one number of a pair and asked to provide its associate. So, if on subsequent trials we present the subject with a list of pairs of the type "FISH-WINDOW,

HAT-BICYCLE, . . ." then on retesting with the original list when "CHAIR" would again be the appropriate response to "FISH", retroactive interference from the second set of learning trials might lead to the inappropriate response "WINDOW". Although paired associate experiments facilitate the study of interference effects, and have been used extensively, the retroactive interference phenomenon has general applications and appears in many situations involving memory. In the recall of a single list, for example, the failure to recall early members of the list may be said to be due to retroactive interference from later members of the list. McGeoch's hypothesis was that response competition between early and later associations was the only source of forgetting, that there should be a perfect correlation between the failure to recall the item B given A, and errors of commission in responding C when B is required. This is not always so, however, and was demonstrated to be false by Melton and Irwin (1940). Their subjects were first presented with a list of eighteen nonsense syllables, one syllable at a time, and the list was presented five times. Each time a syllable was presented the subject was requested to anticipate which syllable would be presented next. Thirty minutes after the end of these trials the subject was required to relearn the original list of eighteen nonsense syllables to a criterion of two perfect anticipations of the whole list. During the 30-minute interval the subjects engaged in an interpolated activity. They were presented with a second list of nonsense syllables during this interval and required to learn the list using the anticipatory response method with up to forty presentations of the list. The interpolated activity allowed a variable amount of retroactive interference to act upon the retention of the original list. The effect of retroactive interference in the experiment is indicated in Fig. 2.7, as a function of the number of learning trials with the interpolated list. The "Absolute R1" in Fig. 2.7. is derived from the difference in recall of the original list before and after the 30-minute interval. The retroactive interference attributable to "overt competition" is the interference predicted to account for all forgetting by McGeoch. The number of intrusions from the interpolated list increases as this list is presented more often, but this is only true up to a certain point. After about ten anticipation trials the number of intrusions in the recall of the test list start to fall off. The recall of interpolated items when original list items are appropriate cannot account for all of the forgetting of the original

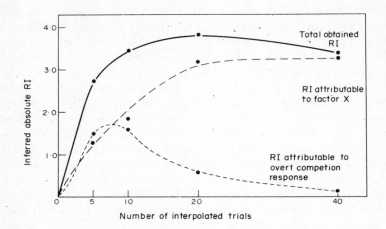

Fig. 2.7. Relationship between the amount of RI and the degree of learning of the interpolated material. (From Melton and Irwin, 1940.)

list, and by subtracting the retroactive interference due to intrusions from the total amount of interference observed Melton and Irwin derive the existence of a second factor which is causing forgetting. This second factor is described rather dramatically in Fig. 2.7. as "Factor X", and can be seen to increase with the amount of interpolated activity. Factor X accounts for almost all of the forgetting when the subject engages in forty anticipatory trials, and is concluded to be the breaking up or unlearning of the associations between members of the original list. Melton and Irwin's two-factor theory of forgetting considers that forgetting is due to competing responses of subsequently learnt material and to subsequent learning breaking up the previous associations.

The mechanism of unlearning was considered by Benton J. Underwood (1948) to be the same mechanism as other workers had described as extinction. Associations which were not reinforced were said to be weakened, and this is the process of unlearning. Evidence of unlearning is provided by an experiment reported by Barnes and Underwood (1959). They presented subjects with two lists of paired associates of the type A-B, A-C. Subjects were then presented with the stimulus word A and asked to recall both B and C, and to indicate which list each response was from. This is a non-competitive response situation: B does not have to withstand competition from C in order to be recalled. The task was not paced, and so a momentarily dominant response needed not to displace a weaker response altogether: if both responses were available then both could have been given. Barnes and Underwood found that the more A-C learning trials were given then the greater was the probability of recall of C, but that recall of B decreased. When more exposure to the A-C association was given, the A-B association became increasingly unavailable, and this loss of availability is said to be due to unlearning.

Although Melton and Irwin (1940) mentioned proactive interference as a cause of forgetting it was left to B.J. Underwood (1957) to demonstrate that it is a major source of forgetting. Items at the beginning of a list cause considerable forgetting of items subsequently presented. If a subject learns a list of verbal items and is retested 24 hours later he will show forgetting of about 75% of the original list. McGeoch's theory accounted for this forgetting by arguing that material learned during the retention interval interfered retroactively with the test list. The interfering material was said to be anything that the subject learned outside of the laboratory. Underwood rejected this notion, arguing that the dissimilarity of the extra-experimental material to the test material could not possibly account for a forgetting rate of 75%, and instead that forgetting was largely due to sources of proactive interference. Proactive interference from earlier laboratory experience with similar material affects the retention of a test list over this interval, or any interval, and this can be demonstrated by using subjects with varying degrees of experience as subjects in verbal learning experiments. In comparing the success of recall with the number of trials given to subjects prior to the list under consideration Underwood's review of the literature led to the observation that a greater amount of prior learning reduced the probability of recalling a subsequent item. If a subject was presented with a single test list and tested on that list 24 hours later then recall would be at the rate of above 75% of the list. If the subject is given twenty trials the twenty-first list will be recalled at the rate of above 25% after 24 hours. Failure to recall 50% of the twenty-first list is thus accountable to presentation of the twenty previous lists, and to proactive interference from these lists.

A further notion which B.J. Underwood has responsibility for promoting is that of spontaneous recovery. If the process of unlearning of early associations is similar to the sources of experimental extinction then characteristics of extinction should be in evidence as unlearning proceeds. Pavlov (1927) reported that if a classically conditioned response is allowed to become extinct, then the response may show signs of recovery after some interpolated activity or rest. The conditioned response is described as having spontaneously recovered, and if unlearning of an association is the same as extinction then the association should also show signs of spontaneous recovery. Underwood (1948) tested the prediction using lists of words in an A-B, A-C, design. At various intervals after learning of the two lists the subjects were presented with the A member of each pair and asked to recall the B or C member, whichever was available to them. Over short retention intervals many more C members were offered in response than were B members, but whereas the number of B responses remained constant over time (up to 48 hours) the number of C responses decreased considerably. Two factor theory predicts that A-B associations should have been unlearnt during the learning of the A-C associations, but after 48 hours there was little difference between the overall recall of B and C responses. Unlearning of the A-B associations should have led to a superiority of recall of A-C associations, which are argued to be responsible for the unlearning. Extinction of A-B associations may be able to account for these data if these associations also undergo spontaneous recovery, as Underwood suggested. Briggs (1954) provided evidence which supports the notion of spontaneous recovery in verbal learning experiments, finding that memory for associations can improve over time without being used. It is the spontaneous recovery of A-B associations which contributes to the proactive interference responsible for forgetting of A-C associations. If A-B associations are unlearnt but do not recover, then they could not interfere with subsequently learnt material.

The empirical flaw with spontaneous recovery is that whereas it correctly predicts the decreasing recall of A-C associations through increasing proactive interference from recovering A-B associations, it should also predict that A-B associations would be increasingly available as they recover. In Underwood's (1948) experiment recall of the original associations remained constant throughout the course of the experiment.

To account for this anomaly Ceraso (1967) has postulated another construct. This leads to an account of the forgetting of paired associates which is intuitively more acceptable. Ceraso describes forgetting not entirely in terms of the interaction between the first and second list, but also as a function of the subject's ability to discriminate between the lists. Shortly after presentation of the two lists the subject is able to differentiate between A-B associations and A-C associations, to think of one list without thinking of the other. Ceraso describes this isolation as being lost over time, and as a result the two lists tend increasingly to merge with each other, a process which he calls "crowding".

If the two lists do merge, then the decline in recall after 24 hours should affect the words in both lists. However, in Underwood's (1948) experiment recall of list 1 remained constant over time, and only recall of list 2 declined. Some factor is needed which counteracts the effects of crowding and accounts for the stability of recall of list 1. This factor is spontaneous recovery.

Interference Theory clearly has difficulty in explaining all of the forgetting phenomena which Interference Theorists are able to demonstrate (see Postman (1969) and Postman and Underwood (1973) for recent developments). The basic processes at work being the items in store becoming indistinguishable from each other with time, or items competing with each other during response, or the associations between items being unlearnt. Interference between associations can account for the failure to recall items which have been stored in secondary memory; it has difficulty in accounting for all failures to recall items and in accounting for the use of some associations which were predicted to have been unavailable.

McGeoch (1932) argued very strongly that interference was the cause of forgetting and that decay was an unsound concept. The Functionalist School of verbal learning theorists, who continued to argue that all forgetting was due to interference with associations, rejected the possibility that the "mystical decay or disuse theory" (Ekstrand, 1972) could account for any recall failures on the grounds that processes which occur over time are not caused by the time itself. Time is not a causal variable but it does allow the activity of other causal variables. To use Kay's (1968) example once more, a coin left in water will change colour over time but time has not caused the change. Time allows causal variables to operate. Some theorists (e.g. Hebb, 1949; Brown, 1954, 1958; Broadbent, 1958) consider that recently presented material may decay autonomously under certain circumstances and that a permanent representation of the material will not then be formed and stored. Decay of the memory trace may correspond to a failure to consolidate a reverberating, dynamic representation and form a permanent, structural representation. If consolidation requires the attention of the subject, as in the model of Waugh and Norman (1965) for instance, and if attention is directed away from the memory trace, then the trace will decay. Interference theorists consider that once acqui- red the trace is always preserved, but that its associations may be lost.

Evidence of the operation of the decay principle in short-term retention has already been presented in this chapter, in the form of the experiment reported by Peterson and Peterson (1959). When rehearsal of a single item was prevented by requiring the subject to perform a counting task then recall of the single item was an inverse function of the time engaged on counting. The interpolated activity involved material which was not similar to the retention material, and interference theory should there- fore predict no interference between the two activities. A more complete check on the amount of forgetting which is due to interference in short- term retention was reported by Brown (1958). He varied the similarity of the interpolated material to the retained material, decay theory pre- dicting no difference in the effect of similar and dissimilar distracting material upon retention, and interference theory predicting more for- getting if the distracting material is similar to the test material. The test material was four pairs of consonants presented visually at the rate of one pair every 1·33 seconds, and the subject was required to read aloud these consonants as they were shown. The distracting material was either three pairs of digits or a further three pairs of consonants, also presented visually and read aloud by the subject on presentation. The interval between presentation and test of the four consonants was held constant regardless of the nature of the interpolated material, and also in a control condition where no interpolated material was presented. With no dis- tracting material, Brown observed 67·3% recall of the test material. With similar interpolated material recall was 25·.6% of the test material, and with dissimilar interpolated material recall was 30·6%. The presence of the distracting material certainly has an interfering effect in this experiment, but the absence of a differential effect of similar and dissimilar material indicates that interference between associations has not occurred to any great extent, but that the process of maintenance of the items in memory has been interfered with: the test items had been allowed to decay. Most of the forgetting in this experiment appears to be due to the presence of an interpolated task, regardless of its nature. Directing attention to the interpolated task serves to permit the unattended memory trace to decay.

This result does not rule out the operation of interference altogether, but it does support the predictions of trace decay theory more clearly. In the same experiment, Brown also observed the effect of preceding redundant information upon recall of the four consonant pairs. Subjects either had to read out three irrelevant consonant pairs or to read out three digit pairs before presentation of the test material. The subjects attempted to recall the test material after the same silent interval used in the control condition. The control condition with no redundant material before or after the text material, led to recall of 67·3% of the test material, and processing of three digits before the test items led to 65·5% recall: no effect. However, presenting three consonant pairs before the test items led to 58·6% recall of the four test consonant pairs. This difference in the effect of similar and dissimilar redundant material indicates that the proactive interference phenomenon does operate in a short term retention situation.

Data reported by Waugh and Norman (1965) may also be interpreted as indicating that interference effects are observable in short-term retention situations. They presented lists of sixteen digits follows by a probe item which was a repeat of a digit presented in the preceding list. On hearing the probe digit the subject was required to respond with the digit that followed it in the list. Two rates of presentation were used, one digit per second and four digits per second, but the two recall curves for this experiment are very similar. The rate of presentation has little effect upon the recall of a single item regardless of the position of that item. Simple decay theory predicts that the forgetting curve for the slower presentation should be steeper than that for the fast presentation. If the presentation is slow then the time between each item permits more decay. On the other hand, interference theory predicts that forgetting will be a function of the number of items presented between the test item and recall. More items intervening between presentation and recall will mean that more retroactive interference will occur. Forgetting was a function of the number of items presented between the test item and its recall, and recall was invariant with rate of presentation. Waugh and Norman's conclusion, that the result confirms interference theory and dismisses decay theory, is quite unsupportable. Decay theory is dismissed because items presented once every second are recalled as well as items presented once every second. The item in serial position twelve (i.e. four from the end of the list) will have been heard 4 seconds from the end of the list in one case and 1 second from the end in the other case. If decay is time dependent then an item in any serial position should be recalled easier with the fast presentation rate, and a shorter delay between presentation and recall. However, the data are not unequivocal, and the design fails to eliminate the possibility of subjects rehearsing the slow digits during the presentation. When items are presented once every second then the extra opportunity for decay may be counteracted by the extra opportunity to strengthen the memory trace. Digits presented every ¼ second may not be rehearsed at all, but digits presented every second may be attended to and more permanent traces formed.

A viable alternative interpretation of the Waugh and Norman result considers forgetting to be a function of displacement from an immediate memory system which has limited capacity (Murdock, 1964). In this memory system the rate of presentation would be inconsequential (over a narrow range, at least) as would the nature of the intervening material. The fixed capacity may be viewed as a store with a limited number of "slots" into which items may be placed, or alternatively as a store which can only encode information at a certain rate. A limitation on the rate of processing information could account for the Waugh and Norman result by arguing that items presented at the fast rate were not encoded optimally but were not forgotten very rapidly. Items presented at the slow rate may have been encoded accurately, but also forgotten more. A limitation on the number of slots in memory, or on the number of features remembered at any one time, could also account for the invariance of recall with rate of presentation. Waugh and Norman found that the probability of recall depended upon the number of items presented between the test time and its recall. Displacement theory predicts exactly this relationship. If an item is still in one of the slots it is more likely to be recalled than if it has been displaced by a large number of intervening items. The absence of an effect of rate of presentation may be described by any number of theories of forgetting.

A distinction between two memory systems on the basis of two forgetting functions is further criticized by Keppel and Underwood (1962) who argued that interference theory can explain the data of Peterson and Peterson (1959), which is one of the principal supportive experiments of decay theory. Peterson and Peterson found that the probability of recall of a single item depended upon the amount of time spent on a rehearsal-preventing task during the retention interval. The material used to distract the subject from thinking about the test item was not similar to the test material, and so retroactive interference was ruled out as a source of forgetting. Keppel and Underwood pointed out that the result was due to proactive interference from previous trials. Trial 1 for each subject showed very little forgetting of a single item in the Brown-Peterson distraction situation, regardless of the length of the distraction interval up to 18 seconds. Retention of a single item for 3 seconds remained high, but as the experiment progressed (and proactive interference built up from previous trials) retention over an 18-second distraction interval declines. The relationships between retention interval, probability of recall, and number of previous trials in the experiment are indicated in Fig. 2.8. The decay curve provided by Peterson and Peterson is therefore only appropriate for a subject who has a maximum amount of proactively interfering material from previous trials. It is not applicable to the recall of a single item in isolation.

The build-up of proactive interference is a demonstrable effect in itself, and has lately been used to demonstrate that interference does not affect forgetting in primary memory. Wickens, Born and Allen (1963) had their subjects recall lists of digits on three trials, and then on the fourth and succeeding trials these subjects either recalled more lists of digits or they recalled lists of letters. Similar groups of subjects started by recalling lists of letters and then either continued with the same material, or were changed to lists of digits. This counterbalancing is necessary so that any differences on the fourth trial are due to a change of material *per se*, and not to differences in the intrinsic difficulty of the material. During the first three trials, with all groups of subjects, interference

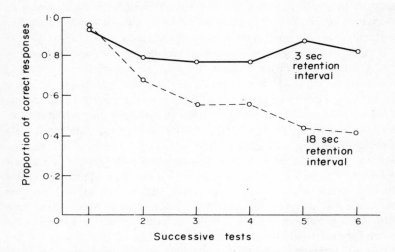

Fig.2.8. Recall of single items following a retention interval during which rehearsal was prevented. (From Keppel and Underwood, 1962.)

theory predicts that recall will decline due to the build-up of proactive interference from the previous trials. This decline is evident in Fig. 2.9. If subjects continued recalling material from the old class of items (whether digits or letters) then recall remained at a low level after the fourth trial. If subjects were presented with a new class of material to remember on the fourth trial then recall was much higher, and approached the level of performance achieved on the first trial of the experiment. The increase in recall ability with a change of material is known as the release-from-proactive-interference effect. Craik and Birtwistle (1971) used this effect to demonstrate that proactive interference does not operate upon the information stored in primary memory. Subjects recalled eight lists, each of fifteen words, and the recall responses were broken down into their primary memory and secondary memory components. Whereas the number of words recalled from secondary memory declined as more trials were completed, the primary memory component

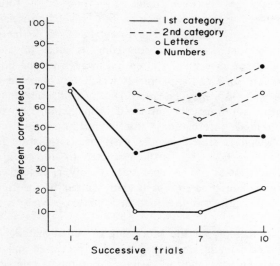

Fig. 2.9. Recall over successive trials as a function of previous trials with the same or different category of items. Trials represented by the dotted lines are the changed category on the fourth trial of the experiment. Recall is improved on these trials in comparison with trials which continue to use the same category of material. (From Wickens, Born and Allen, 1963.)

remained relatively stable at approximately three words. This alone is evidence of the invariance of storage in primary memory when increasing amounts of interfering material are present, but a further condition of their experiment was even more convincing. Subjects recalled lists of fifteen words which were related in meaning for four trials, and on the fifth trial they either recalled another fifteen-word list from the same semantic category or the category was changed. The change of category had no effect upon recall of the words in primary memory, but the number of words recalled from secondary memory increased in the way described by Wickens *et al.* (1963).

Memory Codes and Forgetting

The release-from-proactive-interference experiments indicate that semantic interference between items does not cause forgetting of information stored in primary memory, but only of information being retained in secondary memory. The Brown-Peterson distractor experiments indicate that short-term forgetting is due to autonomous decay following the diversion of attention away from the information. The suffix experiments and experiments which vary the rate of presentation of items in lists may be interpreted as indicating that recently presented information may be displaced from memory by even more recently presented information. Interference operates only upon information which is stored on the basis of its semantic features, a property which we have seen to be restricted to storage in secondary memory (or at least so far as dual trace theory is concerned). Decay and displacement are processes particularly suited to the forgetting of acoustically coded information stored in a limited capacity system such as primary memory.

The role of memory in the processing of verbal material is seen as follows. A visual stimulus may be perceived, processed and responded to without reference to auditory memory, but this is rare (e.g. Baron, 1973). It is more often the case that all stimuli, visual or auditory, are processed using what Posner (1969) describes as the "name code", a process which involves the acoustic or articulatory recoding of the stimulus into a form which may be stored in permanent memory. An aurally presented stimulus may be stored acoustically, as the suffix experiments demonstrate. Acoustical storage is precategorical, and as soon as the stimulus is categorized by the listener it is stored in a phonemic code. This does not mean that all of the acoustical features of the stimulus are lost, for Cole, Coltheart, and Allard (1974) have shown that memory for non-categorical physical features of an auditory stimulus can persist for up to 8 seconds, well over the duration of storage in precategorical acoustic storage. Phonemic storage of a stimulus uses acoustic cues as the basis of storage, but the cues are provided by the subject. Phonemic storage is the result of analysis-by-synthesis in the sense indicated by Neisser (1967) and when the subject retrieves information stored on the basis of phonemic cues he may be retrieving an auditory image of what the word would have sounded like had the subject uttered it himself. It is storage at the phonemic level of processing which leads to the acoustic confusion effect with acoustically (and therefore phonemically) similar materials. If the phonemic representation is not renewed by rehearsal within a certain short interval then features distinguishing it from representations of other stimuli are lost: the item is said to have decayed. More similar representations will require the rehearsals to be more frequent for distinctive features not to be lost quickly, and this is the basis of the acoustic confusion effect. An item is said to be lost by the continuous action of neural noise. If the item is attended to then the signal-to-noise ratio is kept at a high level, but if it is unattended then noise acts to reduce the number of features by which the item may be retrieved.

Displacement effects can be accounted for by this theory without resort to a "slot" approach in the naive sense. Decay is the principal cause of forgetting of phonemic characteristics, and decay is given opportunity to operate by the diversion of attention from the item. Attention is necessary for the maintenance of the representation. Suppose that a list of four items can be just adequately stored on the basis of their phonemic codes, and that the rehearsal rate is one item per ¼ second. Each item will be rehearsed once every second, thus renewing the representation. We can conclude from this that the features of any item are not lost by decay over a 1-second interval. However, if a fifth item is presented rehearsal at the same rate will mean that each item is rehearsed once every 1¼ seconds. Suppose now that decay over a 1¼-second interval leads to the loss of a discriminating feature. We can no longer differentiate between item $i(1)$ and item $i(2)$, and the number of items recalled remains at four: we may be able to recall $i(1)$ *or* $i(2)$. The addition of the fifth item to the list is said to displace one of the other four items, but the cause of the forgetting is the limited rate of rehearsal. If we had been able to rehearse at the rate of one item every fifth of a second then autonomous decay would not have reduced the features of any of the items.

Displacement is also considered to be responsible for the action of an auditory suffix placed at the end of a list of auditory items (Crowder and Morton, 1969). If the suffix is not presented then the final items in the list can be retrieved from PAS and have an increased recall probability. PAS may be argued to have limited capacity and be therefore vulnerable to displacement, but decay can also explain this result. Suppose that unless items in PAS are categorized rapidly they decay: not an unlikely supposition. When the suffix is delayed information about the final items may be read out of PAS into the phonemic code, but delaying the suffix beyond 2 seconds makes no difference to recall of the final items indicating that the life of an item in PAS is less than 2 seconds. PAS need not be said to have limited capacity, for rapid decay is a property sufficient to explain the data, with the action of the suffix being the same as the action of neural noise. If an item is not read out of PAS quickly, and represented phonemically, then it may be overlaid by neural noise or by suffix noise. However, this is a theoretical treatment, and at the present time the issue of whether PAS is a limited capacity system is an open one. Loss of items from PAS may occur through decay or through displacement, the present discussion describes displacement as forced decay or loss of discriminating features. It finds nothing to support the limited capacity proposition, and limits on the extent of recency, etc., are considered to reflect limited readout times.

Limited processing rates may also account for the narrow range of estimates of primary memory. Estimates of approximately three items for the capacity of primary memory may simply be statements of the maximum number of items which can be rehearsed sequentially without loss of discriminating features by decay. Primary memory is thus not a distinct entity or box, but is a rehearsal loop, or phonological memory. The central questions posed by this chapter are whether or not we can reduce categorical memory to a number of discrete components, and what are the functions of the components. It is difficult to conceive of a function of a primary memory which is a much reduced version of secondary memory, with similar coding and forgetting functions but grossly different capacity. It is not difficult to conceive of primary memory as a rehearsal loop which stores words for a certain period after which they decay unless rehearsed again. Such a rehearsal loop would not be vulnerable to information loss by semantic interference because the meanings of the words rehearsed would have little effect upon their recirculation. Retrieval of words from primary memory, in the release-from-proactive-interference experiments and all-list recall experiments would be retrieval of words most recently rehearsed. The words whose phonemic features are most readily available (through least decay) are recalled most successfully, and this is the basis of the recency effect. The finding that auditory presentations give larger recency effects than do visual presentations indicates that either auditory stimuli are transferred to the phonemic code more effectively than are visual stimuli, or that recency is largely governed by precategorical cues. Watkins and Watkins (1973) found that the extent of this modality effect was independent of the length of the words presented, which suggests that recency is a postcategorical effect. It also follows that covert rehearsal rates of phonemically stored information are independent of the length of the words. This is perhaps the most questionable assumption of the present theory, but it is an assumption upon which the theory rests. Craik (1968) found that a fixed number of words could be stored in primary memory, regardless of word length.

This description assumes that humans need only one categorical memory. After storage in sensory memory an item is either categorized or it is lost through decay. If it is categorized it may be permanently stored or the phonemic representation may be lost through decay. When an item is recognized both phonemic and semantic attributes are available about that item, but the longer an item is attended to the greater will be the number of semantic associations generated. Attention may be paid to an item by maintenance of its phonemic representation. The phonemic representation has meaning for the subject, and interference effects may be observed over any duration of storage. If the phonemic representation is attended to then permanent storage is more likely than if it is not rehearsed, but rehearsal is not a prerequisite of permanent storage. Rehearsal, or attention, does increase the strength of the memory trace, and Massaro (1970b) argues convincingly that memory strength increases exponentially as function of the amount of attention given to the item. The semantic component of the memory trace is vulnerable to forgetting through interference, but if the trace is also being rehearsed then forgetting is equally likely to be due to decay of the phonemic representation.

This particular version of the unitary trace view of memory is not very dissimilar to the earlier versions by Kay (1968) and Tulving (1968, 1970), and shares a number of features with the dual trace view suggested by Atkinson and Shiffrin (1968). Kay's view is that all short-term memory experiments are studies of the operation of one memory system over short intervals. The hypothetical memory system holding items which are vulnerable to decay if not rehearsed (i.e. primary memory) is considered to be part of the perceptual analyzing system. Storage prior to analysis, of all inputs, is necessary because of the limited capacity of the analysis process. If the categorization system is otherwise engaged when a new input arrives then the input will be lost unless there is some better facility to hold it until the analyzer can be switched from whatever it was doing. Kay does not describe the fate of these acoustic traces after perceptual analysis has been completed and does not allow for the generation of phonemic traces on categorization, otherwise his model is able to account for much of the available data. One particular finding which causes a problem for the dual trace model is that of Hebb (1961). Hebb's subjects engaged on a series of digit recall trials, 24 lists of 9 digits in each. Unknown to the subjects, however, one list was repeated several times during the 24 trials. Recall of the repeated list improved over the experiment, but a dual trace model with no transfer to permanent storage of material not intentionally transformed would have predicted no improvement. To the unitary trace model the improvement corresponds to the increasing strength of the single memory trace which is used in both long and short retention intervals. Kay's model is incomplete, but it provides a good basis for further model building attempts.

Tulving (1968) has also extended Melton's (1963) position against the dual trace model, and remarked that "the identification of the two types of memory with different storage systems may not constitute the most promising stepping stone to further theoretical analyses". For Tulving the "two types of memory" correspond to two retrieval strategies, and he specifically relates these strategies to the serial position curve of recall, the effect traditionally used as evidence in favour of the dual trace model. Recency, which reflects the output of primary memory in Waugh and Norman's (1965) model, is considered by Tulving to be due to retrieval using additional cues, namely acoustic cues. As each item is perceived a single memory trace is formed, but the information contained in the trace may vary between items. The most recently presented items will have semantic and acoustic information about them available at the time of testing, and so they are recalled more successfully than are items retrieved on the basis of semantic information alone. The extent of recency reflects not the capacity of the primary memory store but the durability of acoustic information in the presence of succeeding acoustic inputs. Any information about a trace which differentiates it from or associates it with other traces may be stored and used as a basis for retrieval, and hence Bruce and Crowley's (1970) result in which acoustic similarity facilitated long-term recall. Temporal marking of items also serves as a retrieval cue in the Tulving model, and position cues are considered to be responsible for the primacy portion of the serial position curve. At the time of presentation subjects may encode information about the position of an item at the same time as encoding the categorical information about the item. There exists no evidence to suggest that a memory trace cannot contain information on more than one dimension simultaneously, and that retrieval of a memory trace may not occur via more than one retrieval cue. Such cues which are non-categorical are described by Tulving as being auxiliary to content information.

A more recent description of human memory by Tulving (1972) distinguishes between episodic and semantic memories. Events are said to be stored in episodic memory on the basis of their temporal and spatial relationships to each other, and may have no other relationship with any event other than where in the sequence of experience they occurred for that individual. This type of memory is ideal for use in the majority of laboratory experiments concerned with human memory, where a set of perceptual events are encoded and, supposedly, retrieved on the basis of the temporal–spatial relationships between them. Semantic memory on the other hand is described as a "mental thesaurus", a store of the meaningful relationships between, and attributes of, objects. Semantic memory also holds the rules for the manipulation of symbols and is therefore necessary for the generation of language. Tulving emphasizes a need for models of memory to account for problem-solving behaviour and the deduction process involved in comprehension, and this is a very necessary emphasis, but the present model sees no reason for the separation of episodic and semantic memory for this purpose. The temporal attributes of events may be stored as attributes of the single representation in memory, just as other attributes are stored. The store of associations in semantic memory could accommodate temporal-spatial associations just as it accommodates more abstract associations.

Tulving's notion of a multi-addressable trace gives an interesting account of the primacy effect, but it appears that stimulus discriminability or perceptual distinctiveness is at least partly responsible. Enhanced recall of the initial members of a list are considered to be retrieved using content information and auxiliary information relating to their unique position in the list. Such auxiliary information is less useful for central items. Underwood (1972, 1973a, b) presented evidence to suggest that a component cause of primacy is differential perceptual efficiency experienced by items in a serial presentation. If the initial members of a list are perceived more accurately than centrally positioned items then the difference in perceptual efficiency would correspond to a difference in the trace strengths of early and central list members, and result in a primacy effect. Primacy might then be a result of the subject attending more to the early list members than to the central items, but the problem then becomes one of establishing why the beginning of the list should attract attention. Perceptual differences may also be considered to be responsible for the recency effect. If acoustic traces of final items persist longer than do the traces of early and central list members then the prolonged lives of these stimuli would lead to longer perceptual processing and stronger memory traces. Evidence in favour of the perceptual processing theory has come from several sources.

Underwood (1972, 1973a) presented subjects with dichotic lists of letters in which a single digit replaced a letter in either the attended list or the unattended list, and in any of the input serial positions. The subjects were required to attend to the letters presented to one ear, but to report the digit whether presented to the attended or unattended ear. Digits occurred equally often in each ear and in each serial position of the list, and were reported either immediately, upon detection, or at the end of the list. As representative of the results in this series of experiments, consider Fig. 2.10. In this experimental condition subjects were required to attend to the designated message by shadowing it, a standard attention-control method. In other conditions subjects either attended selectively without making any overt response or by encoding the attended message and recalling it at the end of the presentation. The effects indicated in Fig. 2.10 hold for these other procedures for controlling the direction of attention. Although subjects were required to detect and retain only one item in each list the success of detection was related to the position of the item in the list. If the digit was pre-

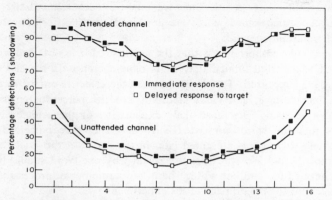

Fig. 2.10. The detection of digits presented in lists of dichotically presented letters, one digit in each dichotic list. The digit was presented in the attended message or in the unattended message, and performance depended upon the position of the digit in the list but not upon the delay of response. (From Underwood, 1972.)

sented near the beginning of the list then it was more likely to be detected than if it were presented in the centre of the list. This relationship was particularly valid for digits presented to the unattended ear. The difference between the extent of the position effects for attended and unattended words may either be due to a ceiling effect whereby all attended digits are so easy to detect that few errors are made, or the difference may be due to a perceptual interaction between the processing capacity available for unattended inputs and the ease of perceiving words in different serial positions. Attended words have been argued to be perceived more effectively than unattended words (Broadbent, 1958; Treisman, 1960) and if early words in a list are perceived more effectively than later words then we might expect a cumulative effect whereby late unattended words are perceived much less effectively than are early unattended words.

Of particular importance is that the position curve is obtained whether the digit is reported immediately or is remembered until the end of the list and then reported. This indicates that the effect is one of reception rather than storage, and lends credibility to the perceptual processing theory of primacy. The most likely explanation of the primacy in Fig. 2.10 is that the words presented early in the list are perceived more effectively than later words then we might expect a cumulative effect whereby late unattended words are perceived much less effectively than are early unattended words.

Of particular importance is that the position curve is obtained whether the digit is reported immediately or is remembered until the end of the list and then reported. This indicates that the effect is one of reception rather than storage, and lends credibility to the perceptual processing theory of primacy. The most likely explanation of the primacy in Fig. 2.10 is that the words presented early in the list are perceived more successfully than words presented later in the list, but this is not a complete explanation. We still have to explain why one word should be perceived better than another word. There are a number of processes which could account for the primacy in the experiment.

Suppose that words are presented at the rate of n words per second, but that it takes the listener, on average, $1/(n\text{-}a)$ seconds to analyse each word where a is a constant. If the processing rate had been $1/n$ seconds per word then processing would have kept up with presentation, but if the processing is slower than the presentation then one of two things can happen. A backlog could build up, with each word being analyzed for $1/(n\text{-}a)$ seconds, that is, as long as is necessary. If the words are analyzed for as long as this then the backlog would be of the form indicated in Fig. 2.11.

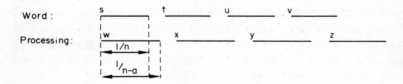

Fig 2.11. A processing backlog resulting from the time necessary for processing being greater than the time occupied by presentation of the stimuli.

Notice the onset asynchrony of stimuli and processing. The first word in the sequence is processed as it is presented — times s and w are synchronous. With later words processing does not start until after the word: times v and z are asynchronous. The consequence of a delay in the onset of processing is that the word would be stored in precategorical memory until it was attended to, and the longer an item is in precategorical memory the more it decays. By time z the characteristics at v may have decayed beyond recognition. The difference between the auditory stimuli "P" and "B" is a 90-milliseconds difference in the onset of the voiced component, and if this differentiating characteristic is lost through decay of the auditory trace then the subject would be unable to say whether a "P" or a "B" had been presented. Recall errors of words in central serial positions may therefore be caused by a processing backlog with consequent decay of these words prior to categorization.

To prevent the formation of a large backlog the subject may decide to curtail processing of the central items even prior to complete analysis. By this model all words in the list might be perceived and categorized, but early words would be processed for longer durations than would later words. With rapid presentation of stimuli the curtailment of processing may mean that some items would not be perceived correctly, and with slower presentations all items would be categorical but early items would be attended to more than later items and hence their trace strengths would vary.

The strategy of directing attention to one part of the list rather than another forms the basis of the rehearsal explanation of primacy, and will be discussed shortly, but it is worth considering why subjects should choose to attend more to the early items than to the central items. The perceptual processing theory would consider that subjects are encouraged to spend less time with the central items due to cumulative processing backlogs. The backlogs may also be a result of an inefficient strategy on the part of the subject, for if he attends to the early items (by rehearsing them) for longer than their presentation times, simply because he thinks that he has more time than he does have, then backlogs will build up.

Further evidence in support of the perceptual processing theory of primacy again comes from an experiment in which the subject was required to respond selectively to a single item presented in a series of items (Underwood, 1973b). This situation differed from the dichotic listening experiments (Underwood, 1972, 1973a) in that attention between messages was not an experimental factor, and only one list was presented at any one time. The item to which the subject was to respond selectively was indicated by a tone presented simultaneously. So, the subject heard a list of ten letters in one ear, and at the same time as one of the letters he heard a tone in the other ear. Perception of tones is quite independent of the direction of attention (Lawson, 1966), and so the subject did not have to direct his attention away from the letters at any time in order to hear the tone. The task was to report which letter had been heard at the same time as the tone, after all of the letters had been presented. Because this task would have been so easy a further task was added which consumed some of the capacity available to the subject. As the letters were presented the subject was required to shadow them. Shadowing ensures that the subject attends to each component of the list as it is presented and that he is unable to selectively rehearse the target item during the retention interval. The data from this experiment are indicated in Fig. 2.12. The word in serial position 1 was presented 6·6 seconds before the end of the list, and was followed by nine semantically-similar items. The word in position 3 was presented 5·3 seconds before the end of the list and was followed by seven similar items.

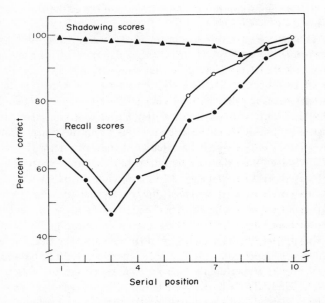

Fig. 2.12. Shadowing and critical item recall scores. ●——● correct recall of critical item; o——o recall of critical item + adjacent recall errors. (From Underwood, 1973b.)

Despite the extra decay and retroactive interference acting upon the first item in the list it was recalled more often than the third item. Aaronson, Markowitz and Shapiro (1971) also found that responses to items when presented as part of a series were more successful to single items at the beginning of the list than when in the centre. In Aaronson's experiment subjects responded immediately on hearing the words, so the effect is quite independent of storage. Perceptual processing theory would argue that the first item had been perceived more efficiently and that a stronger memory trace had been formed. The highly efficient shadowing performances indicate that all items are perceived easily, and so the resultant primacy effect must be a function of processing after initial perception, that is, the attention directed to the categorized form. Theories of primacy which are not supported are those which argue that interactions between items during storage are responsible for higher recall of earlier than of later items. These include the selective rehearsal theory, retrieval tag theory, and proactive interference theory, and relate exclusively to primacy following the retention of the whole list. Primacy may be observed with serial recall (recall in order of presentation), free recall (recall in any order), and with probe recall designs (test only one item, but the subject must remember all items because he does not know which item will be tested until after presentation of the whole list), and the following theories of the effects were designed to account for primacy following retention of the whole list.

The selective rehearsal theory of primacy (e.g. Waugh and Norman, 1965; Crowder, 1969) maintains that more information is available about early items because the rehearsal strategies employed by the subject directs his attention to these items more than to central items. An alternative view using the rehearsal concept (e.g. Atkinson and Shiffrin, 1968) considers that early items enter a relatively empty rehearsal buffer, and are not displaced as quickly as are central or late members of the list. More information about early items would therefore be transferred to the long-term memory store, and their recall probability increased accordingly. The role of the limited capacity rehearsal buffer in the primacy effect is indicated in Table 2.1.

The first item (item *a*) in the list enters an empty rehearsal buffer, and so until the next item arrives the subject rehearses only this one item. When the second item (item *b*) arrives item *a* is already present,

Table 2.1. A simple account of the primacy effect using the rehearsal buffer.

Time from start of presentation:	0 sec	1 sec	2 sec	3 sec	4 sec	5 sec
Presented:	a	b	c	d	e	f
RB1	a	b	c	d	e	f
RB2	—	a	b	c	d	e
RB3	—	—	a	b	c	d
RB4	—	—	—	a	b	c

RB1-RB4 are four "slots" of a rehearsal buffer. "a, b, c, d, e and f" are the first six items of a list, and the table shows the course of the passage of these items through the rehearsal buffer for a particular case where the rate of presentation of the list is 1 item per second. " — " indicates an empty "slot".

and so rehearsal is shared between these two items. The fourth item (item *d*) fills the rehearsal buffer, and rehearsal is divided between four items. Now, the strength of the memory trace depends upon the amount of attention given to the item, and if an item is rehearsed more than another item then it will be more readily stored. Consider the amounts of rehearsal gained by the first items in the idealized situation in Table 2.1. If we make an assumption that it takes ¼ second to rehearse one item (solely for the sake of simplicity of calculation) then item *a* will gain $4 + 2 + \frac{4}{3} + 1 = 8\frac{1}{3}$ rehearsals over the 4 seconds in which it is in the rehearsal buffer before being displaced by item *e*. Item *b* will gain $2 + \frac{4}{3} + 1 + 1 = 5\frac{1}{3}$ rehearsals, and item *c* will gain $\frac{4}{3} + 1 + 1 + 1 = 4\frac{1}{3}$ rehearsals. Subsequent items will gain 4 rehearsals. The number of rehearsals given any item governs its probability of recall, and so this rather simplified model can account for the primacy effect. This particular model fails to take into account the individual rehearsal strategies used by subjects. The presentation of an item to a full rehearsal buffer may or may not displace another item, for the subject may choose to retain an old item rather than acquire a new one. The model does not allow for such strategies and has a mechanical view of the displacement process. Other mathematical models of the primacy effect which employ the rehearsal buffer may be inspected in Norman (1970). Selective rehearsal theories of primacy do not account for the primacy observed in the recall of individual items in the experiments of Aaronson *et al.*

(1971) and Underwood (1972, 1973a, b). There is no reason why the subject should rehearse one item in these experiments any more than any other item. A critical item in the first position of a list is equally as important as a critical item in the fourth position.

The absence of effective rehearsal strategies may be considered to be responsible for the small running memory span (Pollack, Johnson, and Knaff, 1959). In the running memory span experiment the subject is presented with an indeterminate number of items, one item at a time, and is instructed that when the list does stop then he should attempt to recall as many of the most recently presented items as possible. Suppose that a list of digits had been presented, and had ended as follows "... 9, 2, 5, 3, 7, 4, 8, 2, 6, 1", and that the subject could recall "3, 2, 6, 1". In this case his span would be three items as these form a complete sequence from the end of the list. Primacy does not occur in these experiments and the probability of recall is an increasing function of proximity to the end of the list (see Fig. 2.13). Subjects never know whether the item being presented will be required for recall and strategies of organization are futile. Indeed, Crowder and Morton (1969) suggest that organization by the subject may even have adverse effects upon performance, and Hockey (1973) found that at fast rates of presentation (2 or 3 items per second) a passive listening strategy (no organization) leads to greater span than does an active listening strategy (imposed organization by the subject: "rehearse items in groups of three"). Absence of rehearsal, or at least reduced rehearsal, was also associated with a reduced primacy effect in one of the experiments reported by Waugh and Norman (1965). Absence of rehearsal does not always lead to reduced primacy, however, and this has been shown in a running memory span experiment (where rehearsal is assumed to be minimal) by Hockey (1972). Subjects were required to recall either the last six or last eight items presented on each trial, and this generally meant the last few items from a long sequence. On one trial, however, subjects heard a list of only six or eight items according to which experimental condition they were in, and consequently had to recall all items presented. The "normal" running memory trials would have encouraged subjects against using rehearsal strategies in which early members of the presentation are rehearsed more than any other items, and yet the recall curves for lists of six and eight items look remarkably similar to those

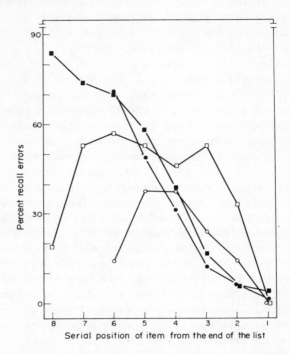

Fig. 2.13. Data from Hockey's (1972) running memory span experiment; recall errors as a function of the position of the item from the end of the list. ■——■ normal running memory span situation, subjects instructed to recall the last eight items presented. ◻——◻ catch trials, instructions as above, but only eight items presented. ●——● normal trials, six items requested. ○——○ catch trials, only six items presented.

in the more usual serial recall experiment. A comparison of recall of the final items in the "normal" running memory trials and "catch" trials is shown in Fig. 2.13. The prominent primacy for the catch trials was obtained for trials where subjects were apparently not rehearsing the early items any more than the central items, and is in support of the perceptual processing theory. The result is not unequivocal, of course, as we have no guarantee that the subjects did not selectively rehearse the first items presented. There is no advantage for subjects to use this strategy, but the distinctiveness of the early items may attract attention.

Without explicit instructions not to rehearse, as in the Waugh and Norman (1965) and Hockey (1973) experiments, subjects may find that the nature of the presentation leads them to attend more to the early items than to the central items. The initial members of the list are distinctive in that they are preceded by nothing. The central items are not distinctive because they follow a series of similar items. Attention may thus be directed to certain members as a function of their distinctiveness (Murdock, 1960; Kintsch, 1970), and this explanation extends to the von Restorff effect whereby an inhomogeneous item in a list (a word typed in red ink when all other words are typed in black ink) is recalled more often than homogeneous items.

Hockey's result may also be explained by the proactive interference theory of primacy (e.g. Glanzer and Cunitz, 1966), which maintains that interference from early items leads to poor recall of later items. In the "normal" trials proactive interference from the earlier members of the long lists would reduce the probability of recall of items in serial positions 4 to 8 from the end of the list, but for the short lists interference would not have been built up, and recall of these early items would be more successful. Proactive interference, like selective rehearsal, cannot account easily for the experiments in which primacy appeared with retention of a single item. In these experiments storage interference effects should have been minimal, because subjects have no reason to retain the lists from which they select the critical item. However, incidental retention of noncritical items may lead to a certain amount of proactive interference influencing the recall of central items more than that of initial items. An experiment reported by Bruce and Papay (1970) suggests that this is not the case. Items which were cued as "to-be-forgotten" had little effect upon primacy, suggesting that proactive interference from incidental material is minimal. Furthermore, an experiment using the release-from-proactive-interference effect confirms the obsolescence of the interference explanation. Wickens, Born, and Allan (1963) found that recall of the fourth series of items returned to the recall level of the first series if the material was changed from letters to digits on the fourth trial (see Fig. 2.9), and Underwood (1975) confirmed the primacy for a single item for lists in which the items preceding the critical item were the same or were different from the critical item. Each list contained ten items, but the structure of the lists differed in two experimental conditions. One group of subjects counted backwards in threes to prevent rehearsal whilst viewing a list of digits, the digits being exposed briefly one at a time. One digit was designated as being critical by having an asterisk shown to the left of the display at the same time. The task was to remember which digit was accompanied by the asterisk and respond at the end of the list whilst performing the distraction task during the retention interval. The digit appeared in each of the possible list positions during the course of the experiment. The second experimental group had the same procedure of events, but all list members prior to the critical digit were letters. The first digit to be presented was always the critical digit. So, when testing recall of serial position 5 the subject would have been presented with four letters, the critical digit, and five digits. When testing serial position 1 the critical digit would have been presented first, and followed by nine digits. If proactive interference had influenced recall of the critical item in this experiment then primacy should have been more prominent with homogeneous lists than with mixed lists. Items in the central serial position should be recalled less successfully when interference from previous similar items is allowed to build up without being released by a change of material. The recall curves for this experiment are shown in Fig. 2.14. The results go in the opposite direction to

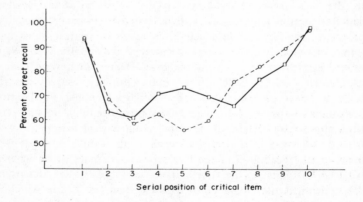

Fig. 2.14. Recall of critical digit from homogeneous and mixed lists. ■ ■ lists of all digits; o o lists of letters followed by digits. (From Underwood, 1975.)

that predicted by interference theory. There is a difference between conditions for recall of the critical item in the central serial positions, but interference theory predicted that a digit following letters would be recalled better than a digit following other digits. In fact for serial positions 4, 5 and 6, a digit following digits was recalled better than a digit in a mixed list. This result certainly does not confirm the proactive interference theory of primacy, but it does raise the problem of why there should have been a difference in recall for the central items. Changing the material during the list may have had a distracting effect upon encoding of the critical item.

Before leaving the primacy effect it is worth making one point for the benefit of those who consider that the effect is nothing more than a small part of verbal memory research. The point is that primacy is a very general phenomenon. In any sequence of events in our lives we are more likely to remember something of the first part of the sequence than the centre of the sequence. The sequence could be yesterday's shopping list or it could be the years spent at school. There is a tendency to remember the events which happened during the first year at school better than the third or fourth year. The first lecture of a completed course may be recalled better than the third or fourth lecture. The first impression which we have of a stranger is the impression which we remember and may be more difficult to change than subsequent impressions. Bull and Reid (1975) have demonstrated that even policemen when recalling information given during briefings tend to produce a primary effect. This general primacy effect may be related to the duration experience of new events. The first year at school is often subjectively longer than subsequent years, and as the more attention we pay to an event the longer it takes to occur (Underwood and Swain, 1973), it seems reasonable to suppose that some aspect of the first event in the sequence is attended to more than that aspect of subsequent events. More attention may be required for the formation of constructs than for their maintenance, to plagiarize the terminology of one view of behaviour (Kelly, 1955). During the initial phases of a sequence of events the analyzers (Sutherland, 1969; Treisman, 1969) or feature "demons" (Selfridge, 1958) may be primed or even formulated, processes which would take more time than would their use alone. Thus the novelty of a new situation, or of the first word in a new list demands more attention for processing of the first event than for subsequent events. Hamilton and Hockey (1970) provide the evidence which supports this view. Over sixty trials of recalling lists the extent of primacy effect decreased. This may have been due to a cumulative effect of proactive interference, but the central serial positions showed no deficit at all. Hamilton and Hockey considered the change to be one of task orientation, and this is the view taken here. During early trials the start of a list was a new event and demanded attention, but after a large number of trials the start of another list was not a novel event and increased attention was not necessary for analysis.

The perceptual processing view of primacy is quite compatible with the unitary base view of categorical memory. Items in early serial positions have higher recall than central items because they are processed into categorical memory more effectively. This may be due to differences in word identification delays or differences in the allocation of attention to different parts of the list, or both, for a well perceived item may attract more attention than a poorly perceived item. Items in the final serial positions, the recency region, have higher recall than central serial positions because at the time of recall not only categorical information is available about them, but also sensory information. Retrieval may proceed with the use of semantic and acoustic cues (at least for auditory presentations). Phonemic memory and semantic memory are functionally indistinguishable. At short intervals however the categorized item may be retrievable using cues retained from the categorization process, and this may lead to an acoustic confusion effect if the phonemic properties of several items are similar. These phonemic cues need not serve any permanent function, they remain from the categorization process and may be lost very rapidly. They are not always lost, however, and may serve a useful role in the retrieval of permanently stored events, as indicated by the tip-of-the-tongue phenomenon.

If "primary memory" does not exist as a memory system built into the processing sequence then we may ask why reports of its capacity have been so consistent. The capacity of primary memory is independent of word frequency, the relatedness of the words, and of the lengths of words stored. The unitary theory would consider that we are able to remember the phonemic features of any words which are presented for as long as it is necessary to understand any word. To understand a word the stimulus characteristics are often insufficient and contextual information is necessary. Consider the sentence:

1.   The man bit the dog.

If this sentence had been spoken to us (as most sentences are) then it is quite possible that we would have misunderstood it but for the lingering acoustic or phonemic traces provided by the categorization of each word. By reconsidering these traces after the initial semantic decoding had resulted in an improbable understanding we are able to check up on the components of the utterance. Postponed processing is also of demonstrable use in what Warren and Warren (1970) refer to as the phonemic restoration effect. When a phoneme is deleted from a sentence spoken to a subject it will be perceived as being present — provided that the sentence contains sufficient contextual information for a perceptual hypothesis to be generated. For instance, the last word in the sentence "It was found that the -eel was on the . . ." determined the generation of the first phoneme of the incomplete word. If no final word was presented, then it was heard as "eel", but if the last word in the sentence was "axle", then "eel" becomes "wheel". If the word supplied was "shoe" then the restoration effect made "eel" into "heel". Similarly, "orange" resulted in "peel", and "table" resulted in "meal". Words which are spoken to us unclearly are not necessarily lost, and the redundancy of language can help the formation of consistent perceptions. Unusual and misheard sentences are not the only time we need some form of buffer store in which the original input may be retained for checking. Consider the following sentence.

2.   The man who came out of the rather grand Victorian style hotel with his hat in his hand bit the dog.

We need to be able to remember the subject of the sentence (the man) whilst the noun phrase (who came out of the rather grand Victorian style hotel with his hand in his hand) is being spoken, otherwise we are unable to relate the subject to the object (the dog). The subject of this sentence is held in a buffer store which may be called primary memory. The purpose of the buffer store is to retain individual categorized words until such a time as the underlying meaning of the sentence may be grasped. The subject here is not being retained on the basis of acoustic cues alone, otherwise the words which follow would have masked it. The subject is retained in a categorical buffer. The capacity of primary memory is remarkably close to the phrase-length which is optimal for retention. Consider Fig. 2.15, which indicates the results of a phrase recall experiment reported by Perfetti and Goodman (1971). Subjects were presented

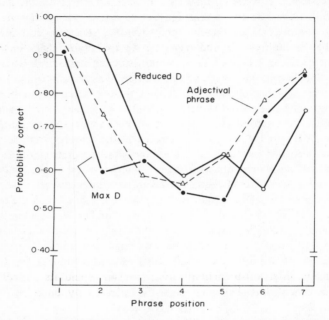

Fig. 2.15. The probability of correct word recall as a function of position within a phrase. (From Perfetti and Goodman, 1971.)

with phrases of three types which varied according to one grammatical model (Yngve, 1960), and recall was after a short interval. The differences in recall predicted by Yngve grammar are discussed in subsequent sections of this chapter, and the differences between these three curves are inconsequential so far as the present discussion is concerned. This particular set of recall curves could have been from any recall experiment using nonsense syllables, unrelated words, or geometrical shapes, and the presence of primacy and recency in an experiment using meaningful material vindicates the study of these effects with other materials. If Perfetti and Goodman's phrases had been four words in length a very different set of recall curves would have been obtained, with very few errors in any serial position. The basic unit of an idea is usually formalized in a sentence using no more than three or four words. Basic units in this sense being a noun and its complements, and correspond to phrases, for example sentence 1 is composed of two basic units, "the man" and "bit the dog" being the noun and verb phrases respectively. If a phrase exceeds three or four words in length then we may have difficulty in understanding the whole sentence. We need to be able to decode each phrase into its underlying notions at the time of listening otherwise relationships *between* notions cannot be formed. If the related components of ideas are separated by the formal structure of the sentence then comprehension becomes difficult because one component must be retained for several words until the completing components are presented. The components of an idea need to be heard together in sequence, without disruption of the sequence, and for optimum comprehension the sequences must not be more than three or four words in length. The importance of continuity of words forming each idea in comprehension of sentences is indicated by the following examples.

3. If the usually safe but currently very thin ice is walked across by the boys the keeper will be annoyed.
4. The rabbit the hawk the hunter shot swooped upon disappeared.

These sentences are described as being left-branching and self-embedded respectively. In a left-branching sentence a word and its complements (e.g. the definite article and noun) are separated by qualifiers, or the qualifiers may even start the sentence, as below:

5. Almost but not all of the current top-class track and field athletes available last month went on tour.

The qualifiers are written to the left of the noun as the sentence is written and processing of the noun is postponed until the qualifiers have been presented. A self-embedded sentence is composed of several dependent clauses each of which postpone completion of the previous notion. In sentence 4 "the rabbit disappeared" is interrupted by "the hawk swooped upon" which in turn is disrupted by "the hunter shot". Each of these interruptions mean that a noun must be remembered until a further clause is heard before the idea is complete and ready to be related to other ideas. Easily understood sentences are often right-branching in form, and the right-branching equivalents of sentences 3 and 4 would be:

6.   The keeper will be annoyed if the boys walk across the ice which is usually safe but is currently very thin.
7.   The hunter shot the hawk which swooped upon the rabbit which disappeared.

The easily understood right-branching sentence is so-called because the qualifiers are added to the end of the notion, or to the right as the sentence is written down. The noun is presented before its modifiers. The difficulty with both the left-branching and self-embedded examples above is that one component of a notion must be retained in its formal state until the qualifiers have been presented. After the qualifiers have been presented all components of the notion are related and the underlying meaning derived. The system for holding words in their formal state (i.e. exactly as presented in the sentence) is the phonological code, and this code has the properties which are otherwise said to represent primary memory. Thus, if the number of qualifiers exceeds the "primary memory span" the first component of the notion will no longer be available in its phonological form when the second component is presented. If the phonological form of a component is not available then decoding of the meaning is difficult because contact with the lexicon is not available without regeneration of the phonological form. Word analysis is subject to a limited processing channel and we can only analyse the meaning of (or modify the meaning of) a limited number of words at any instant. To be certain of the meaning of "usually safe" in sentence 3 we need to know that the speaker is talking about ice. If the phonological code of "usually safe" is not available then it will have to be regenerated before the meaning of the whole phrase can be understood.

The problems faced in understanding complex sentences have been investigated by comparison of the ease of retention of sentences of various forms, and in the following discussion three particular explanations will be mentioned.

Remembering Sentences

The difficulties in understanding complex sentences are not dependent entirely upon their length, for the self-embedded sentence (4) is, if anything more difficult to unravel than the left-branching sentence (3). Yngve (1960, 1962) suggested that the surface structure of a sentence affects its retention because each word commits the speaker to continue for at least a certain number of words. The speaker commits himself to utter certain words in order to complete the sentence in a grammatical form. Consider the sentence:

8.   The newly formed ice broke easily.

On uttering "the" the speaker is committed to at least two further words in order to produce a grammatical sentence: a noun phrase and a verb phrase. If the noun and verb follow promptly then the memory load will be slight and the sentence may be described as not being embedded, or having a low depth of surface structure. The self-embedded and left-branching sentences used earlier may be said to have high depth of surface structure. To return to sentence 8, if "the" commits the speaker to at least two more words it is said to have a depth of 2. Uttering "the newly" commits the speaker to at least three further words, the adjectival, noun and verb phrases requiring completion. "Newly" therefore has a depth of 3. "Formed" commits the speaker to complete the noun and verb phrases, having a depth of 2. On completion of the noun phrase by the utterance "ice" the commitment is reduced to one word, which is all that is necessary for a verb phrase. The depth of "ice" is therefore 1. Presenting the verb "broke" completes a grammatical utterance (and this is where Yngve stretches the imagination) but the intonation used to utter the word indicates to the listener that the sentence is incomplete, and at least one more word is to come. "Broke" therefore also has a depth of 1. When the adverb "easily" is uttered with an intonation characteristic of terminal words the commitment to continue the sentence is released, and "easily" has a depth of 0. Sentence 8 has depth numbers of 2,3,2,1,1,0, and the mean depth of the words of the sentence is 1·5. The greater is the depth rating of any individual word, the greater is the memory load, and the less is the likelihood of comprehension and recall. Embedded sentences have poor recall, according to the Yngve model, because the listener must remember more commitments made by earlier words in the sentence whilst processing words which are intermediate between commitment and fulfilment.

Martin and Roberts (1966) presented subjects with a list of six sentences after which they attempted to recall each of the six sentences. Each sentence had equal length and different syntactic form (kernal, passive, truncated passive, negative, passive negative, and truncated passive negative), and was unrelated semantically to the other sentences in the list. Two levels of sentence depth were used, sentences having a mean Yngve depth of 1·29 or of 1·71. Subjects recalled 51·2% of the high depth sentences, and 64·3% of the low depth sentences, and there was little variation in this ordering for the six types of surface structure. The one exception to this result was with passive negative sentences, when the high-depth version was recalled slightly more often than the low-depth version. This experiment does suggest that Yngve depth is an important factor in sentence retention, and it is probable that retention is guided in this situation by ease of comprehension. A sentence with high depth is said to be harder to understand because the listener must retain incomplete ideas for longer than he does with a low depth sentence.

An alternative account of why we have difficulty in handling complex sentences has been proposed by Miller (1962) and Miller and Chomsky (1963), and is based upon Chomsky's (1957) views of the application of transformation rules to kernal sentences. Whereas the Yngve model accounts for psycholinguistic phenomena using surface structure assumptions, Chomsky points to differences in the expression of deep structure as being important. That similar surface structures can have very different deep structures should be sufficient to justify this view.

9.   I saw the sparrows flying to the trees.

10.   I saw the Grand Canyon flying to New York.

These sentences have very similar surface structures, but our knowledge of the word enforces very different interpretations: they have different deep structures.

11.   I saw a Jumbo Jet flying to New York.

Sentence 11 is ambiguous, and by this we mean that at least two interpretations are permissible with the given surface structure and our knowledge of the properties of objects. Not all of the relationships between components of sentences are expressed by the surface structure trees. For Chomsky the surface structure is a product of transformation rules which are applied to the deep structure, or psychologically meaningful idea behind the linguistic expression. The fewest number of transformation rules applied to the deep structure result in a kernal sentence (12), which may be expressed as sentence 13 by performing the passive transform.

12.   The boy hit the ball.

13.   The ball was hit by the boy.

Now, when we remember a sentence as we heard it we retain the deep structure and information of the transformation of the deep structure in which the sentence was presented. So given sentence 13 to remember we would encode sentence 12 plus a passive transform marker. Hence we get the common observation that the general meaning of a sentence may be understood and remembered, but we are often unable to remember the exact wording, the exact syntactic structures (Mandler and Mandler, 1964). In these cases the deep structure is retained but the transformational markers have been lost. Miller and Chomsky explain the greater incidence of errors in the recall of embedded sentences as being due to a limited amount of storage space available in our memory systems. Complex sentences are more difficult to remember than simple sentences because there is more transformational information to be remembered about them. Wang (1970) asked listeners to judge sentences for comprehensibility, and more transformations led to a greater probability of a sentence being judged as more difficult to understand. This result does not support the Miller and Chomsky view exclusively, however, for linguistic depth as measured by Yngve's method was also correlated with ease of comprehension.

Mehler (1963) also provides evidence in support of storage being affected by transformational complexity. Mehler tested the recall of kernal sentences (or what he considers to be kernals, e.g. "the man has bought the house", which may be described as a simple active affirmative declarative sentence), and recall of a number of transformations of these kernals. There was a general tendency for complex sentences if not recalled correctly, to be recalled as the kernal form. If a passive sentence was recalled incorrectly it was more likely to be recalled as a kernal than as anything else. This tendency did not hold for all transformations, the negative passive interrogative, for instance, was rarely recalled as a kernal, but quite often as the negative interrogative or passive interrogative. In this instance one transformation marker is being lost during the retention interval, but quite often a marker would be added. Simple interrogatives were recalled in error more as negative interrogatives than as kernals, and simple negatives quite often as negative interrogatives. Most of the errors in Mehler's study were due to syntactic confusions, however, suggesting that the deep structure of the sentence is retained more accurately than are the syntactic markers which are required for performance.

One of the points arising from Mehler's experiment has been questioned by Martin and Roberts (1966) who consider that the result is explicable entirely within the framework of the Yngve model. Martin and Roberts re-analyzed Mehler's data, calculating the mean depth of each of the sentences, and finding that depth increased with transformational complexity. The result of increased error probability with increased complexity could therefore be due to either postponement of processing or to transformational complexity. Table 2.2 indicates an almost linear relationship between the number of transformations and structural depth. As the number of transformations increases the structural depth increases and the number of sentences correctly recalled decreases.

Table 2.2. The reanalysis of Mehler's (1963) data by Martin and Roberts (1966).

Sentence type:	Kernal	Passive	Negative	Passive-negative
Number of transformations:	0	1	1	2
Number of sentences correctly recalled:	300	243	234	191
Yngve depth:	1.17	1.38	1.43	1.67

On a slightly different tack Perfetti (1969) introduced a further measure of sentence complexity. He maintained that previous studies had ignored the proportional amount of semantic content. In general sentences are composed of two types of words: lexical or content words (nouns, adjectives, etc.), and grammatical or function words (pronouns, articles, etc.). In sentence 14 the function words are in italics:

14.   *The* men *have* taken *the* nets *to the* boat.

The lexical words convey the semantic information of the message, and function words are largely redundant. The utterance "men taken nets boat" is still meaningful, if ambiguous, but "the have the to the" conveys nothing. An analogy between the usefulness of grammatical and lexical words and of vowels and consonants may be appropriate:

15.   C*n y** r**d th*s?

Grammatical words in sentences and vowels in words convey little information, but they do resolve certain ambiguities of interpretation and allow the listener to operate at a lower rate of processing. In a test of the psychological validity of the lexical-function distinction Perfetti used four types of sentences, combining high and low lexical density (the ratio of lexical to function words) and high and low structural depth. Examples of the four sentence types are given in sentences 16-19.

16.   The family has accepted an offer to purchase the house.
          (low lexical density, low structural depth)
17.   The use of credit by the customer has obviously increased.
          (low lexical density, high structural depth)
18.   The police watched nearly every move made by the clever thief.
          (high lexical density, low structural depth)
19.   The almost never used machine is too expensive to keep.
          (high lexical density, high structural depth)

Whereas structural depth had little effect upon recall (39% for both depths), lexical density was effective (44% for low lexical density, and 35% for high lexical density).

Perfetti and Goodman (1971) continued the criticism of the Yngve model by investigating the immediate recall of sentences with very high depth in comparison with their untangled forms. In the left-branching sentence (20) "clearly" has a structural depth of 7. But in the right-branching

20.   When a clearly less than carefully concealed weapon was noticed by the detectives, the man was arrested.
21.   The man was arrested when detectives noticed a weapon which clearly was less than carefully concealed.

version (21) "clearly" has a depth of 3. These depth ratings are evident in the ease of comprehension, but structural depth was found to have no effect upon recall. The probability of recalling either version was 0·72, whereas the Yngve model predicts that sentences with higher depth incur more processing postponements and should be recalled less well than their low-depth equivalents. Memory for noun phrases with varying depth was also largely invariant, and Fig. 2.15 (p.114) indicates that the major factor which governs recall is the position of the word in the phrase. three types of phrase used by Perfetti and Goodman were a high depth adverbial noun phrase (max D in Fig.2.15), the same phrase with reduced depth (reduced D), and a low-depth adjectival noun phrase (adjective) phrase). Instances of these three phrase types are given in examples 22-24, respectively.

22.   A considerably less than well disciplined child.
23.   A child disciplined considerably less than well.
24.   A friendly confident really happy small child.

Small differences were obtained in the recall of these phrases, against the Yngve prediction. The probability of recalling any particular word from a high depth phrase was 0·66, but from either of the low depth phrases the probability of recall was 0·70. Fig. 2.15 indicates that this effect is particularly evident for the second word in the high-depth phrase, which was typically the word with greatest depth. In phrase 22 "considerably" has a depth of 5. The Yngve model cannot be rejected totally by these data, but it has only weak predictive value. Perfetti and Goodman suggest that a better description would include consideration of the organization of the phrase around the noun.

Another approach to the investigation of short sentences, which are by themselves easily remembered, has been described by Savin and Perchonock (1965). They used a technique similar to the residual processing capacity methodology described in more detail in Chapter 4. Briefly, to compare the difficulties of two tasks which may both be performed ideally we can assess the two primary tasks indirectly by adding another task and observing performance on this secondary task. Primary task a is performed at the same time as the secondary task, which is again checked for error. The comparison of secondary task errors is a measure of the difficulties of the two primary tasks. An easy primary task will permit more attention to be directed to the secondary task whereas with a difficult primary task more errors will be committed in the performance of the secondary task. The rationale of this method is not dissimilar to that of comparing the volumes of two objects by the Archimedian method of observing the amount of water which each displaces. In both methods an assumption of limited capacity is made. By dropping an object into water we are displacing water from a space which is limited in volume, and by adding a second task to a well-performed primary task we incur errors because the human operator can only perform a limited number of tasks at any one time.

Savin and Perchonock presented a short sentence of the type in example

25, or any of a number of transformations, followed by a list of eight words. The subject had to recall the sentence (primary task) and then

25.   The boy hit the ball.

recall as many of the list of words as possible (secondary task). The number of words recalled would then indicate the difficulty of remembering the sentence. Subjects recalled between 3·48 and 5·27 words in addition to the sentence, but in general the greater the number of transformations then the fewer was the number of words recalled. This relationship is indicated in Table 2.3, and the result has been interpreted as giving direct support for the Miller and Chomsky model.

Table 2.3. The mean number of words recalled in addition to a sentence of varying transformation complexity.

Number of transformations:	0 (i.e. kernal)	1 (e.g. passive)	2 (e.g. passive negative)	3 (i.e. passive negative interrogative)
Number of additional words:	5·27	4·55	3·91	3·85

The means for the sentences with one and two transformations change to 4·52 and 3·74 when the negative interrogative is considered as one transformation — Katz and Postal (1964) give support to this view. Data from Savin and Perchonock (1965).

The syntactic markers indicating the presence of a transformation are argued to take up space in the limited capacity storage system. Again, however, the result is not unequivocal, and Savin and Perchonock's experiment has been criticized on methodological grounds.

The recall of one set of items has been shown to impair the subsequent recall of other items still being held in memory (Kay and Poulton, 1951; Brown, 1954), and Epstein (1969) attempted to implicate the Savin and Perchonock experiment with an extra condition to control for possible effects of output interference. Subjects were required to remember a sentence and a number of words, and then either recall the sentences and then the words or alternatively recall the words and then the sentence. The Savin and Perchonock result was confirmed for the sentence-words order of report, more complex sentences reducing the number of words recalled, but the result was not confirmed for the words-sentence order. We must conclude that in the original experiment the recall of the sentence interfered with the storage of the words, because when the words

124   Attention and Memory

are recalled first the transformational complexity of the sentences did not affect the number of words recalled.

Alternative explanations of the Savin and Perchonock result have also been supported by Glucksberg and Danks (1969) and Boakes and Lodwick (1971). If complex sentences are recalled slower than simple sentences the difference in the amount of information retained would be accountable to increased forgetting due to decay or opportunity for interference. This supposition has been confirmed. The onset latency for the recall of the sentence is dependent upon the transformational complexity of the sentence, as indicated in Table 2.4. With more complex sentences not only is the onset of recall of the sentences slower

Table 2.4. The mean number of words recalled in addition to a sentence of determined transformational complexity, and the onsets of sentence recall and word recall as a function of sentence complexity. Data from Glucksberg and Danks (1969).

Number of Transformations:	0	1	2
Number of additional words recalled:	4·93	4·69	4·54
Onset latency of sentence recall (sec):	1·28	1·33	1·42
Onset latency of word recall (sec):	4·32	4·62	5·02

but onset on recall of the words is also slower. The extra delay in recalling the words could explain entirely the differences in the numbers of words recalled without reference to a limited capacity notion of memory. Transformationally complex sentences also have an effect upon the recall of secondary material, but the effect is not one of displacement. Transformations are difficult to process, and this is reflected in the latency data provided by Glucksberg and Danks and by Boakes and Lodwick, but the view is not supported that sentences are stored as a kernal plus a number of syntactic markers.

The Savin and Perchonock technique has also been used to test the structural depth explanation of the difficulty of handling complex sentences. Wright (1969) found that increasing the structural depth of a kernal sentence (26) by adding an adverbial phrase (sentence 27) the effect upon the number of additional words recalled was similar to the effect of transforming the sentence to the passive negative form (sentence 28), as indicated in Table 2.5. The difficulty in handling a transformed sentence appears to be similar to the difficulty in handling a sentence of high structural depth. An objection to this view is that the deep structures

26. The cat watched the bird.

27. The cat very soon watched the bird.

28. The bird was not watched by the cat.

Table 2.5. The number of words recalled in addition to a sentence of varying transformational complexity, and varying structural depth. Data from Wright (1969)

Number of Transformations:	0	1	2
Yngve depth:	1.00	1.42	1.36
Number of additional words recalled:	3.34	2.93	2.99

of the sentences used were not held constant. Wearing (1972) found that the semantic contents influenced retention more than transformational complexity, unpredictable sentences being recalled more accurately than predictable sentences, and although Wright's sentences were balanced for lexical content, the deep structure of sentence 27 is very different from that of sentence 28. This objection was considered in a further experiment reported by Wright in which the depth and transformational complexity were varied with smaller differences of meaning. Examples of the material used in this experiment are given in sentences 29 and 30.

29. The guard who was looking through the window watched the prisoner.
    (active, high depth)

30. The prisoner was watched by the guard who was looking through the window.
    (passive, low depth)

Transformation theory predicts that sentence 30 would be more difficult than sentence 29, and Yngve structural depth theory makes the opposite prediction. Using the Savin and Perchonock method with sentences of this type Wright reported that 3·52 additional words were recalled with the active, high depth sentence and 3·23 words with the passive, low-depth sentence. This result both supports transformation theory and contradicts the prediction made by structural depth theory. The discrepancy between the two experiments reported by Wright is concluded to be due to inadequate control of the deep structure in the first experiment. Controlling the transformational complexity, the structural depth, and the lexical content is just not enough in experiments investigating sentence retention. This criticism also applies to Wright's second experiment, however, because sentence 30 has a lower lexical density than sentence 29, and Perfetti's (1969) analysis would have predicted the direction of the results in terms of the ratio of lexical to grammatical words. Transformation theory predicts the result, but it is not the only theory to do so.

It should be noted that Wearing and Crowder (1971) have reported a dissimilar result to that of Wright (1969) in a modification of the Savin and Perchonock design. Digits were presented interleaved between the words of the sentence, which was either active or passive, and of either low or high depth. Both transformational complexity and structural depth affected recall of the digits, and in Wearing and Crowder's experiment the lexical density of the sentences was held constant.

Why do we have difficulty in recalling complex sentences? The conclusions from this sketchy review are that transformational complexity, the limitations imposed by the postponement of associated ideas, and the informational content (lexical density), may all affect recall under appropriate conditions. If we impose a greater load upon the rate of processing or upon the retention of words then performance is affected adversely. By incurring a commitment to produce a particular word or phrase and then postponing presentation of that word or phrase we impose a load upon the psychological representation of the word: an isolated adjective must be retained as a word rather than giving a qualified meaning to a noun. Splitting an infinitive serves to postpone processing of the verb until after presentation of the adverb (e.g. "to blatently argue") and as such imposes a load upon memory. The alternative version ("to argue blatantly") qualifies the verb after presentation of the verb, and as such results in no postponements and is easier to process. As someone who is particularly prone to produce split infinitives I apologize to the reader for over-using his memory.

This chapter has dealt with the processing of information and storage of categorized units in a somewhat mechanical fashion. Words are described as being processed from one storage code to another with little consideration of the selective processing of words, except in relation to the primacy effect, and with little consideration of the interactions between items, except in relation to the effects of similarity upon forgetting. We have been concerned here with an issue which has engaged, and is still concerning psychologists, the issue of how many memory systems humans have. This does not appear to be a very fruitful approach to the problems of how we use the information presented to us, and takes no account of the integration of information into the individuals' schemata (Bartlett, 1932). The schemata, which are in a sense conceptions of all aspects of the environment, are constructions based upon selected information and modified by subsequently selected information. The approach to the study of memory should be that of the pragmatist, for as psychologists we need to know how information is analyzed and responded to so that we know how best to present it. The search for one, two, or thirty-two memory systems is in itself inconsequential. We do need to know which factors influence the perception, storage, and response to information, and their investigation has led to the documentation of a number of stages of processing. But to equate these stages with storage systems is a step which is possibly invalid and positively unnecessary. There does appear to be a phonological memory which lasts for a few seconds, has very limited capacity and which has been equated with primary memory. However, these characteristics do not apply exclusively to very recent memory, and phonological coding is not always essential for processing, facts which should make dichotomists suspicious of their theoretical position. We do have evidence of memory for different attributes of items in store (e.g., structural, phonological, categorical) being available under different experimental conditions, but it is an invalid step to conclude that different memory stores are operating in these situations. The characteristics of storage in primary memory have been shown to apply to storage in secondary memory under certain circumstances and vice versa for the characteristics of storage in secondary memory. These systems do not appear to operate independently of each other, a fact which led Kay (1968) to suggest that very recent memory shows the properties of a long-term memory system operating over short intervals. Phonological memory, or primary memory, is seen here as one of the functional characteristics of the word-recognition system. To recognize a verbal stimulus categorically we usually produce a phonological representation, and because we produce this phonological representation and use it to influence behaviour we also remember the representation. We need to be able to remember it, otherwise it would be useless immediately after being produced. It is these representations which form the basis of categorical memory, but production of a phonological representation is by no means essential for lexical analysis. The longer a word is in what Neisser (1967) described as active verbal memory, and is being used, the more associations will be formed and recognized between it and other words. Words at this stage of processing undergo elaboration coding in the Tulving and Madigan (1970) sense and associations between categorizations and other forms of memory will be evoked. For instance, a word may conjure up visual images previously associated with that word, but it is debatable whether non-verbal stimuli are stored noncategorically. We may recognize a smell without knowing the name of the substance causing that particular sensation, but we are able to categorize and code phonologically the surrounding circumstances of the original sensation. Phonological encoding of nonverbal events may mediate recognition, but it is obviously not the sole basis of visual, tactile, auditory or olfactory memory. The problems of nonverbal memory are more difficult to investigate than those of verbal memory, and accordingly have received little attention. One of the major problems of verbal memory is that of the unique organization of information constructed by individual subjects. Ebbinghaus recognized that words have different meanings for individuals, and attempted to avoid the problems of organization by using nonsense syllables. This is one problem which memory research has faced during recent decades, and is one of the subjects of the next chapter.

CHAPTER 3

CONTROL PROCESSES

When we present a list of words to a subject and ask him to recall it, it is quite likely that the list will not be recalled in the same order as it was presented. Such behaviour in the free recall situation has been described by Atkinson and Shiffrin (1968) as being indicative of the operation of control processes in memory. One of the more formidable problems in experimental psychology is to describe the strategies available to us in the performance of specified tasks. Recall does not usually proceed along the lines of a uni-dimensional filing system, but rather the words presented to a subject are assimilated into his schemata and retrieved according to the interpretations and organizations imposed by these schemata. These two approaches typify studies of what Tulving (1972) refers to as episodic and semantic memory, with the enormous number of reported verbal learning experiments generally being studies of episodic memory. Bartlett (1932) described a system of remembering in which subjective organization was responsible for the errors of recall by the attempts we make to fit information into these schemata, and the problem here is to describe the strategies of processing by which we actively manipulate information in encoding and retrieval. We must be prepared to describe why two subjects recall the words of the same list in different orders or recall different words, and why the same subject may recall two similar lists of words not only with varying overall success, but also with varying order of report. Some of these descriptions have been provided in the previous chapter in terms of the forgetting due to similarity of material, the number of retrieval cues available, the limitations in retaining words using their phonemic codes, perceptual limitations, etc. A feature common to these factors is that they are limitations of the processing system which we have available to us. The present discussion will centre around recall differences produced within the limitations of the system, involving processing strategies which are, or which could be controlled by the subject. For example, control processes have been postulated to account for the primacy effect in the recall of a list. The subject may choose to attend selectively to the beginning of the list at the expense of the items in the centre. This strategy would serve to produce stronger memory traces of early items than of central items. The commonly held explanation of the recency effect does not rely upon subject-dependent processes in the sense that recency is not a strategical phenomenon but is a result of the persistence of auditory information after presentation. The subject may choose whether or not to use that information but given that he is attempting to remember the list he will do so.

The control processes to be considered here are the direction of selective attention as indicated by rehearsal, the mnemonic grouping of words on the basis of certain features, the selective scanning of words in memory as a part of the retrieval process, and the phenomenon of selective forgetting of information no longer needed.

Functions of Rehearsal

From a theoretical view it has been argued that rehearsal serves two purposes. When an item is rehearsed, vocally or subvocally, it is maintained in primary memory and is also more likely to be transferred to the more permanent secondary memory (Waugh and Norman, 1965; Atkinson and Shiffrin, 1968). A simpler account, which does not resort to the postulate of independent memory traces, considers that when an item is rehearsed the strength of the unitary memory trace is increased and that the act of rehearsal provides additional features by which the trace may be retrieved subsequently. In general it is true to say that additional rehearsal increases trace strength, but it should be noted that repetitive rehearsal is not sufficient to produce major changes of recall probability. Jacoby (1973) had subjects recall lists of five words either immediately or after a 15-second interval filled with overt rehearsal. The recall of lists following rehearsal was no better than immediately after presentation. This result could be interpreted as meaning that rehearsal does not increase trace strength, or that rehearsal acts only to postpone the onset of autonomous decay processes, as Brown (1958) suggested. Alternatively, the extra opportunity for forgetting could counteract the extra opportunity for increasing the trace strengths of those items rehearsed. Using the Brown-Peterson paradigm Meunier, Ritz and Meunier (1972) gave subjects single consonant-vowel-consonant trigrams of low association values with retention intervals varying between 0 and 18 seconds. One group was permitted to rehearse the trigram during the retention interval whilst a second group engaged in a backwards counting task which prevented rehearsal. After twenty-five such trials the subjects were required to recall as many of the trigrams as possible. The result was surprising, for in the "immediate" recall test (i.e. 18 seconds or less between presentation and recall) vast differences appeared between the rehearsal and no-rehearsal groups, with rehearsal ensuring almost perfect recall, but in the final recall test the groups performed equally poorly. Repetitive rehearsal was sufficient to retain a meaningless item adequately whilst being rehearsed, but the absence of elaborative coding or reconstruction (Tulving and Madigan, 1970), Craik and Lockhard, 1972; Weist, 1972) meant that once the item was not retrievable on the basis of phonological cues then it was hardly retrievable at all. Repetition in itself serves little function other than to regenerate the phonological code of the word, but it is with this function that classrooms of schoolchildren recite lists of foreign nouns and multiplication tables. Repetition is quite pointless unless it gives opportunity for interaction between the words being rehearsed and between those words and others in memory. The effects of organized or elaborative rehearsal have been shown clearly by Weist and Crawford (1973). Subjects who were allowed to organize their rehearsal of a list of related words performed better than a group of subjects who were forced to rehearse the list sequentially. Organization was evident in the clustering of related words in recall, and was more frequent for the organized-rehearsal group than for the sequential-rehearsal group. Phonological repetition allows opportunity for subjective organization of the list of words but is not sufficient for permanent retention, a point raised by Brown (1958) when he concluded that "it is not impossible that the moderate strengthening of learning which did occur was due, not to rehearsal as such, but to finding interpretations of the letters". A word must be integrated into the subject's own memory system for effective long-term retrieval to be possible, and by rehearsing the word or list of words associations are formed which will outlast the phonological cues as a basis for retrieval. If the phonological cues themselves have some relationship, as with a tongue-twister for instance, then the organization may be as much around acoustic similarity as around the semantic attributes of the utterance.

The importance of the phonological code has already been discussed in some detail, and will be considered here only briefly. One of the primary points concerning the phonological representation of an item is that vocal rehearsal (saying an item over aloud) has a different effect upon recall from subvocal rehearsal (saying an item to oneself, or thinking about it), and this is just as our examination of acoustic storage would have predicted. A direct comparison of these two strategies, which are operable during input, was made by Conrad and Hull (1968). They presented sequences of seven digits visually and at a reasonably fast rate, so there was little opportunity for repeated rehearsal of individual items. Subjects were instructed to read the digits silently or to read them aloud, and written recall followed immediately after the presentation finished. The errors in recall are indicated in Fig. 3.1 as a function of the serial position in the list and the vocalization strategy imposed upon the subject. Comparing the serial recall curves for the two vocalization conditions it is apparent that the final three serial positions yield fewer errors for

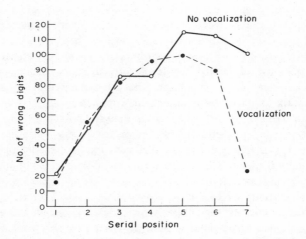

Fig. 3.1. Effect of input mode on serial position of errors. The presentations were visual. (From Conrad and Hull, 1968.)

vocal rehearsal than for silent rehearsal. In statistical terms only the final serial position differs between conditions, but the effect is quite definite. With transcription of a visual presentation into an overt phonological code the recency effect is improved. Recall in this case was written, that is, silent, but in an experiment reported by Murray (1966) this factor was also varied. Lists of letters were presented visually and subjects either read the letters aloud or silently as they were shown, as in the Conrad and Hull experiment. Half of the subjects in each of these groups recalled the letters aloud, and half recalled them by writing the letters on slips of paper. The modality of recall had an effect upon neither the overall number of letters recalled nor upon the serial positions of the letters in the lists. The major factor was whether or not the list was vocalized during the presentation, but vocalization in itself provides little advantage. It is the setting up of acoustic traces which enhances the recency effect and these traces must be set up at the time of presentation of the display as a part of the encoding process.

Without diverging too far from the main theme here there are one or two points which are worth making about vocalization and the recency effect. The first point is that the modality effect (which is another description of the difference between the recency effects with visual and auditory presentations) is not dependent upon a voiced component from the subject. The difference in the recency region of the serial position curve is just as easily obtained using a visual presentation or an auditory presentation with the subject looking or listening passively, as it is with a visual display and the subject sitting passively in one condition and vocalizing in the other condition. Strictly speaking there are several "modality" effects in the comparison of visual and auditory displays. For instance Mackworth (1964) varied the presentation rate for auditory and visual display. Whereas faster rates (4 words/second against 1 word/second) decreased the recall of visual presentations, speeding up the auditory presentations increased recall. A possible explanation of this effect is that in the case of visual displays the decreased presentation time per word reduces the time allowed for phonemic categorization, and the recognition and subvocalization rate may have been exceeded in the faster conditions. The rate of silent rehearsal of a recognized item has been estimated at 1 item per 100 msec (Landauer, 1962), and Mackworth's fastest rate was 1 item per 250 msec. So, although the rehearsal rate is not exceeded we are getting pretty close to it once the initial recognition is taken into account. The increase in the recall of spoken items would then be due to items already being coded in the form in which they are to be used, and hence there would be no decrement due to a fast presentation. The increase itself was possibly due to less decaying of acoustical information than with a slow presentation. This interpretation is probably applicable to all of the "modality" effects, each of them being an interaction of the slower decay of auditory rather than visual material, and of auditory material being presented in the same code as that used for storage whereas a transformation is required for visual information.

So far as the modality effect of recency is concerned it should be made clear that the higher recency for the final auditory items is not simply because they are at the end of the presentation and are therefore not followed by more information. An effect can still be found if the list is continued, but continued visually. Murdock and Walker (1969) presented lists of twenty letters with the modality of presentation changing a number of times in each list. The first five letters were auditory, the next five visual, the next five auditory, and the last five visual. The presentation rate was fixed for the whole list, and in a second condition the visual and auditory blocks were counterbalanced with the first to have the form visual, auditory, visual, auditory. Increased recall of auditory letters over visual was obtained for the final few items at the end of an auditory block whether or not more letters followed. The advantage of an auditory presentation appears when the particular presentation terminates and is not dependent upon the arrival of new information provided that it is not in the auditory modality. The recency effect is therefore a function of the survival of acoustic cues, and is not determined by the state of the categorical processes. If it were so then the processing of further (visual) information would have eliminated the recency effect of auditory items presented in mid-list.

The activity of the subject is not critical for the modality effect to appear, as it may seem from the Conrad and Hull and the Murray experiments alone. Murdock and Walker provide evidence of a modality effect with experimenter controlled auditory and visual presentations. The source of the vocalization of visual presentations is similarly inconsequential to the effect. Crowder (1970) presented lists of nine digits to subjects with the use of a film strip. Recall was always written so in a control condition with visual presentation and written recall subjects had no need to use acoustic coding other than for their own purposes. Crowder had two experimental conditions which he termed active and passive vocalization. In the active vocalization condition the subjects read out the letters as they were presented, and in the passive vocalization condition the experimenter read out the letters as they were shown. Crowder found little difference between the conditions in which the visual display was read aloud by the subjects or by the experimenter, but in both of these conditions there is produced a larger recency effect than with the silent visual presentation. Apart from the recency portion of the curve there is little difference due to the vocalization component, and the effect upon recency of the addition of voicing the display was interpreted by Crowder in support of PAS theory. The availability of acoustical information about the final items for a few seconds after the end of the list is said to increase recall because there is more information available about these items. This extra information is used during the prolonged readout time enjoyed by the undisplaced acoustic trace.

The experiments discussed so far concern manipulated rehearsal strategies and, in the case of the Brown (1958) and Peterson and Peterson (1959) experiments, situations in which rehearsal is prevented for at least part of the retention interval. Other studies have observed the effects of rehearsal in situations where the subject was free to rehearse whichever items he chose.

Corballis (1969) presented his subjects with lists of eight digits visually and at a rate slow enough to allow a fair amount of activity between items. Subjects were asked to rehearse aloud, to vocalize any thoughts which they had during the presentation, and to recall the list immediately after the display terminated. Whether vocal rehearsal of this type is effectively different from silent rehearsal is debateable, but Corballis observed two general strategies which may be termed cumulative rehearsal and rehearsal by grouping. For a subject employing the cumulative rehearsal strategy each time a new digit is presented all items previously presented are rehearsed. The subject attempts to rehearse the whole of the presented list each time a new item appears. If the sequence is "47136259" then when the item "7" is presented the subject would say "47"; on seeing "1" the subject would say "471", and so on. In effect rehearsal is identical with recall when this strategy is used. This strategy requires a fast rehearsal rate, and is only efficient with slow presentations. Corballis and Loveless (1967) also suggest that cumulative rehearsal may not occur with auditory presentations. With the grouping strategy the items "47" might be rehearsed as a pair at any point during the presentation and similarly for items "13" and so on. Even further processing might lead to this particular list being encoded as "forty-seven", "thirteen", etc., but a more common observation is that subjects tend to impose their own structure on the list by using changes of stress and rhythm as the groups are rehearsed. Rhythmic organization of this sort has been argued to form a basis of verbal memory (Neisser, 1967, 1969), and is undoubtedly a popular mnemonic in short-term memory experiments.

Although very different strategies were used by the subjects in the Corballis experiment there was very little difference in the mean recall scores from the two main strategy groups. Provided that the subject engages in some organizational activity as the list is presented then a certain level of performance is attained.

Rundus (1971) also requested his subjects to rehearse overtly, and compared the number of times an item was rehearsed with the probability of its recall. Subjects were free to choose their own strategies of rehearsal. Twenty common words were presented visually at a very slow rate, and the comparison of frequency of rehearsal with probability of recall is indicated in Fig. 3.2. The mean number of rehearsals gained by each item does appear to be related to the probability of recall, except for the recency part of the serial position curve. This relationship provides support for an explanation of the negative recency effect in terms of absence of rehearsal (Craik, 1970; Craik, Gardiner, and Watkins, 1970). When subjects immediately recall a list of words the serial position curve shows the characteristic primacy and recency effects, but if at the end of the experiment the subject is asked to recall words from all of the ten lists then the items recalled least successfully are those from the recency positions. The negative recency effect may be accounted for by supposing that rehearsal aids permanent storage and that subjects tend not to rehearse the final few items in the list. The extensive recency effect in Fig. 3.2, in the absence of extensive rehearsal, vindicates the use of this strategy for the case of immediate recall. If we only need to rehearse an item when the previous phonological representation is decaying and becoming less retrievable then an adequate strategy is that of not rehearsing the final items to any extent.

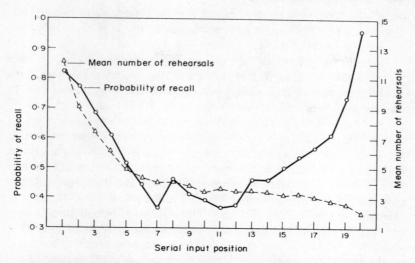

Fig. 3.2. The mean probability of recall and the mean number of rehearsals of an item as a function of its serial imput position. (From Rundus, 1970.)

At the time of recall the final items will have been rehearsed recently and the traces still retrievable.

The high correlation between the primacy effect and rehearsal in Fig. 3.2 may suggest that rehearsal is responsible for the increased recall of the early members of the list. Rehearsal undoubtedly can be instrumental in producing a primacy effect, and rehearsal may be viewed as an overt indication of attention. Directing one's attention selectively to one member of series does lead to increased recall of that member on a subsequent test (Waugh, 1969), but rehearsal theorists still have the problem of establishing why the initial members of a series are rehearsed more than the central members. The availability of empty slots in the fixed capacity rehearsal buffer is one explanation (Atkinson and Shiffrin, 1968), but we now have many instances of primacy in experiments where selective rehearsal is inappropriate (Aaronson *et al.*, 1971; Hockey, 1972; Underwood, 1972, 1973 a,b, 1975). Fischler, Rundus and Atkinson (1970) also noticed a slight primary effect when subjects were permitted to rehearse "only the item currently being presented, preventing rehearsal of earlier items". With rehearsal equated in this way the persistence of primacy suggests that perceptual distinctiveness contributes to the enhanced recall of the early members of the list.

One of the prominent rehearsal strategies mentioned by Corballis (1969) is that of grouping, and rhythmical grouping by the subject forms a substantial part of the recoding process as described by Neisser (1967). Recoding or organization into what Miller (1956) called "chunks" is necessary in order to overcome the capacity limitations inherent in the human information processing system, and rhythmic grouping is perhaps the simple form of organization. By recoding sets of relatively unrelated items into groups the memory span can be increased dramatically. If the basic limit to our ability to relate information to other information is governed by the magic number 7 ± 2, in Miller's terms, then the way to overcome the limit is by chunking. Three pieces of information become one unit or chunk, and the span is increased by a factor of three. The chunk is a subjective unit of recoding, it is the information remembered by the individual himself by whatever mnemonic is available. One of the characteristics of categorical memory is that the information is recoded and this organization also serves to increase the amount of information stored. Categorical memory exists only as an organized structure, and a prediction from this view was tested by Neisser (1969) using serial order intrusions. Consider the following two lists which might be presented successively in a serial recall task:

List 1:	Stimulus:	*a*	*b*	*c*	*d*	*e*	*f*	*g*
	Response:	"a	b	c	-	e	-	g"
List 2:	Stimulus:	*h*	*i*	*j*	*k*	*l*	*m*	*n*
	Response:	"h	i	j	-	e	-	-"

On recalling list 1 immediately after presentation the subject makes two errors of omission, failing to recall the items in serial positions 4 and 6. List 2 is then presented and the subject commits three errors of omission (positions 4, 6 and 7), but also an error of commission. An item is recalled in serial position 5 which was not a part of the list which was presented. However, this same item was presented in the previous list, and recalled correctly, but of especial importance is that this item was presented and recalled in the *same serial position* in the previous list as it was erroneously recalled in the final list. The response "e" in list 2 is a serial order intrusion because this item was presented and recalled in the same position in the previous list. Now, Neisser's views about the structure of categorical memory, or active verbal memory specifically, predict that the serial positions of items in a list are defined for the subject only by the rhythmic organization imposed upon it. Serial order intrusions should only appear when successive lists have the same rhythmic pattern. Neisser (1969) presented subjects with a large number of lists of ten digits with recall following auditory presentation of each list. Half of the list had the same rhythmic pattern as the preceding list, and two patterns were used, as follows:

$$3\text{-}3\text{-}3\text{-}1, \text{ for example}, 794 \quad 051 \quad 632\ 8$$
$$4\text{-}4\text{-}2, \text{ for example}, 6571\ 8039 \quad 42$$

The rhythm was established by longer pauses between groups of words than between the words of any group. The prediction made from Neisser's views of rhythmic organization was confirmed by this experiment: significantly more serial order intrusions appeared in lists which followed lists of similar structure than when there was a change of structure. This experiment demonstrates convincingly the importance of rhythmic grouping for verbal memory.

Mnemonic Organization

Tulving (1968) described discrepancies between input order and output order in free recall experiments as being a function of "primary organization". The tendency to report items from the end of the list first is not dependent upon the semantic attributes of the words in the list. "Secondary organization" is so dependent, and may or may not be determined by any organization imposed by the experimenter. A list may be composed of two sublists of related words, the sublists being unrelated to each other, and the imposed organization of this list would be reflected in the clustering of words from the sublists in recall. Alternatively a list of apparently unrelated words may be organized into a semantically meaningful configuration unique to that subject. This subjective organization would also be evident in the pattern of recall, for a group of 4 or 5 words may be more meaningful to an individual in an order different to that in which they were presented. The ordering of the words in recall would indicate some subjective organization, but the ordering alone would tell us little about the particular organization used. The present discussion of the organization of memory will centre upon the grouping of items in rehearsal and recall.

One of the experiments reported by Rundus (1971) observed the rehearsal strategies, and hence an organizing process itself, when the subject was presented with a list containing sets of related words. Bousfield (1953) found that when subjects were given a list of 60 words composed of 4 groups of 15 related words, then recall was clustered into the 4 groups much more than would be expected by chance, and Rundus's technique allowed the observation of the clustering process during the presentation of such a list. Words were presented visually and at a slow rate, subjects being encouraged to rehearse overtly during the whole of the presentation. The lists contained 24 words in which 12 words were unrelated to each other, 6 words belonged to one semantic category, and 6 words to another category. The order of the words within each list was randomized. Recall of a particular word was related to the number of times which that item was rehearsed, but the semantic relatedness of a word to other words also increased the likelihood of recall. Category words were recalled more often than unrelated words even for those words which were rehearsed equally often. The clustering of category members was found in recall, with related words tending to be recalled together. Subjects also tended to group similar items together in rehearsal. When a new item was shown the subject was more likely to rehearse a related item than any other. When a non-categorized item was shown it was more likely that another non-categorized item would be rehearsed than one of the category words. The organization of the lists during rehearsal clearly can play an important part in ensuring a higher level of recall than when this organization does not occur. Weist and Crawford (1973) have emphasized this point in showing that organization during rehearsal is necessary for organized recall, as indicated by the overall level of recall and an index of clustering. In this group of experiments a possible organization is provided by the experimenter in the words he selects to include in the lists. The organization task for the subject is to notice the relatedness between some of the words and others, and when these relationships are made explicit retention is made much easier.

Bower, Clark, Winzenz and Lesgold (1969) had their subjects attempt to learn a list of 112 words which were either organized by the experimenter or presented in random order. The organized set of words took the form of four groups, with 28 words in each. The 28 words were arranged in a taxonomic hierarchy with examples, as in Fig. 3.3. The ran-

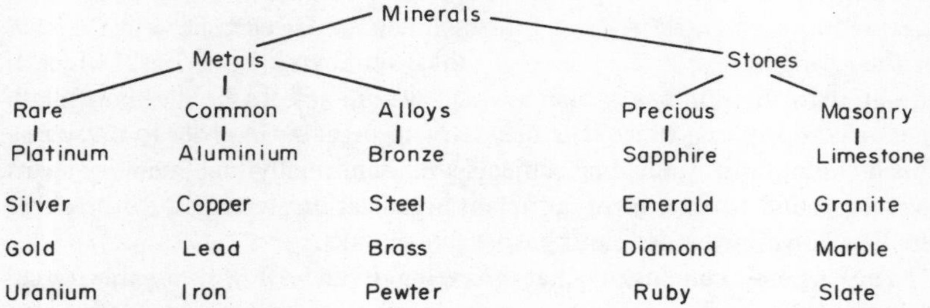

Fig. 3.3. An example of a taxonomic hierarchy as used by Bower *et al.* (1969). All words, including the category headlines, were required for recall.

domized set of words were also presented in four groups, but the words in any group were chosen randomly from the 112 words in the total set. With both conditions subjects were shown the four groups of words for about 1 minute per group, and subjects then recalled as many of the 112 words as possible. Subjects recalled 65% of the words when they were explicitly organized and 19% when they were randomized. On the second trial subjects recalled almost all the words in the organized condition. When recalling the organized words, subjects tended to reproduce the hierarchies as shown, first recalling the nodal words in the hierarchy and then the words below them. If a nodal word was not recalled then an entire section of the hierarchy below the node might be irretrievable. Systematic organization of the type used by Bower *et al.* is clearly a very powerful mnemonic aid, the main benefit of which appears to be the retrieval plan which it provides. Rather than attempt to remember and then retrieve 112 words independently, the subject need remember successive sets of category headings, each of which leads to another set. For example, in the hierarchy illustrated in Fig. 3.3 suppose that the individual has remembered that "minerals" is the taxonomic heading, he need only remember that there are two subheadings at the next level and that these are "metals" and "stones". The "metals" group have three subheadings, and so on, successively deriving groups from previous groups. This is, in effect, a retrieval plan based upon "chunking", in that a list which exceeds the memory span is broken up into chunks which are well within the span. There are four hierarchies, two main categories within the hierarchy, two or three headings within each category, and four members under each heading (at least in the example in Fig. 3.3). None of these numbers exceed 7 ± 2, which is the limit to the number of items which we are able to hold in immediate memory at any one time. It is necessary to organize in order to overcome this inherent limit. Individual subjects with abnormally high memory spans may be found to have highly efficient organization strategies, for breaking the lists down into more easily retrievable chunks.

The general conclusion that grouping is an efficient organizational strategy because it reduces the load placed upon the retrieval system is also applicable to a result reported by Mandler (1967). Two groups of subjects were presented with 52 index cards, each with one word printed on it, and the two groups were given very different instructions. One group was told to organize the cards into a number of piles in whatever categories the individuals chose. A restriction was that at least two piles were used, but not more than seven. The other group were told to place the cards into seven columns, the first card into the first column, the second card into the second column, and so on. Organization in this case was based upon the ordering within the pack of cards rather than the meaningful relations between the words on the card. Half of the subjects in each group were told to learn the words, and the other half were given no such instruction. Whether subjects were told to remember or not, after five sorting trials they were given a recall task. Subjects who were given the organization instructions alone remembered about the same number of words as subjects given the learning instructions alone. Giving an additional instruction to organize and learn led to no advantage over either instruction alone. Subjects given neither instruction recalled fewer words than subjects in the other three groups. Organization of the material is a sufficient process to ensure retention of that material, but more interestingly specific instructions to learn the material led to the same overall level of recall as instructions to organize. This result suggests the hypothesis that learning is the equivalent of organization. When we attempt to learn a list of words a useful technique is to attempt to organize them into meaningful units with the relations between words serving an organizational function, and in Mandler's experiment organization appears to serve the same purpose as learning.

The importance of stable organizations has been indicated in a series of experiments reported by Bower and his colleagues. It is not enough to organize items in one way but once a particular order has been made and a particular set of relationships generated then this order must be maintained. Changing the ordering with the same words does not aid recall nearly as much as repeated trials with the same ordering. Bower, Lesgold, and Tieman (1969) showed subjects a group of four unrelated nouns, and instructed them to visualize a scene employing these four nouns. For example, with the stimulus words "dog, bicycle, cigar, hat", a suggested image is a *dog* wearing a *hat,* smoking a *cigar* whilst riding a *bicycle.* Thus four items were organized into one scene, or chunk. Imagery is a particularly efficient mnemonic device (see Bower (1970), and Luria's (1969) account of a mnemonist who used imagery extensively), and Paivio (1969) has argued that the concreteness, or imagery rating, is the most useful predictor as to whether or not a word will be remembered. Twenty-four words were arranged in groups, and subjects allocated to one of two conditions. In one condition the same word groups were presented over three trials, with recall tested after each presentation of the complete sets of words. Subjects in the second condition were shown the same twenty-four words on each trial, but the words appeared in different groups each time. The results of this experiment are indicated in Fig. 3.4. Whereas recall of a changing organization increases only slightly with repeated presentation, when the same organization is available then recall benefits considerably from repetition.

Effects of changed groupings are similar with serial recall of lists of digits. Bower and Winzenz (1969) presented a series of digit strings, each of 5 digits, which were grouped on presentation. For example, 17348 might be read as "seventeen, three hundred and forty eight". Each time a string was presented subjects had to say whether or not it had been presented earlier in the experiment. When a string was repeated after a variable number of interpolated strings it either had the same organization as its original presentation (i.e. in the example above, "17" and "348"), or the organization was changed (e.g. "173" and "48"). The

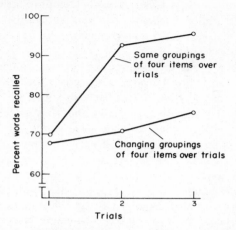

Fig. 3.4. Mean recall errors over four trials for noise items and for items repeated with the same grouping or with different groupings. (From Bower, Lesgold and Tieman, 1969.)

probability of recognizing a repeated item was much lower when the grouping was changed, suggesting that the grouping is part of the identity of a remembered string. The grouping of a string of random digits into a pair of numerical quantities is related to the rhythmical representation of the string in "active verbal memory", or phonemic memory if we must dichotomize, and this result would be expected from Neisser's (1967, 1969) views of the subjective representation of verbal information.

A second experiment reported by Bower and Winzenz (1969) investigated the effects of changed groupings upon the cumulative learning of digit strings. Subjects were presented with a particular string of 12 digits four times in each trial, and with new digit strings between the repeated items to check on the base-line recall of new items ("noise items"). The task for the subjects was to recall each string of digits immediately after presentation. Repeated strings either had the same grouping, or the grouping was changed on each presentation. Lists were presented in blocks of eight, with four repeated lists and four new lists per block, and four trials with each block were tested with each subject. Over the four trials recall of new strings did not vary, but recall of repeated strings increased from about 50% accuracy to about 75% accuracy, as indicated in Fig. 3.5.

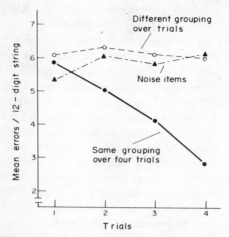

Fig. 3.5. Mean percentage of words recalled over trials for lists repeated with the same or with changing quartet groupings. (From Bower and Winzenz, 1969.)

This is a typical learning curve for repeated presentations, with repetition serving to strengthen the memory trace of the subjective representation. If the grouping of the list changed, but the digits kept the same then recall did not improve over the sixteen presentations of this one list. These lists were recalled at much the same level as were new lists, suggesting that re-organization of the grouping produced a new list. A similar result was reported by Tulving (1966) who first had his subjects learn a list of nine common words, and then a list of eighteen words. For half the subjects the nine words were included in the eighteen, and for the other half new words were presented. A large number of trials with the second list indicated different learning curves. The group with new words were initially at a disadvantage in comparison with the group who experienced the repetition, but after a few trials the group with new words performed better than the other group. The conclusion from this experiment and from the Bower and Winzenz experiment is that subjects were generating particular associations between words which were inappropriate with changed orderings. When more words were added to the nine already learnt then new subjective organizations may have offered themselves to individuals, and these may have competed with the established organizations.

We cannot rely upon subjects in memory experiments to sit passively and shunt information from one "slot" to another as certain flow-charts may imply, but subjects will attempt to give meaning to the material presented whether it is prose or a list of nonsense syllables. Only by imposing a unique structure upon the material perceived can individuals form a representation of their experiences, and these schemata will in turn influence subsequent perceptions. Isherwood was quite mistaken when he claimed that he was "a camera with a shutter open, quite passive". Human memory cannot act as a camera or a tape-recorder even though some of the component processes (sensory memory) may have this function. To remember effectively we need to organize and to integrate material into our existing memories. When organization is imposed upon material by subject or experimenter then retention benefits. Whenever material is categorized into subgroups then learning proceeds along an easier course than when it is left uncategorized.

Having established that the organization of material aids its recall we have yet to conclude which of the stages of processing are involved in this advantage. Which stages are aided when the material is well organized? Asch and Ebenholtz (1962) suggested that "availability" cues govern the free recall of individual items, but Tulving (1968) notes tersely that "availability seems to be another descriptive label for recall probability". Availability or accessibility of items may aid recall by facilitating efficient retrieval. If an item is described as having high availability all we may be saying is that it has available sufficient retrieval cues to ensure recall. The organization of a list serves to increase availability by clustering related items, for instance. An item in a cluster is more available because group membership would be one of the cues on which retrieval might operate. The importance of organization for the retrieval process was indicated in the experiment reported by Bower, Clark, Winzenz and Lesgold (1969) in which subjects learned quite rapidly a total of 112 words which had been organized hierarchically. Subjects organized their recall of retrieving words under headings. The headings were retrieved first, and then the words categorized under them. When words were under a particular heading this increased their availability, or to put it slightly differently, categorized words have an additional retrieval cue in comparison with uncategorized words (Tulving and Pearlstone, 1966; Tulving, 1968). The problem of how we search through memory for information in store will be considered in the following section.

Memory Search: Organization of Retrieval

How do we search through memory for an item previously encoded, and what are the effects of organization upon such a search? The line of investigation prompted by Sternberg (1966, 1969) will be discussed here as an introduction to the subject of retrieval and recognition.

In the experimental investigation of recognition the subject is typically presented with a set of test items, and at some later time a probe item is presented and the subject is required to respond according to whether or not the probe was present in the test set. The process of interest here is that of how information from the stored ensemble is gathered before the recognition decision is reported. A solution to this problem was provided by Sternberg (1966) who maintained that a search through memory is both serial and exhaustive. By "serial" it is meant that items in storage are compared with the probe item one at a time, rather than in parallel. So, if four items are in store and if it takes n seconds to compare any of these items with the probe item then Sternberg's model would expect the total search time to be $4n$ seconds if each item is compared. It is, however, a debatable point whether or not each item is compared with the probe in a memory search. Sternberg considers that the total test series is scanned, and this is what is meant by the term "exhaustive". Opposing models suggest that the search through memory is terminated when a match is made between the probe and a stored item (e.g. Anders, 1973; Theios, Smith, Haviland, Traupmann, and Moy, 1973). If the test set is the digit series "517239" and the probe item is "2", then Sternberg's model argues that each and every item in the test set is compared with the probe regardless of where the "2" is located in the list. If the search proceeds in an orderly fashion comparing the probe with items in the same order as they were presented to the subject, as is almost certainly *not* the case, then the "2" would be compared with first the "5", then the "1", then the "7", and then the "2". At this point a match would be made, but the exhaustive scan says that all items are compared, and the "3" and the "9" compared with the "2" before a response is available.

This counter intuitive search strategy must be used for reasons which outweigh the seemingly more efficient strategy of terminating the search once a match is found. The self-terminating models of memory search argue that once a match has been found then enough information is available for the recognition decision to be made and the search discontinued at a point related to the position to the test item in the search order. Perhaps a decision to stop searching when a match is made would take up more time and be less efficient than not making such a decision and simply proceeding with the scan.

Sternberg's (1966) model of an exhaustive scan is so controversial that it is worthwhile to look into the supporting evidence in some detail. His subjects were presented with a series of digits at the rate of one digit every 1·2 seconds, and the series contained between 1 and 6 digits. Two seconds after presentation of the final member of the series a probe digit was presented. If the subject thought that the probe was a member of the original series then he pulled one lever, and if not he pulled another lever. The independent variable was the number of digits in the series and the dependent variable was the recognition response latency: how long did it take the subject to decide whether or not the probe was part of an encoded series? Each probe in the 144 trials had an equal probability of being in the positive set (i.e. presented) or in the negative set (i.e. not presented). No digit in the series was a repeat, and subjects were encouraged to make their responses as quickly as possible but without losing any accuracy. The error rate was in fact very low. In Fig. 3.6 the open circles are correct negative responses and the closed circles are correct positive recognitions. The linear regression here accounts for 99·4% of the variance of positive and negative responses — there is no difference in the slopes of "yes" and "no" response times with memory set size. The equation for the regression line is:

$$RT = 397·2 + 37·9S$$

This means that the slope intercepts the y-axis (response latency) at approximately 400 msec, and that the response latency is a composite of this constant and a value determined by the number of items searched (S). It takes almost 38 msec to scan one item, twice this time to scan two items, and so on, with the search time increasing linearly with increasing search sets. The intercept of 400 msec represents the time taken by the various processes which are independent of the number of items scanned,

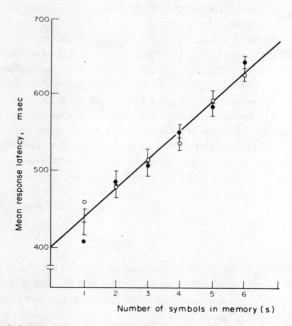

Fig. 3.6. Relation between response latency and the number of symbols in memory for positive (filled circles) and negative responses (open circles) from Sternberg (1966).

for instance, time taken to encode the probe, to start the search, to reach a decision and to execute the motor response. The linear function of response latency against the number of items searched suggests that a series of comparisons are made, one after the other. The addition of another item to be searched would then add a constant period to the total time taken by this search, and this period would be the time to make one comparison. If more than one item could be compared at the same time then adding items to the search set would not add a constant period to the total search time. The mean time per item with large sets would be less than the mean time per item with small sets. However, Sternberg concludes that "an internal representation of the test stimulus is compared successively to the symbols in memory, each comparison resulting in either a match or a mismatch". The time from the beginning of one comparison to the beginning of the next has the same mean value for successive comparisons.

The similarity between the functions for positive and negative responses suggests that the memory search is exhaustive rather than self-terminating. The self-terminating scan stops the comparison of probe against memory set as soon as a match is detected. With this strategy the subject would have only to scan the whole of the memory set when the match was with the final item scanned (or when a negative response was appropriate). With six items in the memory set this would occur, on average, one in six trials with positive response. On average the subject would only have to scan half of the items in the memory set, and with a self-terminating search the mean response time for positive responses should be considerably faster than for negative responses because in this case the whole of the set must be scanned on each trial. The slope of the function should be half of that for negative trials:

$$RT = 397 \cdot 2 + 37 \cdot 9(S/2)$$

However, the slopes of the two functions in Fig. 3.6 are identical. indicating that exhaustive scanning is operating. Even if the match is made with the first item selected in a set of six items the remaining five items are still scanned before the response is made.

Although the experiment reported by Sternberg (1966) involved a short-term memory process, with the subject being presented with a set of items and being tested immediately, it should be noted that essentially similar results have been reported for recognition scanning in long-term memory. Juola, Fischler, Wood, and Atkinson (1971) had their subjects learn lists of 10, 18 or 26 words, engage in a distraction task to ensure that the lists were not being retained with the rehearsal buffer, and then respond to a test probe. A linear increase in response latency with increasing memory set size suggested a serial search, but whereas Sternberg reported that the mean search time was about 38 msec per item the search time was 5 msec per item for an item in the long-term store. The search of the permanent store may have similarities with the search of recently presented information.

A number of problems have arisen with the interpretation of the serial-exhaustive search, and these will be mentioned before the consideration of the organization of search processes.

The exhaustive nature of the search is questioned by the appearance of serial position effects in response to individual members of the search set. Items at the ends of a set gain faster responses than items in the centre (e.g. Corballis, 1967; Clifton and Birenbaum, 1970; Corballis, Kirby and Miller, 1972; Forrin and Cunningham, 1973). If all items in the list are scanned before a response to a match is available, then it should make no difference to the response latency where in the sequence the match occurs. The recognition time decreases with proximity to the end of the list, but with a slightly decreased recognition time for the first item in the list. The serial position effect in memory search is not compatible with the simple exhaustive scan, but it is generally found with faster presentation rates than that used by Sternberg, and with a shorter delay between test set and probe. Burrows and Okada (1971) found primacy and recency at both fast and slow presentation rates however. Serial position effects are reduced considerably when the delay between the end of the test series and presentation of the probe is increased (Clifton and Birenbaum, 1970; Forrin and Cunningham, 1973). A modification of the exhaustive scanning model is in order if it is to explain these data, and an account based upon differing trace strengths, or accessibility (Burrows and Okada, 1971), meets these requirements. If the traces of the items in the search set are not uniform then we might expect that items with distinctive representation will be compared with the probe faster than will items which have lower trace strengths. The more recently presented items have stronger traces than central items as they would have longer read-out times from precategorical storage, and initial items have stronger traces due to their perceptual distinctiveness. Initial items in a list are processed more efficiently than central items, but the final items remain in the phonological representation for longer than any item and these traces are vulnerable to autonomous decay for the least time. Slowing down the rate of presentation would give subjects more encoding time for items which are perceived poorly, and so equalize the trace strengths. Indeed, Burrows and Okada (1971) report less pronounced serial position effects with their slower rate. Imposing a delay of testing may also act to afford opportunity to the enrichment of weak traces, thereby reducing the serial position effects.

A trace strength analysis is also appropriate to an experiment reported by Baddeley and Ecob (1973) in which items in the memory set were repeated. For example, in the digit sequence "2919" a recognition response to "9" would be faster than to "1", and to "9" in the sequence "2916". The repetition serves to increase the strength of the repeated item, and to increase accessibility for the probe item. Items which are less accessible through poorer encoding or greater decay will be more difficult to reach a decision about, and this is reflected in the response latency. Repeating an item serves to increase the trace strength and facilitate a faster decision.

The general principle of a sequential search which terminates not when a match is reached but when all items in the memory set have been scanned may be appropriate to experiments in which the set is small and well defined, but it does not seem likely to be the strategy which would be employed out of this context. For instance, when asked the question "What is Montpellier?" would it be profitable to search through all the proper names held in the lexicon, or would it be quicker to extract a set of possible categories from the probe and search only these categories? An exhaustive search of all names may be less efficient than an exhaustive search of certain categories of names even though the strategy would necessitate an extra categorization process. If categorical memory is organized into a series of hierarchies, as it may be (e.g. Segal, 1969; Collins and Quillian, 1972; Wood, 1972), then a memory search may be restricted to one of the categories of the hierarchy if a highly efficient retrieval plan is operating. Naus, Glucksberg, and Ornstein (1972) tested the generality of the exhaustive scanning strategy in the case of categorized word lists, and in particular tested between two processing strategies, the Directed Entry search and the Random Entry search. These two strategies describe how the search is started, and of course this has implications for how quickly it is completed.

The Directed Entry search specifies that the probe is categorized and that category entered purposively. With a self-terminating facility in addition this would imply that only the category indicated by the probe would be searched, and the number of comparisons made would be equal to the number of items in the probed category. This would lead to a reduction of 50% in the mean processing time per item when two categories are presented with equal numbers in each. With one category of n items the mean processing time would be kn msec/item, but with two categories each of $n/2$ items the mean processing time would be $kn/2$ msec/item with a Directed Entry search. This saving would be reflected in the slope of the function of response time against total number of items presented, and should be 50% of the slope for a one-category search.

The Random Entry search strategy proposes a random choice of the category first selected for scanning. If the category entered in a two-category search is the same as the category probed, and if we again add a feature of termination after searching the appropriate category, then the slope of response latency against total set size will be reduced by 50%. However, if the inappropriate category is searched first, as will happen on half of the trials, then there will be no slope reduction. With the Random Entry strategy the slope will be reduced by 50% on half of the trials, and not reduced at all on half of the trials. Hence the slope reduction would be 25% less than the one-category search on average. The advantage of this strategy over the Directed Entry search is that the category of the probe does not have to be estimated before the search is started.

Naus *et al.* investigated these strategies by comparing searches of one-category and two-category lists. The two-category searches were through blocks of animal names and girls' names. The positive set was composed of 2, 4, 6 or 8 words with equal proportions of words from each category when a two-category search was tested. One word was presented every 2 seconds and 2 seconds after the final words a warning light was presented and was followed by the probe. The dependent measure was how quickly the subject responded "yes" or "no" to the probe, according to whether or not the probe word had been in the original memory set. The subjects were well versed in the items which were likely to be presented in that they had learnt the total set of twelve animal names and twelve girls' names from which each test set was taken. The subjects were therefore well aware of the categorical nature of the presentation. The obtained slope for the one-category search was:

$$RT = 490 + 31 \cdot 9S$$

The obtained slope for the two-category search was:

$$RT = 499 + 24 \cdot 2S$$

Comparison of the averaged processing times per item gives a slope reduction of 24% for the two-category search, a result which corresponds closely with the prediction derived from the Random Entry model. The Random Entry model predicts that 75% of the items are searched when the memory set is categorized into two equal halves, and when processing times are estimated from the effective set size rather than the presented set size then the obtained slope for the two-category search was:

$$RT = 501 + 31 \cdot 7S$$

where S in this case is 75% of the total number of items presented. This search rate of 1 item every 31·7 msec is comparable with the search rate with one-category set.

Not all of the evidence is in favour of a Random Entry search, however, and when the data from individual subjects are analyzed it appears that whereas most subjects used this strategy one subject had an average slope reduction of 40% for the two-category sets. This indicates at least some use of a Directed Entry strategy, and that strategies are optional. They may be influenced by the material being handled but strategies are to some extent open to individual choice. Naus *et al.*, invoking a "net savings" hypothesis, suggest that Random Entry rather than Directed Entry strategies are preferred because of the matching operations necessary with Directed Entry. The additional process of finding the category of the probe and matching that category against the category of the appropriate set may lead to extra processing time which would outweigh the advantages of a shorter scan. The subject who had a slope reduction of 40%, and thus appeared to use the Directed Entry strategy some of the time, also had the greatest difference in intercept times for the one-and two-category searches. The intercept time is a measure of the time taken by processes common to all searches, as occupied by categorization, motor response, etc. Most subjects had a reduced slope consistent with the Random Entry strategy, and little increase in the time taken by constant processes, but this subject had a slope reduction consistent with the Directed Entry strategy and a greater increase in the number of constant processes required. The trade-off between number of items searched and number of constant processes appears to be a matter of individual preference. If a situation could be devised such that the trade-off would greatly benefit one or other strategy then presumably all subjects would employ one strategy rather than the other. For instance, if the Random Entry strategy forced the scanning of very large numbers of irrelevant categories then an additional categorization process may be the economical strategy to employ, as with the example of searching one's memory for the nature of

Montpellier. Rather than scan the names of all items in the lexicon it would seem more efficient to make a guess at the possible attributes of Montpellier and scan the names given under these locations. This categorization procedure may save time in comparison with a search which starts quicker but which may go on for longer because of the greater number of items searched.

This experiment as much as any other shows the variety of control processes which are available for operation upon our memories. In a situation where a clear-cut distinction was sought between two alternative strategies not all subjects employed the same strategy and furthermore individual subjects did not employ one strategy exclusively.

The generality of the use of Random Entry strategies in the search through short lists was tested by Underwood (1974b) in an experiment where unequally sized categories were used. Naus *et al.* presented lists composed of items from two categories, with equal numbers of items from each category in every list. This type of search set led to a strategy of entering the two-search sub-sets on a random basis: the subjects tended not to match the category of the probe with the category of the items in store. In this case the matching process was not economical, and category membership was not established. Suppose, however, that the search set had consisted of grossly unbalanced categories, as is the case with the items in our memories (do you know the names of more towns than you do the names of flowers, or of pieces of cutlery?). Would it still be economical to enter the categories on a random basis, or would it now be faster to extract the category of the probe and only search the most likely items? Lists of names of birds and of foodstuffs were first learnt by subjects, and then test lists presented and probed. The test lists were composed either from one of the categories, or from both with equal numbers of items from each, or from both with unequal numbers from each. Four, six or eight items were presented, and with unequal categories the composition of these lists was 3:1, 5:1, or 7:1 respectively, such that the smaller category always contained only one item. Positive and negative probes were presented equally often, but for purposes of simplicity only the regression lines from the trials with positive probes are presented in Fig. 3.7. First observe the difference between the two regression lines for the unequally categorized lists. The linear regression equation for the smaller category (one item) was:

$$RT = 728 + 2 \cdot 5S$$

The regression equation for the larger category (3, 5 or 7 items) was:

$$RT = 733 + 14 \cdot 7S$$

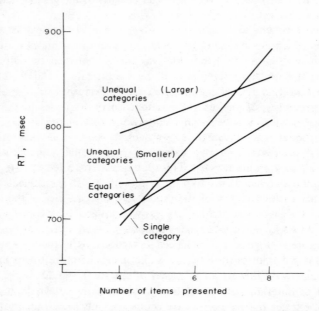

Fig. 3.7. Best fitting linear regression lines from memory search with positive probes. (From Underwood, 1974b.)

Whereas the latency in responding to the smaller category was almost constant regardless of the *total* number of items presented, the latency for an item from the larger category did vary with the number of items presented. Note also the high intercept times which suggest the presence of processes common to searches with all lists and which are invariant with the number of items presented. The longer intercept items indicate that subjects were extracting and matching the category of the probe with the categories of the search set, and entering only the appropriate sub-set. The regression equation for the equal categories was:

$$RT = 597 + 26 \cdot 1S$$

This also indicates a Directed Entry search, even though the intercept time is faster than for the unequally categorized lists, because the search time per item is reduced by 46% in comparison with the one-category lists, whose equation was:

$$RT = 496 + 48 \cdot 5S$$

The presence of a Directed Entry search with equal categories in this experiment, in contrast with that of Naus *et al.*, may have been due to the advantage of this strategy in other trials of the experiment. Once subjects started to use the Directed Entry strategy they may have applied it throughout the experiment. Apart from demonstrating the use of the strategy when conditions are favourable, supporting the "net savings" hypothesis, the data raise two problems. A difference of approximately a tenth of a second appears to be necessary for a Directed Entry to the appropriate sub-set, as indicated by the intercept times for one-category and equally categorized lists. Why then should a further increase in intercept time be necessary with unequally categorized lists? Further processes are evidently necessary with unbalanced lists, but their identification will require further investigation. Secondly, a Directed Entry search of the larger category of an unbalanced list should have produced a saving in the mean search time per item of approximately 18%, but the observed slope reduction was 70% in comparison with the one-category search, perhaps indicating that a categorized probe may be compared with the items in store faster than may be an uncategorized probe. The mean search time for equally balanced lists does not support this hypothesis, and there are clearly a number of differences between the Directed Entry strategies used with the balanced and unbalanced lists in this experiment.

Before leaving the area of memory search it may be worth mentioning one or two points raised in a theoretical paper presented by Cavanagh (1972). Sternberg (1966) found that digits were scanned at the rate of 38 msec per item, and since the experiment many replications have been reported, but not all of them have used digits. Where different materials have been used different scanning rates have been found. Cavanagh compared the scanning rate with the memory span for a variety of materials —

digits, colours, letters, geometrical shapes, words, random forms, and non-sense syllables — and the result of this startling comparison is present in Fig. 3.8. This shows an inverse linear relationship between processing rate

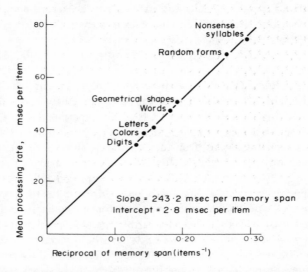

Fig. 3.8. The relation between short-term memory processing rate and the reciprocal of the memory span for seven classes of stimuli. (From Cavanagh, 1972).

and the memory span for the material processed: the fewer the number of items in the memory span the slower is the scanning rate. If the memory span is high, as with digits, then these items are scanned quickly. The slope of this function is of interest and indicates that the time taken to process a full memory load (whatever the material) is constant at approximately ¼ second.

In other words, if the memory span for a particular type of material was one item, then it would take ¼ second to scan it in a memory search task. This result of varying processing rates to give a constant periodicity of memory availability may be related to the view of memory suggested in the previous chapter. This view is based upon the unitary trace notion and abandons the dualist constructs of short-term memory and long-term memory. Examples of the operation of primary memory are considered to result from the decay time of the unrepeated phonological representation of a word. The immediate memory span may also be a product of limited rehearsal rates, the memory span being the number of items that can be reported before the phonological trace fades. Cavanagh's review indicates that the time to process a full memory span is constant, regardless of the type of material stored. Whereas the primary memory span appears to be constant regardless of the length of the words (Craik, 1968), the immediate memory span is subject to variation. The scanning rate appears to be a constant number of features per unit time, with individual items containing many features being scanned at a slower rate per item than are items with fewer distinctive features. The invariance of primary memory capacity with length of words can also be accounted for by considering the number of retained distinctive features to vary according to the time allowed for decay. Decay will strip off a constant number of features, but if the word has more features then it will appear to be less affected by decay than will be a shorter word. The short word will have been rehearsed more recently and so will have decayed less, but the decay will have stripped off a certain number of features. The long word will have been rehearsed less recently, will have been open to more decay and will have lost more features. The long word will still have a certain number of features remaining however, and will still be retrievable in its phonological form. Long and short words will therefore lose the same proportion of their features and the phonological representations will be equally retrievable despite being in relatively more or less decayed form. The immediate memory span may be composed of items retrieved on the basis of their phonological codes but items will as often be retrieved by their elaborated or semantic features. If two or three words can be related subjectively into one chunk then the span can be increased two or threefold. The span is a measure of the number of chunks that can be constructed during the presentation of the list, and it is evidently easier to form unrelated items together into chunks if the items are familiar (digits, letters) than if they are unfamiliar (nonsense syllables, random forms). Hence the memory span is not constant for all materials, as it would be if it were totally dependent upon the rate of rehearsal and retrieval of the phonological representation. The constant scanning rate of a full memory span, indicating a constant rate of processing of distinctive features, supports the view that retrieval is dependent upon the number of available features regardless of how they are distributed into long and short words. The more features an item has the longer it will take to compare the item with another during memory search, and the longer it may take to set up the appropriate programme for phonological recirculation. The more features an item has, the slower will be the processing but the more resilient the trace will be during the period of inattention, and consequent decay.

Intentional Forgetting: Organization of Retrieval

The retrieval of information from memory is dependent to a certain extent upon individual differences; retrieval strategies are control processes selected by the individual. If information is potentially available but not retrieved then it is said to be forgotten whether it is retrievable at a later time or not. Given that humans have a system which can efficiently (or at least moderately efficiently) perceive and store verbal material, then we must also have a function in this system by which information which is no longer needed can be ignored. We have to know which information is useful for the task in hand, and we have to be able to both dispense with information which will not be required after immediate processing and inhibit the retrieval of information irrelevant to the task in hand. A function is needed whereby old information is selectively prevented from interfering with new information otherwise the processing would simply be overloaded. A number of case studies are available to indicate what happens when the forgetting process fails to operate selectively and two studies will be mentioned here. Luria (1969) reports the case of an individual with a very persistent iconic memory and strong visual imagery. This subject was able to perform remarkable feats of memory and eventually took a job as a professional mnemonist. Long lists of unrelated digits or letters would be remembered perfectly, as could complex and meaningless mathematical formulae which had been invented. In the summer of 1936 he was given a long series of nonsense monosyllables to learn. He reproduced them perfectly on immediate testing, and again in April 1944 when he had no reason to expect to be tested. Such a "perfect" memory may seem very desirable to us, but it led to considerable problems and it seems more desirable to be able to forget, or at least inhibit the retrieval of all but the most relevant information at any one time. The mnemonic technique which Luria's subject used was to visualize the symbols around a story. Words very easily conjured up their images but this concrete memory also led to concrete thinking. The surface image of a metaphor, for example, would prevent comprehension of the deeper meaning. The life of this individual was largely dictated by the visual images of words which he came across. Images became reality and distracted him from whatever task he was engaged with, and Luria described him as a daydreamer who was engulfed by images that were all too vivid. This failure to lose sight of the distinction between reality and fantasy, which was a consequence of a very powerful mnemonic tool caused him to change jobs dozens of times before becoming a stage mnemonist. Even then his memory was a handicap because material remembered from previous performances tended to interfere with the material which was required. He had to train himself to forget images which were no longer needed, and he did this by visualizing the blackboard with the unwanted material written upon it and then erasing the material and covering it with an opaque film. Another technique was to jot down on paper the message he wished to forget and then burn it. If we do not have a system for forgetting then it seems that we have to learn one.

Hunt and Love (1972) also describe a remarkable mnemonist who at the age of 5 memorized the street map of a city with a population of half a million, and memorized railway and bus timetables. As an adult he was able to play up to seven games of chess simultaneously whilst blindfolded. He gave perfect performances on a number of experimental tasks administered by Hunt and Love, and on a memory search task of the Sternberg type he was able to scan all members of the search set in parallel. Adding items to the search set made very little difference to his response latency. However, this subject does not appear to have used visual imagery exclusively as a mnemonic technique, although he did score higher than other subjects on an imagery test (Paivio, 1971). He does not suffer from the problems of distinguishing reality which Luria's subject was troubled with, although he is an under-achiever in that he did not finish his college education and now works as a store clerk. A remarkable memory is not a sufficient qualification for economic success. This subject claims to have acquired the ability to remember long passages during childhood, and that he practised the use of mnemonic techniques. His outstanding memory is therefore due to active attempts to learn information rather than to the spontaneous appearance of visual images, as with Luria's subject. Whereas Luria's subject was unable to select between relevant and irrelevant information Hunt and Love's subject did have this selectivity, and the importance of this discriminating function is evident in the differences in their personalities.

One of the ways in which experimental psychologists have looked at the question of selectivity in the elimination of information from consciousness is with the phenomenon of intentional forgetting. The general paradigm here is to present a series of items and to cue the subject that part of the series will not be tested for recall. By a number of measures it might appear to be the case that these items, cued as to-be-forgotten, are indeed erased from the subject's memory: there is little interference with the recall of to-be-remembered items, and when at the end of the experiment the subject is asked to recall the to-be-forgotten items he is able to remember remarkably few of them.

Bjork, LaBerge, and Legrand (1968), in one of the first studies of intentional forgetting, were concerned to discover whether cueing subjects to forget earlier items in a trial was sufficient to reduce the proactive interference operating upon later items in that trial. Each subject was presented with a series of digits which were to be shadowed, and amongst these digits were either one or two consonant quadragrams (e.g. "SBLV"). The aim of the experiment was to assess the effect of proactive interferences from the first quadragram upon recall of the second quadragram, and the effect of instructions to forget the first quadragram upon this source of interference. The three conditions necessary for this comparison were (i) presentation and recall of both quadragrams (with recall of the second quadragram first, to minimize the effects of decay and response interference); (ii) presentation of both quadragrams with instructions after presentation of the first quadragram that it may be forgotten, with recall of the second quadragram only; (iii) presentation and recall of only one of the quadragrams, with no possibility of proactive interference from an earlier source in any trial. The purpose of the shadowing task was to equalize the amounts of rehearsal given to the quadragrams in all conditions. Without the shadowing task the forget cue could serve to reduce the amount of rehearsal given to the to-be-forgotten quadragram. The forget cue might otherwise act to manipulate the trace strengths of the items rather than their interference effects *per se*.

When only one quadragram was presented recall was more successful than when two quadragrams were presented and recalled, indicating an effect of proactive interference from the first quadragram when it is required for recall. When the subject was instructed that the first quadragram was not required for recall then recall of the second quadragram increased, though not as much as when it was presented alone. A certain amount of proactive interference was present even with the forget cue, though not nearly so much as when the subject had to remember the earlier material.

A number of alternative explanations suggest themselves from this experiment to account for the effect of to cue to forget. Subjects may be able to erase completely the to-be-forgotten items from memory. This would leave no memory trace and recall of the cued items would then be impossible. The proactive interference from to-be-forgotten items, although less than that from to-be-remembered items, is still effective, and suggests that total erasure is not the forgetting mechanism in use here. Selective rehearsal is also a possible mechanism for the effect. Items which are cued to-be-forgotten may not actively be forgotten, but more simply their traces may not be strengthened by rehearsal. Manipulation of this control process may allow more or less amounts of interference to act upon subsequently presented material. The presence of the shadowing task in the experiment reported by Bjork, LaBerge, and Legrand would tend to reduce the amount of rehearsal after presentation of the first quadragram, but the shadowed digits were presented at the rate of only one per second. Subjects may therefore have rehearsed the first quadragram between uttering the shadowing responses. The third explanation of the effect also relies upon control processes available to the subjects. The forget cue may serve to categorize the two quadragrams and this differentiation would serve to reduce interference between them. If one of the quadragrams can be encoded or tagged differently then different retrieval cues would be available about the consonant items. The quadragrams would interfere with each other less if they were categorized differently due to a "release from proactive interference" effect (Wickens, Born and Allen, 1963). Interference results from similarity, and so the more easily two items can be differentiated the less will be the interference between them.

The organisation theory has been supported by an experiment reported by Bjork (1970) using a paired-associates task. Each trial proceeded as follows: (i) two pairs of items were shown on a yellow background;

(ii) an explicit instruction was then given to remember *or* to forget the "yellow" items; (iii) two pairs of items were shown on a green background; (iv) an instruction was given to either forget *or* remember the yellow *or* the green items; (v) the subject recalled the second members of to-be-remembered pairs upon presentation of the first member. The five conditions may be abbreviated as follows: (a) remember yellow — remember green (RY:RG); (b) remember yellow — forget yellow (RY:FY); (c) remember yellow — forget green (RY:FG); (d) forget yellow — remember green (FY:RG); (e) forget yellow — forget green (FY:FG), in which case no recall test was given. Comparisons between these conditions are apparent in Fig. 3.9. The FY:FG condition was necessary so that the FY:RG was not totally predictable on presentation of the FY instruction. Only when an instruction was given did the subjects know whether to retain an item or not. One of the most striking effects in Fig. 3.9 is that of the delay of the forget cue. Performance with the green items is much better when the subject is told to ignore the yellow items before being given the green items (FY:RG) than when he was told afterwards (RY:FY). When subjects were told to ignore yellow items (following storage) until after encoding of the green items (RY:FY) then performance is not much better than when they have to remember both pairs (RY:RG). Bjork argues that these

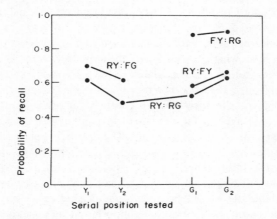

Fig. 3.9. Correct response proportions as a function of forget and recall instructions. (From Bjork, 1970.)

data support a theory of intentional forgetting which postulates both the rehearsal and organization processes to be operating. Organization could be on the basis of the forget cue, which would differentiate between sets of items and reduce the interference between them, but organization is inadequate to account for the results on its own, otherwise performance in the RY:FY condition should equal performance in the FY:RG condition. In either case the subject has only to search one set of items at the time of recall.

The account of intentional forgetting which is based upon differential rehearsal has been given support by an experiment reported by Roediger and Crowder (1972) in which rehearsal strategies were manipulated. In each trial the subject was presented with a consonant trigram and a three-digit number, and always had to count backwards in threes from the number given at the same time as the trigram. The counting task lasted for 3, 9 or 17 seconds, after which a dashed line indicated that the subject should attempt to recall the consonants. Three sets of instructions were used to modify the strategies used for retaining the trigram during the counting task. The instructions were: (i) "try to remember and rehearse the item while still counting quickly"; or (ii) "try to remember the item during the retention interval, but without covert rehearsal"; or (iii) "attempt to forget the letters between the time you see them and read them aloud and the time the dashed line appears after your backward counting". One problem with this design is that in the "forget" condition the subject knows that he will have to remember the item after some interval. The item will not be intentionally forgotten as it was with the Bjork *et al.* (1968) and Bjork (1970) experiments, and this experiment is therefore not directly comparable. Its value is in the demonstration of the importance of rehearsal strategies for retention, for the forget cue would not have been so potent as in the earlier experiments. Two measures were taken from each trial, and they were the success of recall and the number of counting responses made. The forget cue clearly had an effect upon recall, and the effect was to decrease recall as the retention interval increased. When subjects were instructed to rehearse while counting backwards they performed better than all other subjects, and the effect of an increased retention interval was slight. The number of counting responses made in each condition might be an indication of the amount of attention paid to the memory task, rehearsal being a manifestation of attention. More attention paid to the counting task would mean less attention paid to the retention of the consonant trigram, assuming that we have a limited amount of attention available for distribution. If the number of counting responses is inversely related to the number of rehearsal attempts, then the same rank ordering of conditions appears as it did with retention performances. In general, the less was the opportunity for rehearsal the lower was the final recall score. The results indicated that the effects of forget instructions can be explained by non-rehearsal of the cued material, and Roediger and Crowder concluded that the instruction to forget was interpreted by subjects in the same way as the instruction not to rehearse. Differences between these two conditions are said to be due to differences in the initial encoding of the trigram.

Altered strategies of rehearsal may account for the effect of the forget cue, but an equally credible explanation argues for organization of material as the mechanism. Woodward and Bjork (1971) presented lists of common words to subjects for immediate recall after presentation of each complete list of 24 words. After each word in the list a cue indicated to the subject whether that word was to-be-forgotten or to-be-remembered. After recalling the to-be-remembered words (half of each list) from six of these lists the subjects were then required to recall all of the words presented in all lists regardless of how they were cued. In a second condition the lists were categorized into six groups each with four words. This stimulus clustering improved the final recall of both to-be-forgotten and to-be-remembered words. The more to-be-remembered words there were in a category the greater was the chance of the to-be-forgotten words in that category being recalled. If a category was composed entirely of to-be-forgotten words then the chance of any one of these words being recalled was much less than that of a to-be-forgotten word in a group composed mainly of to-be-remembered words. Although subjects did rehearse the to-be-remembered words more often than they did to-be-forgotten words a large effect of organization is apparent in this experiment. If the subject has a retrieval cue, derived from the category of the adjacent to-be-remembered words, then forgotten words may be recalled. It appears to be the case that to-be-forgotten words are not excluded from memory altogether, but that they are not retrievable unless aided by specific cues, such as semantic category. The availability of "forgotten" words is indicated by an experiment reported by Elmes, Adams, and Roediger (1970) in which a delayed recognition test showed little difference between the recognition of to-be-remembered and to-be-forgotten words.

Support for the selective retrieval hypothesis of intentional forgetting also comes from an investigation of what Epstein and Wilder (1972) describe as the "only effect". This term refers to the superior recall of to-be-remembered items, in the intentional forgetting paradigm, when a particular set of items is cued rather than any set. Given two sets of items to remember the subject might be cued to retrieve set A or set B, or either, but he performs better if informed that a probe will test a particular set. This effect is interpreted to be due to a strategy of selective search: the cue "Set A" excludes set B from the search, but the probe "Either" means that the subject has to search through both sets. Epstein and Wilder varied this design slightly in order to test the non-cued set, the set which the subject is to regard as useless. Subjects were always presented with four pairs of stimuli, and a pair consisted of a nonsense syllable associated with a common word. Two of the words were semantically related by some category, and the other two words were from another category. Four such pairs might then be BAF-DOOR; TEV-WALL; CEB-SPIDER; QYT-ROACH. To emphasize the categorization the pairs were presented in two blocks, with an interpolated distraction task performed between the blocks. After the four pairs had been presented a cue indicated to the subject whether the probe would relate to the first block, the second block or to either of them. After a pause a single syllable was shown and the subject was required to respond with its paired associate. Following a number of trials with this procedure the subject was unknowingly presented with inappropriate search cues. The subject would be informed that the test would be of one block, but a nonsense syllable from the other block would be presented. At the time of presentation of the nonsense syllable the subject would either be informed that the cue was inaccurate, or given no information about its validity.

In the trials where the cue was accurate the "only effect" appeared in the comparison between cues to specific blocks, and cues to either block, with "only" cues 83% of the words were recalled on presentation of the syllable, and with "either" over 50% of words were recalled. If subjects were informed that the "only" cue was inaccurate then they were able to recall 46% of the words which had been designated as to-be-forgotten by implication. If subjects were not informed of the inaccuracy of the "only" cue then they recalled 13% of these words. Given an inaccurate search cue words have the appearance of being forgotten, but when subjects are informed that the cue is inappropriate they could redirect the categorical search and recall was equal to that of lists in which no forget cue was given.

The results of Epstein and Wilder may be interpreted to indicate that "forgotten" material is not forgotten at all, and that failures of memory are often due to inappropriate search plans being used. This conclusion is supported by work on the effect of another factor in remembering — the factor of ageing. Performance on memory tasks declines from maturity to old age (Welford, 1958; Kay, 1968), but Schonfield and Robertson (1966) found that the age decrement is restricted to recall. They found no large age differences with a recognition task, and it may be that where memory decrements appear they result from inappropriate search strategies. Words may always be available, but not necessarily accessible.

This discussion of control processes has concentrated upon strategies of rehearsal, organization, and retrieval. These three functions of memory are quite inseparable even though they have been dealt with in some isolation here and elsewhere. When given meaningful information subjects rehearse together items which are related, and when relatively meaningless information is used the subject imposes his own organizations by rhythmic grouping. Organized rehearsal serves to organize storage and retrieval, for items which are categorized together facilitate the retrieval of each other in the search of memory. Organization may be on the basis of previously learnt associations but it is just as likely to be on the basis of temporal grouping, as in the case of rhythmic rehearsal of random strings of digits. Using the description of Gordon Bower (1970), "what we remember is our cognitive autobiography, not stimulus and response events", and any associations which arise during the period of presentation and storage may be used as a cue upon which retrieval may be based. Bartlett (1932) showed that material to be remembered will be selectively integrated with the subjects' existing schemata, and not as material to be remembered *per se.* Studies of human memory appear at last to be moving away from the sterile approach of verbal learning theory, and towards a less segmented view of cognitive organization.

CHAPTER 4

ATTENDING AND REMEMBERING

One of the most effective processes which control how we perform on recall cases was not dealt with in any detail in the discussion of Control Processes, and this is the process of attention. In general it is true that unless we attend to a stimulus we are unable to remember and respond to it. After making such an over-statement as this we must immediately qualify it by saying that this is largely the case for stimuli about which we are uncertain, and less true for stimuli which we can predict. We need to attend to a list of digits which form a telephone number if we intend to use that number, but we can walk down a street without attending to every bump in the pavement. The difference between these two activities is that the information contained in the telephone number is largely un-predictable, but the information necessary to walk down the street is very small and may be handled by automatic activities, following extensive practice (see Welford, 1968). Only when we are given an unpredictable input is attention necessary, for instance if we turn a corner and are faced with an open man-hole. Attention is not essential for all activities, even apparently complex activities. When driving a car we frequently find that we have negotiated a section of the route involving a number of bends, gear changes, and in which a certain amount of traffic had been present, but that we cannot remember having driven along that section. We may be so engrossed in our conversation or our thoughts that the realization that we are some distance from the last point we can remember may be quite surprising. There are two alternatives to the explanation of this phenomenon. One is that we did not attend to the "missing" section of the route and that our driving was controlled by automatic activities, and the other is that we did attend but on performing each manoeuvre we for-got it completely and rapidly. Both of these are viable explanations and will be examined in more detail later, but for the present purposes attention is considered to be necessary for the processing of unpredictable information. A similar phenomenon then occurs when reading large sections of text. We may find that we have "read" a complete page in that each of the individual words may have been recognized, but that we cannot remember any of the meaning of the text, and may be able to remember few of the isolated ideas presented. Whilst involved with one's own thoughts sufficient processing capacity may be available for the analysis of individual words and phrases, but to integrate these ideas with each other and with other schemata one's attention (meaning the bulk of the available processing capacity) is required. In order to remember information we must attend to it, even though we need not attempt to remember it intentionally. Perception is equivalent to encoding, and so whenever we process information we will remember it unless we take steps to forget it. The perception of unpredictable events requires attention, and so if we need to remember an event then we need to attend to it. A further debatable issue here is whether attention operates upon perception, or whether all events are perceived regardless of the direction of attention. This point will also be discussed in a later section. The present discussion makes the assumption that attention is required for remembering, and that it is not possible to study memory without taking account of the process of attention. Attention is directed towards the material to be remembered in memory experiments by instructions given to the subject, but these instructions may be implicit or explicit. If we engage the subject on another task while a list of digits are read out aloud, with instructions to attend to the task in hand then the subject would recall few of the digits, certainly fewer than if he had listened intentionally and attended to the digits alone. We find difficulty in reading a book and listening to the radio at the same time, and our difficulty in comprehension necessarily results in a decrement when attempting to recall what we have heard and what we have read. This very technique of diverting attention between two tasks has been used to investigate mnemonic processes with some success in recent years, and has been referred to as the residual processing capacity methodology. The dependent measure in memory experiments may be the number of items recalled, or it may be the latency of response to a probe item as in the memory search experiments, but a second measure may also be taken in the case of an accurate response, and that measure is the level of accuracy on a subsidiary task which is performed at the same time as the memory task.

Dividing Attention to Study Memory: Residual Processing Capacity Methods

This is a methodology derived from man-machine design problems where the designer needs to evaluate the processing load imposed by alternative systems. A problem here is that under normal conditions the operator may not make any errors even though the alternative systems may impose different loads. One system may be more difficult to operate than another, but only under stress would faults in the systems become apparent. To find which system produces the most faults the operator may be placed under induced stress, but an alternative is to occupy the residual processing capacity of the operator under normal running conditions by using a simultaneous subsidiary task, and measure performance on the subsidiary task when performance on the main task is optimal. This method is based upon a view of human perception and response in terms of the transmission of information through a communication system, and has come to be known as Information Processing Theory (Craik, 1948; Welford, 1952, Broadbent, 1958). With this body of theory the common experience that humans cannot perform several tasks at the same time as well as we can perform them individually can be described as demonstrating that the processing capacity available to the human is limited. The strong form of this theory argues that two independent messages cannot be handled concurrently, and this is supported by the phenomenon of the psychological refractory period. A single response to one signal may be delayed if that signal is presented soon after a first signal (Telford, 1931; Vince, 1948), and the single channel theory of information processing considers that the delay is caused by the processing of the first signal. The response to the second signal is postponed until after the processing of the first signal is cleared. A weaker version of the limited processing capacity theory considers not that the human has a single processing channel of fixed capacity, as the refractory studies imply, but that he is a processor who may handle many channels provided that the total fixed amount of capacity is not exceeded (Moray, 1967). In this way well practised or highly compatible responses are said to be easier because they require less processing time and capacity compared with novel or incompatible responses. Many tasks can be performed simultaneously provided that the sum of the capacity available to the processor is not exceeded by the sum of the capacity required for each task. Thus in our example of walking along the street whilst holding a conversation these two tasks are said to require a total amount of processing capacity which is within the means of the system. If the conversation turns to a discussion of some obtuse concept, then more capacity will be required for the maintenance of the conversation. If the sum of the capacities is now exceeded, or close to being exceeded, then any input to the walking activity which requires extra capacity will lead to a breakdown in the performance of one or other of the tasks. The main feature of this analysis is that man has a limited amount of processing capacity available — he is able to perform only a limited number of tasks at the same time. Instances where this generalization is seemingly contradicted (e.g. "one-man" bands) may arise through some or all of the activities being overpractised and so consuming minimum amounts of capacity.

To compare the capacity consumed by two different tasks (E1 and E2) each of which may be performed perfectly under optimal conditions, residual processing capacity methodology adds the same loading task (L) to each of the experimental tasks. With the capacity limit now exceeded errors occur, and the combination (E1 + L; or E2 + L) which produces the most errors has the most difficult experimental task. This method is related to that involved in the application of Archimedes' principle, in which the volume of a solid is not measured directly, but by the amount of water it displaces when immersed. The combinations of experimental and loading tasks are indicated in Fig. 4.1. Brown (1965) used a loading task to obtain objective measures of the performance of car drivers. The processing capacity required for driving is difficult to measure directly because the driver is usually self-paced and motivated to avoid errors, especially when his performance is being watched. He tends to maintain his activity at a level below that which would occupy all of the available processing capacity, thereby keeping in reserve a certain amount of residual capacity to meet unpredictable events. Brown instructed his subjects to drive as well as they could (the primary, or experimental task) whilst performing an auditory short-term memory task (the subsidiary, or loading task). The subsidiary task consisted of listening to lists of digits and reporting whenever the sequence odd-even-odd was presented. As would be expected, errors on the subsidiary task were more frequent in heavy traffic conditions than when driving was straightforward. Driving performances would have been very difficult to assess directly, but the errors

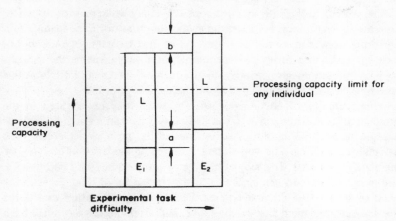

Fig. 4.1. Using a loading task to assess the relative difficulty of two experimental tasks. E1 and E2 are the experimental tasks which, when performed alone, require less capacity than is available and so are performed perfectly. Only when the loading task (L) is added to an experimental task do any errors appear as a result of exceeding the processing capacity limit with the processing capacity requirement.

produced on the memory task indicated clearly which of the driving situations occupied the most capacity.

Johnston, Greenberg, Fisher and Martin (1970) have demonstrated the usefulness of the residual processing capacity method in the study of memory, where performance on a loading task was measured as a function of the processing demands of a memory task. The loading task in their series of experiments involved the tracking of a moving line on a screen with a lever on the armrest of the subject's chair. The subject was instructed to attempt to follow the movement of the line by adjusting the lever, which was connected to a second line on the screen. This is a continuous task and is therefore preferable to intermittent tasks involving the presentation and response to digits because if the subject is engaged continuously on the leading task it is impossible for him to switch between tasks. With an intermittent task the subject may have been able to switch his attention back and forth between the primary and subsidiary tasks, and although the subsidiary task would have reduced the amount of available processing time performance would have been a measure of the success with which the subject could switch his attention as well as a measure of the difficulty of the primary task. With a continuous subsidiary task errors occur whenever the subject directs his attention away from that task. The loading task performance was measured as a function of the processing of a number of memory tasks in a series of experiments. In all experiments the subjects were instructed to give priority to the memory tasks, and an incentive scheme of reward was employed to encourage this priority.

The difficulty of encoding words for recall was investigated in the presence of the loading task, when difficulty was manipulated by increasing the rate of presentation, or by presenting the material under poor listening conditions. The verbal task involved the extraction of category members from a list. The subject heard a category name (e.g. "furniture"), and was required to remember as many instances of that category as possible from a list of mixed items. During the presentation of the list the subject performed the tracking task, and after the last word had been presented tracking stopped and the subject recalled all of the category members which had been heard. Adding noise to the list as it was presented produced a disruption of the tracking task, but rather surprisingly the rate of presentation had little effect and when the rate was increased *and* noise added the number of tracking errors did not increase above that number for poor listening conditions alone. Increasing the rate of presentation was only effective when noise was added to the list.

The retention load was also found to be related to the number of tracking errors made. Words forming lists of varying lengths were presented, and tracking performances monitored during a 21-second retention interval prior to recall. Longer lists produced more errors on the subsidiary task, but a feature of interest for the errors over the retention interval was that fewer errors were made during the first few seconds than over the last 16 seconds of retention. The ease of short-term retention may be due to the presence of sensory information or clear phonemic representations shortly after presentation and to the increased necessity for rehearsal during longer retention intervals.

The activity of recall also affected the performance of the subsidiary task, which was measured as a function of a number of recall tasks. Subjects were presented with five words, and they then started tracking. After 5 seconds, the subjects were given a cue instructing them to recall the words in one of four ways. These cues indicated free recall (in any order), serial recall (in the order of presentation), backward recall (opposite order to presentation), or alphabetic recall (alphabetical order of the first letter of the words). Tracking errors were measured from the presentation of the recall cue, and indicated no difference between the processing of free and serial recall, but these modes were easier than backward and alphabetic recall, which did not differ between themselves.

Comparisons between these three experiments are not strictly valid because different tasks, memory loads, retention intervals (etc.) were used between experiments. It is, however, tempting to look at subsidiary task performances over encoding, retention and retrieval, and this comparison indicates that more tracking errors are produced during retrieval than during the other two stages. Perhaps this is because more capacity is required for overt recall than for the other stages, but another possibility is that all three stages require similar amounts of capacity but that recall permits less simultaneous processing with tracking than do the other stages. It may be more difficult to organize and execute two overt activities than one overt activity plus one covert activity. This view is consistent with an effect reported in an experiment where subjects listened to lists of letters and responded selectively to a digit embedded in the list (Underwood, 1972). Subjects responded to the digit either immediately or after presentation of the list, and were required to remember the list or to shadow it during presentation. When engaged in the continuous overt activity of shadowing an overt report of a detection produced a slight decrement of the performance of the shadowing task in comparison with the condition in which subject remembered the digit until after completing the shadowing task. An immediate overt response had no such effect upon the covert encoding task, as indicated by the recall of the whole list. The overt shadowing response also led to a decrement in the number of targets detected, although it made little difference whether they were reported overtly or encoded and reported at the end of the list.

The amount of processing capacity required for overt recall was investigated by Martin (1970) using a situation similar to that of Johnston *et al.* (1970). The subsidiary task was the tracking of a moving line on a screen, and the dependent measure was the number of errors produced during memory tasks. Tracking was observed during the whole of each trial in this experiment, during the presentation and recall of each list. An additional variable which Martin looked at was the organization of the lists of words during input. Words were presented in blocks of semantically related words, or the same words were presented in random order. Presentation was at the rate of one word per second, and two blocks with four words in each were used in one of Martin's experiments. Each list of eight words was presented three times to observe the effects of organization upon demands of processing capacity. Tulving (1968) suggested that learning is the result of efficient organization, and so with added trials organization should require decreasing amounts of capacity and hence allow greater tracking accuracy. Tracking errors, which are an indirect measure of the capacity allocated to the memory task, indicated that retrieval did demand more capacity than did encoding, and that repeated presentation and recall of the same items served to increase the efficiency of recall rather than encoding. The organization of items in memory, which decreases with increased familiarity appears to occur at retrieval. Increased familiarity had little effect upon the capacity required for encoding, although the conclusion that organization is a retrieval effect was not supported by a subsequent experiment showing that lists which could be organized by categorization required less processing capacity than lists which could not easily be categorized, and this advantage was gained by the encoding, storage and retrieval stages (Martin, Marston and Kelly, 1973).

An alternative method of determining the amount of processing capacity allocated to a primary task has employed occasional responses to a simple signal. This method, used notably by Posner and his colleagues (Posner and Boies, 1971; Posner and Klein, 1972), does not reduce the total amount of capacity available during the complete performance of the primary task, but tests the amounts of residual capacity at various stages. The subject is instructed to perform the primary task as well as possible but also to press a button whenever he hears a burst of noise. Fast responses to the noise are taken to indicate that the primary task is not consuming all of the available capacity whereas slow responses indicate that there is little capacity residual from the primary task. One particularly interesting result from this series of experiments is that the process of encoding a stimulus appears not to demand capacity. Posner and Boies (1971) presented a probe stimulus at various points during a letter-matching task. The primary task was for the subject to indicate whether two letters were the same when they were presented one after the other, separated by several seconds. The subject was also required to press a button whenever he heard a tone.

Immediately after presentation of the first letter the response to the tone
was no slower than when the subject gave full attention to the tone in a
control condition. The response latency to the tone started to rise about a
quarter of a second after presentation of the first letter, and started to decrease again after presentation of the second letter. A cumulative record of
the latencies to probes presented at various points during a number of trials
is given in Fig. 4.2 as a function of two exposure durations of the first

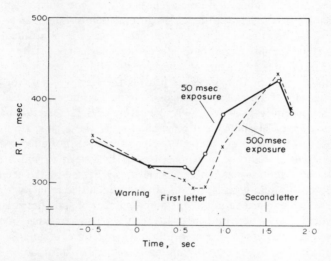

Fig. 4.2. Probe RTs compared for exposure durations of the first letters of 50 and
500 msec. (From Posner and Boies, 1971.)

letter (50 msec, and 500 msec). The second letter was exposed until the
same-different response was made. During the period following presentation of the first letter the subject is assumed to actively encode the stimulus in preparation for the matching response when the second letter is
presented. The encoding process does not affect the response to the probe
whilst a sensory representation may be assumed to be present. Only when
the subject relies upon his own representation, phonemic or visual, is response to the probe delayed. A methodological problem inherent in the
probe reaction paradigm for assessing the available processing capacity is

that a second variable confounds the interpretation, and this is the temporal expectancy of the subject. When the subject is aware that on some trials he will be tested with a single probe he will not necessarily expect to be tested an equal number of times at each of the possible points during the trial sequence. Certain events during the sequence may lead to an expectation of being tested at certain points and not at others. Test uncertainty, as well as capacity availability, and preattentiveness of encoding may have been affecting performance in the Posner and Boies experiment. If the subject is expecting to be tested at some points more than at others then a probe presented at this time will gain a faster response than other probes. The variability of response latency here may not be totally accountable to preattentive processing of aspects of the primary task.

Subsidiary task performances are proving themselves as a useful tool in the assessment of the attention demanded by various mnemonic tasks, and they also indicate very convincingly the nature of the interaction between the processes of attending and remembering. If we do not attend to a stimulus, and this is to say that processing capacity is not allocated to it, then we have difficulty in remembering it. The extent to which we do attend to storage, organization and retrieval is reflected by the decrement recorded on subsidiary tasks. We do not have unlimited capacity available and we are able to attend to only a limited number of activities at any one time, whether these activities are overt, such as pursuit tracking, or covert, such as organizing items in memory into meaningful configurations. The necessity of attention when attempting to remember information is also demonstrated by a series of experiments in which two messages are presented simultaneously to subjects. If one of these messages is attended to then subjects can recall very little of the other message, but the validity of this claim is considered in the following discussion.

Memory for Unattended Information

The "early-selection" theories of attention described by Broadbent (1958), Treisman (1960, 1964a), Neisser (1967), and Moray (1969) argue that the selection of a message for processing is based upon the physical characteristics (location, intensity, voice pitch, etc.) of the message, with meaning extracted only from those signals which are selected. Reports of highly probable or important words (Moray, 1959; Treisman, 1960) in the non-selected, and therefore unattended messages, are considered to result from low recognition thresholds or from occasional sampling of the unattended messages, which then becomes the attended message.

The "late-selection" theories of Deutsch and Deutsch (1963), Reynolds (1964), Norman (1969), and Keele (1973) consider that all incoming signals undergo analysis of semantic content but that attention is required for the selection, organization, and execution of the response. Selection takes place with the aid of both meaningful and physical information, the most pertinent signal gaining further processing.

Although theories of attention can be placed crudely into these two groups it should be noted that intermediate theories have been offered, notably a capacity model which considers that analysis of many signals is possible provided that their analysis would not consume the total amount of capacity available (Underwood and Moray, 1971; Kahneman, 1973). Activities demanding a large amount of the available capacity would not be attended to in addition to similar activities, but several activities which demand smaller amounts of capacity may be attended to simultaneously.

One way of looking at the distinctions between these classes of theories is by testing for retention of unattended material. Early-selection theories (also known as perceptual selection or filter theories for reasons which will become apparent in the next chapter) predict that because unattended messages are not perceived there can be no categorical memory for them. Late-selection theories (also known as response selection theories), and Norman's theory in particular, consider that all messages are processed into primary memory, and so unattended messages should exhibit all of the characteristics of this level of storage. The capacity theory makes predictions specific to each situation. If sufficient capacity is available for categorical processing then categorical storage will be in evidence, otherwise only precategorical storage will result. The amount of capacity available for analysis of secondary messages depends upon other demands upon attention, notably the complexity of analysis of the primary message.

Not only does work on memory for unattended messages throw light upon the function of the attention process but also, of course, upon a major control process of memory. If we are able to remember unattended messages then it follows that attention is not necessary for encoding the storage, and the Posner and Boies (1971) experiment goes some way in supporting this counter-intuitive suggestion. Experiments which have reported evidence relating to the storage of attended and unattended messages must be considered in relation to theories of attention and theories of memory; the view here is that such theories cannot be mutually exclusive. We cannot account for the phenomenon of memory without considering the phenomenon of attention, and vice versa.

Much of the early work tended to suggest that subjects have no memory for unattended material. Cherry (1953) presented his subjects with spoken passages from newspapers to one ear, with instructions to shadow them (repeating each word as soon after hearing it as possible). To the other ear was presented one of a variety of signals: normal spoken English, reversed speech, or a continuous tone. After the presentation subjects were questioned on their memory of the non-shadowed (that is, unattended) message. Subjects were always able to comment on the unattended message if it had been the tone, and normal speech was identified as such. Subjects were unable to comment on the language spoken in the unattended message, however, and were unable to identify and remember any words heard in that message. Reversed speech was sometimes considered to be "normal", and by other subjects to "have something queer about it". If the passage presented to the unattended ear was changed from being spoken by a male, and then spoken by a female, then the change was noticed. It appears from this experiment that whereas the physical characteristics of the unattended message were perceived and remembered, the semantic content was not.

Moray (1959) supported this conclusion with an experiment which again used the shadowing technique to ensure that the subject directed his attention to the required prose message. To the other ear in this dichotic listening task was presented a list of seven common words, over and over again, a total of thirty-five times. Thirty seconds after the end of the shadowing task a recognition test was given. Whereas subjects recognized words presented in the shadowed message they were unable to recognize unattended words despite the constant repetition.

A failure to remember unattended words was also a feature of an experiment reported by Mowbray (1964). His subjects shadowed a list of fifty words which were common and randomly selected. For most of the time the second auditory channel was silent, but on a number of occasions a single word was presented to the unattended ear. Subjects were instructed to shadow the word list and to remember any words presented on the second channel. The recall task proved to be impossible without disruption of the shadowing. Whether the target words were recalled or not the words presented at the same time in the "attended" message were not shadowed on 80-90% of occasions, and all other words were missed on less than 40% of occasions. A control condition with no single words presented in the second channel led to approximately 20% of the to-be-shadowed words being missed. The relationship between the recall and shadowing of simultaneous words is indicated in Fig. 4.3. The success of recall of words in the second channel depended largely upon their position in the trial, and also upon the number of words presented. A single word near the end of the list was recalled on 75% of occasions, but recall was generally between 35% and 55%. However, this is not particularly meaningful to the present discussion because these words were only arguably unattended: only if shadowing had not been disrupted could it be argued that they had formed part of the unattended message. Disruption of shadowing, for instance, may have been due to the silent rehearsal of target words between the shadowing responses.

The three experiments of Cherry, Moray and Mowbray lend consider-

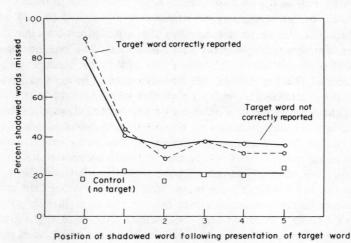

Fig. 4.3. Percentage of shadowed words missed as a function of the position of the shadowed word following presentation of the target word. (From Mowbray, 1964.)

able support to the early-selection theories of attention, which are based upon an assumption that the perceptual system has single channel operation. These experiments indicate that we have no memory of events to which we do not attend. If material in the unattended message is recalled then it is at the expense of processing of material in the attended message. Apparently we cannot perceive two words presented simultaneously when a continuous response is required to one message. The presence of the continuous response is important to this conclusion, because if a subject hears a single pair of words dichotically there is little difference between the recognition of the attended and unattended words (Brown, 1970).

The necessity for caution in the interpretation that there was no evidence of retention for unattended messages was demonstrated by Peterson and Kroener (1964). Subjects shadowed lists of 14 digits presented to one ear whilst another series of digits was presented simultaneously to the other ear. A letter was substituted for one of the digits in each non-shadowed list and immediately after the end of each dichotic presentation and completion of shadowing the subject attempted to recall the unattended letter. With a 6-second retention interval (that is, the letter was presented at the beginning of the list) subjects were able to recall the letter on 32% of the trials, and the response rate increased to 53% with an "immediate" test. A possible problem of interpretation here is that subjects were instructed that whereas they were to shadow one message they would always be tested for recall of part of the other message: we cannot be certain that the message which is designated as being "unattended" is not being attended to. Indeed, perfect shadowing might have indicated that the subjects had been attending to the "attended message", but even after several hours of shadowing practice large numbers of lists had to be eliminated from the analysis because of shadowing errors. Extensive shadowing practice is known to lead to highly efficient strategies of the division of attention between dichotic inputs (Underwood, 1974a), and Peterson and Kroener's subjects may have been distributing their attention between the two messages rather than attending exclusively to one of them. Whereas this experiment does indicate some memory for (possibly) unattended inputs the subjects did know in advance which message would be tested, knowledge shown to be extremely effective by Murray and Hitchcock (1969). When subjects are precued as to which message will be tested recall is more successful than when no cue is given.

It is important to note that the Peterson and Kroener experiment does not give unqualified support to the late-selection theories of attention, which predict that unattended messages are perceived and therefore may be remembered. If the unattended message had been perceived then recall of a target letter with a minimum retention interval should have approached 100%. The 53% recall of letters tested immediately after presentation indicates inefficient perception of the non-shadowed message.

The delay of testing for recall after presentation was an effective variable in the Peterson and Kroener experiment: a delay of 6 seconds between presentation and recall reduced the probability of recall considerably, and this could account for Moray's finding of no memory after 30 seconds. Norman (1969b) used a similar design but tested for recognition after short and long intervals. Subjects shadowed prose for a few minutes, and while they were still shadowing a list of six numbers was presented, with two digits in each number. The presentation rate was a digit pair every second. Two conditions were tested, one in which the list was immediately followed by a signal to stop shadowing and a test pair of digits, and in the other condition the signal to stop shadowing and the probe were not presented until 20 seconds after the presentation of the six numbers. The subjects responded as to whether or not the probe number had been presented in the previous list. To check on the disruptive effect of shadowing two further conditions were used. The probe was presented immediately after presentation of the six numbers, with no shadowing at all, and in the other condition the subject attended to the six numbers, and then shadowed for 20 seconds before being given the recognition probe. The first of these two control conditions tests for the effect of attending to the shadowing task whilst the list is presented, and the second control condition extends this comparison for the case of delayed recall. The results from these conditions are presented in Table 4.1. The "recognition" probabilities must be judged in relation to the false alarm rates in each condition. If a subject has a high false alarm rate then a large proportion of his correct recognition responses are likely to be guesses. Only when a subject has a much lower false alarm rate than correct recognition rate can we conclude that he is recognizing the probe rather than responding indiscriminately.

In the two immediate tests the false alarm rates were well down on recognition rates for the most recently presented numbers, but the number

Table 4.1 Recognition probabilities and false alarm rates from Norman (1969b).

	Serial position of test numbers		False alarm rate
	1	6	
(i) Shadowing prose: immediate test of digits	48%	83%	48%
(ii) Shadowing prose: delayed test of digits	70%	66%	62%
(iii) Listen to digits: immediate test	43%	100%	24%
(iv) Listen to digits: interpolated shadowing and delayed test of digits	60%	75%	69%

presented at the beginning of the list (hence with a test delay of more than 6 seconds) was not recognised at a rate greater than the false alarm rate, except when the subjects were able to attend to the numbers of presentation. When the subjects did not attend to the presentation of digits they were unable to recognize them at an interval of approximately 6 seconds. With a delayed test similar results appear. If the subjects did not attend to the presentation then recognition was not possible, and even when distracted by shadowing after attending to the digits recognition was still impossible. Recognition of unattended digits was possible only if the probe was presented within a few seconds, supporting Peterson and Kroener's result, and also explaining the Cherry, Mowbray and Moray results which found no memory for unattended inputs when tested after several seconds. Norman also demonstrated no memory after such a delay.

The experiments of Peterson and Kroener (1964) and Norman (1969b) provide some evidence of temporary storage for unattended material while shadowing another message, and it follows that attention is not required for storage over intervals of a few seconds. However, it is not clear from these experiments at which point the words in the unattended message were categorized. Unattended words could be perceived on arrival and stored in their categorical form, and the retention interval, which was filled with the shadowing activity, would act to reduce the trace strength of the categorical representation. This is the view taken by Norman (1969b), but an alternative explanation is that unattended words were not categorized until the shadowing task stopped. Until this point the un-attended words would reside in a precategorical store of the form described by Crowder and Morton (1969). The delay between presentation and test would then give an opportunity for decay of the precategorical memory trace, and the recognition score would be an indication of the state of the trace at the time when attention was directed towards it. This interpretation, which is in support of early-selection theories of attention, may also be concluded from a number of other experiments which will be discussed here.

Glucksberg and Cowen (1970) used a technique similar to that des-cribed by Eriksen and Johnson (1964) in their attempt to establish the existence of a sensory store of auditory events. Subjects shadowed prose in Glucksberg and Cowen's dichotic listening task, and at various delays after the presentation, of a digit in the unattended prose message, a cue light came on and the subjects were required to say whether or not

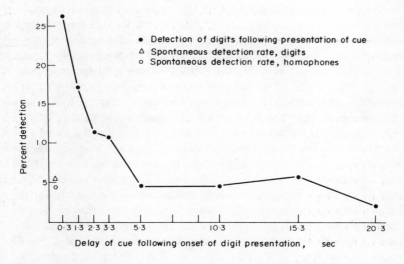

Fig. 4.4. The detection of a digit embedded in prose as a function of the delay of the response cue. (From Glucksberg and Cowen, 1970.)

they had heard a digit "recently", and what that digit was. If they heard a digit without being post-cued then subjects were required to respond immediately. This spontaneous detection rate was 5·7% of the total number of digits presented in the unattended message. The cue light was presented up to 20 seconds after the digit, and the relationship between the delay of the cue and the probability of recall is shown in Fig. 4.4. Although the detection rate was 26·3% of all digits if the cue was almost immediate, a delay of only 5·3 seconds results in a drop of the detection rate to less than 5% where the function becomes asymptotic with delay. This result is entirely in line with Norman's (1969b) result, but the low spontaneous detection rate indicates that the limitation in one of perception rather than storage. The 5% "detection" rate with delays greater than 5 seconds coincides with the number of digits which would be reported by chance when the cue light is shown, as obtained by multiplying the probability *that a digit* had occurred (0·5) by the probability of guessing correctly *which digit* had occurred (0·1). There is no evidence in this study of any memory for unattended events with retention intervals greater than 3 seconds. The issue is still open to question whether or not unattended messages are represented precategorically in an echoic store or categorically in a semantic store. Evidence on this issue come from the Glucksberg and Cowen experiment in the form of detection reports of homophones. Subjects occasionally responded to homophones of digits ("for", "too", "to") as if they were digits, and the spontaneous detection rate of these items is similar to that for digits. Now, only if semantic context is ignored would homophones be mistaken for digits, and so we may conclude that the context of the unattended message was not analysed. What subjects may have been responding to was the sound of the stimuli rather than their meanings. Unattended stimuli may activate their lexical representations, but only when attention is directed towards them may ambiguous stimuli such as homophones be interpreted. Unattended stimuli may be recognized as words, but attention is necessary for their integration into concurrent behaviour. It is, however, possible to argue that only when the cue light appeared was attention directed to the sounds held in precategorical memory for analysis of the presence of digits. The duration over which unattended digits could still be reported corresponds roughly to the duration of precategorical storage as measured by Crowder (1969) and Darwin *et al.* (1972).

A possible problem for this interpretation is provided by Klapp and Lee (1974) who replicated Glucksberg and Cowen's experiment but found that subjects were also able to estimate accurately the duration of storage of the digits. Time-of-occurrence cues may be indicative of categorical analysis, but could alternatively have been deduced by the subjects from the state of the trace. A highly decayed trace of an unattended input may indicate to the listener that it had been presented some time ago, whereas a particularly strong trace would indicate recent presentation.

Differences between the storage of attended and unattended items have also been shown by split-span studies of memory in which subjects hear lists of three or four items in each ear (hence a total of six or eight items per dichotic list), and recall all items presented. By giving instructions to listen or rehearse the items presented to one ear the effects of attention may be observed, and such instructions were used effectively by Bryden (1971). Subjects heard lists of four pairs of digits but were instructed to attend to and rehearse the four digits presented to one ear (for half the

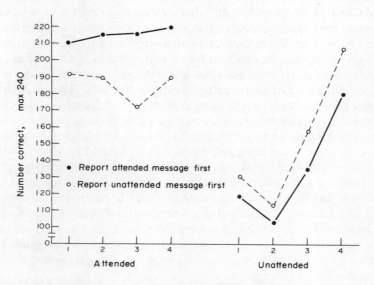

Fig. 4.5. Recall accuracy as a function of attention and report instructions. All subjects were required to report both the attended and unattended digits. (From Bryden, 1971.)

subjects this was the left ear, and for the other half it was the right ear). The eight items were recalled in ear groups, either all of the attended digits first and then the unattended digits, or the unattended and then attended digits. Fig. 4.5. indicates the effect upon recall of attentional strategies and order or report. There are two main features of interest in Bryden's data: the shapes of the serial recall curves for attended and unattended digits, and the effect of order of report upon attended and unattended digits. Whereas the serial position curves for attended items are relatively flat, the curves for unattended items indicate a substantial recency effect, with the items towards the end of the list being recalled more successfully than items at the beginning. Note, however, a small primacy effect which, if these items are not being rehearsed, might be due to the perceptual distinctiveness of initial members of a list (Underwood, 1972, 1973b, 1975). The different serial position curves for attended and unattended lists indicates that these lists were processed very differently, and that attention can be redirected to an unattended input very soon after presentation. The importance of presentation for the recall of unattended inputs may be due to the rapid decay of precategorical traces, whereas the categorical representations of attended inputs are less susceptible to rapid decay. The effects of order of report of the two sub-lists pose a problem for the simple interpretation of Bryden's data in terms of early-selection theories of attention. Fig. 4.5 indicates that reporting the unattended list second has less effect upon recall of that list, than does reporting the attended list second upon recall of that list. Delaying recall is more disruptive on attended than on unattended digits. If the categorical traces of attended inputs were more stable than the precategorical traces of unattended inputs then exactly the opposite result would have been expected. Evidently the echoic trace is not disrupted by output interference but the categorical trace is so affected. An alternative explanation suggested by Bryden is that in the unattended-attended order of report the activity of categorizing the echoic traces of unattended digits disrupts the storage of the attended list, rather than the output of these digits. Once an item has been processed into its refined categorical state it is more susceptible to subsequent processing or output interference than when it is being stored as a raw, sensory representation.

This experiment provides a clear demonstration of the effect of attention in studies of memory, and of the effect of instructions to attend.

Although we cannot be certain that subjects did not attempt to encode the "unattended" message, because they knew that both messages would be tested on each trial, the data indicate that whereas the "attended" message was encoded the "unattended" message was certainly not fully encoded.

The problem of encoding "unattended" messages in these experiments has been met successfully by a technique used by Davis and Smith (1972). In all of the other experiments mentioned here the subjects have been aware that at some point they would be tested of their recall of the unattended messages, and this may have resulted in attempts to encode these messages. The Davis and Smith experiment provides an ingenious test of the prediction of late-selection theories that unattended inputs are stored in primary memory. Primary memory is said to have a definite limited span, and the number of items necessary to fill a primary memory store has been put at between two and four words. Now, if both the attended and unattended messages are stored in primary memory, then when dichotic lists are presented and memory of the attended message tested primary memory should appear to have a span which is one-half of the estimate of the span with monaural lists. With dichotic lists primary memory will fill up with items from both the attended and unattended components, but with monaural lists items for only one source will be present. If attended and unattended messages are tested then the primary memory span would appear constant, but if only one component is tested then the span would appear to be reduced. Davis and Smith only ever tested the attended message to reduce the benefit to the subject of occasionally listening to the "unattended" message, a possible strategy operable in other attention experiments. Subjects listened to a list of six items, and were then probed for the recall of one word from that list. At the same time as the list subjects were presented with unattended monosyllabic words or nonsense syllables either simultaneously with attended words or temporally staggered between them. In a control condition no unattended words were presented. The interesting feature here is that the recency effect, used to estimate the primary memory span by the Waugh and Norman (1965) method, was not reduced by the presence of an unattended input. For the control condition, simultaneous words, simultaneous nonsense, staggered words, and staggered nonsense the estimates of the span were 2·2, 2·0, 2·0, 1·9 and 1·8 words respectively. This amounts to no effect upon the span by unattended inputs, and suggests that unattended items are not stored in primary memory, at least not at the expense of attended items. The late-selection theories are not supported by this experiment, which indicates that storage in primary memory is a feature which does not follow for words which are not coded phonologically.

Each of the experiments in this series can contribute to the same conclusion, that attended inputs are categorized but unattended inputs are stored only in precategorical memory. If attention is not switched towards a word within a few seconds of its presentation then it becomes irretrievable. The attended message of a dichotic presentation is represented phonologically, each word being categorized shortly after arrival, but unattended words are not represented in a phonological code and reside only in echoic memory. This is not to say that unattended messages do not influence behaviour, for Posner and Taylor (1969) and Baron (1973) have shown that phonological coding is not essential for analysis of verbal stimuli, but in most cases attention and a resultant phonological representation are necessary. This is a very general rule, and the capacity model allows for at least partial encoding of the "unattended" message if analysis of the attended message is not demanding. With highly predictable sequences of words in the attended message, for instance, processing capacity may be allocated for analysis of the secondary message. When spare capacity is available it may be spent on the elaboration coding or subjective organization of the attended message, or on the categorization of the unattended message, but experiments which claim to test the level of analysis of an unattended message should ensure that all available capacity is devoted to the attended message.

Conscious and Automatic Access to Semantic Memory

Collins and Loftus (1975) have recently provided an extended version of Quillian's (1967, 1969) model of semantic memory which takes account of some examples of automatic access to the lexicon. The structure of semantic memory suggested by Quillian is that of an associated network of concepts. The network is composed of units and their properties, much as a dictionary might be organised. Thus, some of the units in the network would be "table", "bird", "mat", "tram", and other objects, whereas properties are structures which specify the units; accordingly, "solid", "flying", "dirty", and "obsolete" might be properties associated with these units. Units and properties need not be represented in semantic memory as words, but they may be more abstract structures which might correspond to these words. The units and their properties are organised hierarchically with the concepts at each level connected by pointers (or associations) both subordinately and superordinately. For example, the unit "bird", which has properties "lays eggs", "has feathers", "can fly", etc, is connected both to the general unit "animal" (which: "has skin", "moves", "eats", "reproduces", etc) and to the most specific unit "ostrich" (which: "can't fly", "has long legs", etc). Quillian's computer model was intended to comprehend language, which is done by searching through the network to relate the words in the sentence in a grammatically permissible order. To comprehend the sentence "the canary has skin" we trace the path (i) a canary is a bird, (ii) a bird is an animal, (iii) an animal has skin. Collins and Quillian (1969) established the plausibility of the model with an experiment in which subjects were required to understand sentences and judge them true or false. The sentences combined units with possible properties which would be stored at the same hierarchical level or at another level. Collins and Quillian assumed that it takes time to move from one level to another, and so it should take longer to respond to "a canary has skin" than to "a canary is yellow". They confirmed the prediction, and found that the more distant were the units from the properties on the semantic network, the longer was the verification time. It is necessary to assume here, that properties are only stored once in memory, or "has skin" might be stored on the same hierarchical level as "canary". This is the assumption of cognitive economy, and has been criticised thoroughly by Conrad (1972) and Anderson and Bower (1973) who cite instances of multiple storage, and instances of subjects being unaffected by hierarchical distance when judging whether or not two units share a common property. Collins and Loftus (1975) distinguish between the weak version of the theory of cognitive economy, and the strong version. The strong version, clearly unacceptable, is that properties are stored only once, whereas the weak version argues that the addition of an instance to a category does not lead to all of the properties of that category being stored with the instance in memory. There may be examples of category properties being particularly useful in connection with subordinate members, but we rely generally upon inference to decide whether or not a canary has skin. The strong theory requires that once we have learnt

(i) that robins can fly, and (ii) that birds can fly, then "can fly" must be deleted from "robin". Replication is not permitted by this version of the theory, but in some cases it will be inevitable. The experiment reported by Collins and Quillian (1969) clearly relates only to the weak version of the theory, and demonstrates that cognitive economy does operate for part of the network.

Of particular interest to the present discussion is the capacity of Quillian's model (and of the Collins and Loftus revision) to take account of a wide variety of phenomena of semantic processing. Words facilitate each other under some processing constraints, and interfere with each other at other times, whether or not we intend the interaction and whether or not we are aware of it. Loftus (1973), for example, asked her subjects to generate an instance of a category (e.g. "fruit") given an initial letter (e.g. "P"). The category-letter pair were shown together, and the measure of interest was the subjects' response latency. When the subjects had named an instance of the same category on the previous trial then the responses were faster. When the subjects responded to "fruit-P" in the absence of prior context the mean response latency was 1.50 seconds, but if the previous trial had also required a fruit (but with a different letter) then the mean latency was 1.22 seconds. Collins and Loftus (1975) account for this result with an assumption of spreading activation of the semantic network. When one category is activated by use all instances of the category will be activated, and so more easily retrieved if required within a certain period. The activation decreases over time, and in Loftus' (1973) experiment probing of the fruit category two trials back lead to a response time of 1.29 seconds. The facilitation effect is time-dependent.

The generality of this semantic interaction effect is now well documented. Meyer and Schvaneveldt (1971) used a lexical decision task to establish the effects of semantic association when the semantic attributes of the words were not of primary importance. Two strings of letters were presented on each trial and the task was to respond "yes" if both strings were words, and "no" otherwise. On seeing "KNIFE — SMUKE" the response would be "no", but "yes" to "BREAD — DOCTOR". If the two letter strings formed words which were related (e.g. "BREAD — BUTTER") then the response was an average of 85 milliseconds faster than when they were semantically unrelated. It is easier to access information in semantic memory shortly after processing related items, and this result lends itself neatly to the spread of excitation hypothesis. The meanings of words appear to be influential even when we do not need to use the meaning, but only the legality of the word. Meyer and Schvaneveldt's subjects may have been using the existence or non-existence of semantic attributes to direct their lexical decision however, and so this experiment cannot be interpreted in terms of preconscious access to semantic memory. A number of other experiments do provide data to support this conclusion however, and will be mentioned here, although they are of considerable importance for the discussion of the function of attention contained in Chapter 5.

Jacobson (1973) presented words tachistoscopically for recognition, with an exposure duration of 8 milliseconds, followed at some interval by a masking stimulus to disrupt readout from iconic memory. The masking stimulus, another word, was either related or unrelated to the target word, and influenced dramatically the success of report. The dependent measure, minimum onset asynchrony of the target and mask required for recognition, varied as a function of semantic association. When the two words were related ("TOWN – CITY") a mean interval of 28.5 milliseconds was necessary between onsets of the two words, but if they were unrelated ("TOWN – FOOT") then a mean of 55.0 milliseconds was necessary before identification was possible. There are some problems of guessing strategies with this paradigm, but in another of Jacobson's experiments guessing is clearly inappropriate. Subjects saw a word presented in a tachistoscope, and simply read it out. This was followed by a second word which was to be read out as quickly as possible. When the words were semantically related the response to the second word was 58 milliseconds faster than when the words were unrelated.

A similar effect of spreading excitation has been reported by Warren (1972). Subjects first repeated three instances of a category which were presented aurally (e.g. "robin, canary, sparrow"), and then named the colour of ink of another word (the Stroop test). The coloured word was either a word from the spoken list (e.g. "robin"), the category of the words in the spoken list (e.g. "bird"), or a semantically unrelated word (e.g. "pencil"). Category words and list members slowed the colour naming response by about 100 milliseconds in comparison with unrelated words, even though use of these words was not necessary for performance on the Stroop test. Conrad (1974) has extended this result for the curious case of ambiguous words. If words access their lexical representations automatically then how many representations are activated when we are presented with such words as "light", or "race", or "mint"? If access is pre-attentive then all possible representations should be activated regardless of prior context, and this was demonstrated by the Conrad experiment. Subjects first listened to a sentence, with instructions to remember it, and then named the colour of ink of a single word. The final word of the sentence was critical in the sense that it was occasionally a word with more than one meaning (e.g. "we made tea in the pot"). The Stroop word reflected this ambiguity on a number of trials, and the colour naming latency was affected accordingly. When the coloured word was related to the non-sentential meaning of the final word (e.g. "marijuana") the response was retarded by 50 milliseconds in comparison with the same coloured word following an unrelated sentence (e.g. "the man owns a sailboat"). Regardless of the context imposed by the sentence, both meanings of "pot" had been accessed, and the activation of the non-sentential representation was available to interfere with a subsequent task. When the Stroop word was related to the sentential meaning (e.g. "utensil") the interference was only slightly greater than with a word related to the second meaning.

Ambiguity may also be resolved by words which gain access to the lexicon pre-attentively. Bradshaw (1974) presented an ambiguous word at a fixated point for 125 milliseconds with a letter string to either side. One of the letter strings was composed of randomly selected consonants, the other a word related to one of the meanings of the centrally fixated ambiguous word. After presentation the viewer was given the choice of which of the two possible meanings of the fixated word was most applicable. Subjects were biased towards selecting the disambiguating peripheral word, even when they were unable to report these words. Similar reports have been made of the effects of words of which we are unaware. The meanings of words which we are unable to report do appear to be available occasionally (Allport, 1976), and unreportable words influence the naming of simultaneously presented pictures when the tachistoscopically shown picture and word are semantically related (Underwood, 1976a,b). .

These experiments do not support exclusively Quillian's hierarchical structure of semantic memory, of course, they merely establish the plausibility of the notions of spreading excitation and automated lexical access, features of the Collins and Loftus revision of Quillian's model. Alternative models have been offered, together with considerable criticism of hier-archical structures, and of particular interest are the comments of Smith, Shoben and Rips (1974) concerning the association of semantic features, and Johnson-Laird (1975) concerning semantic organisation by utility.

When lexical entries are activated by directed use, this activation appears to spread to associated entries. Even when we do not attend to a word, or when there appears insufficient stimulus information for the threshold of recognition to be exceeded, words may still produce semantic effects upon the processing of other words. However, such pre-attentive activation would correspond to a low depth of processing in the Craik and Lockhart (1973) model of the operation of memory, and as such would not render the items available for recall. If we do not direct attention towards an item then the item will gain no elaboration coding and fewer attributes will be associated with it. The more attributes an item has in memory, the more likely it will be to be recalled, and the deeper the level of processing (from structural analysis to categorical analysis) the more attributes will be available. There are several associated implications of this view, not the least of which is that memory here is seen as a by-product of the perceptu-al system, following Kay (1968), and Craik and Tulving (1975) go further to say that "episodic memory is an automatic by-product of operations carried out by the cognitive system, and that the durability of the trace is a positive function of 'depth' of processing, where depth refers to greater degrees of semantic involvement". Craik and Tulving (1975) prefer a "spread" of encoding metaphor rather than "depth", in which the percept may be elaborated in a variety of ways rather than the fixed order of pro-cessing implied in the Craik and Lockhart (1973) model. It is a matter of the strategy of elaboration employed by the subject which determines which attributes will constitute the memory trace. The experiments of Meyer and Schvaneveldt, Loftus, Jacobson, Warren, Conrad, Bradshaw, Allport, Underwood and others, suggest that lexical activation can be pre-attentive — a logogen may be excited by semantically associated logogens becoming excited (spreading excitation) — but such activation may lead to no awareness and no record in memory. To achieve a stable memory trace of an event it must be allocated a spread of encoding of a variety of attributes, and this is a function of the encoding strategy in operation. We can contact lexical memory without the use of the attention process, but new entries require attention to elaborate the associations.

Memory for Dichotic Inputs

An advantage of using dichotic messages in the investigation of acquisition strategies is that with similar, competing inputs we can look directly at the question of whether simultaneous stimuli can be encoded simultaneously. Although decay time is reduced by parallel inputs, twice as many stimuli are being presented per unit time, and decay of the echoic trace is sufficiently rapid to be apparent even with short retention intervals. The supposed use of the precategorical store for retention of the second of two simultaneous inputs was tested for the case of single pairs of words by Treisman and Fearnley (1971), and before discussing the case of series of dichotic pairs their experiment should be mentioned. They asked the question of whether simultaneous speech is processed serially, with use of the precategorical store, or in parallel, with each input being categorized on arrival. In each trial subjects heard either two simultaneous nonsense syllables or a nonsense syllable at the same time as a digit, the task being to indicate whether a digit had been heard. With parallel processing the response time to simultaneous inputs should be the same as that to single items, whereas with serial processing the mean response time should be slower for simultaneous than for single inputs. Treisman and Fearnley found that the response time to simultaneous inputs was in fact approximately 80 msecs slower than for a single item, thus indicating that serial processing was operating and subjects were first testing the stimulus heard with one ear and then switching their attention to the other ear. The data were not unambiguous, however, and a further test resulted in support of the notion of parallel categorization. On some trials the subjects were informed which digit would be presented if one was to be presented at all. Precueing the identity of a target digit would reduce the decision time by converting the task into one of physical matching rather than semantic classification. Precueing with a single item results in the same processing advantage by serial and parallel processing, hypotheses, but with simultaneous items the advantage over non-cued trials should be more apparent by the serial processing hypothesis where successive gains would accumulate. With the parallel processing hypothesis the precueing advantage would be gained by both items at the same time. So, parallel processing of simultaneous items would lead to the same precueing advantage for single items as for simultaneous items, but serial processing would lead to a greater advantage for simultaneous items. With an auditory cue as to which digit would be presented if one was to be heard at all the mean response time to a single item was 441 msec, and to a pair of items 504 msec. Without the cue the latency of response to a single item was 532 msec, and to a pair of items 613 msec. Cueing produces an advantage of 109 msec for a pair of items, and 91 msec for single items, and this small difference argues against the serial analysis hypothesis.

Although performance is less efficient with simultaneous inputs than with single inputs it appears that we are able to listen to items presented to different ears, under some circumstances at least. The data from experiments requiring a division of attention between longer messages indicate that simultaneous processing is possible only if continuous attention is not required for one message. If the listener is able to respond immediately to both items then parallel processing strategies may be operable, but if one message must be stored until after responding to a series of other items then serial analysis after storage in echoic memory may be the most efficient strategy. With this general hypothesis as a framework we shall now consider the evidence from studies of dichotic listening which have used sequences of words.

The basic paradigm was first reported by Broadbent in 1954, who presented his subjects with three pairs of digits in fairly rapid succession. One digit in each simultaneous pair of items was presented to the subject's left ear, and the other digit in the pair to the subject's right ear. After all six items had been presented the task was to recall as many as possible. The principal feature of the results from this experiment is that if all six items were recalled then it was more likely that recall was organized by the ear of presentation than by the temporal order of presentation. All of the items from one ear tended to be recalled in a group, rather than two digits heard simultaneously being recalled together. For instance, if the subject heard these digits:

Left Ear:	5	9	1
Right Ear:	4	3	8

then recall would tend to be organized in the order 591,438 rather than 54,93,18. Broadbent formulated his interpretation of the processes involved here in his book *Perception and Communication* (1958), where it was argued that the ear-order mode of recall is preferable to temporal recall because of the limited capacity of the information transmission system, and the nature of this limitation is indicated in Fig. 4.6.

The limited capacity of the processing system is evident in the number of words which can be analyzed at any one time. Of the three messages *a*, *b*, and *c* in Fig. 4.6 which are presented to the listener only message *a* is

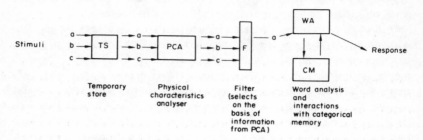

Fig. 4.6. Broadbent's (1958) filter theory of the limit of attention.

analyzed for semantic content: it is the perceptual system which is said to have limited capacity, and only words to which we attend are said to be perceived. The message to be analyzed is selected on the basis of its physical characteristics, and may be selected on presentation, or from the temporary store (sensory memory). The outcome of the analysis of physical characteristics determines which message is to be attended to, and which messages are to be filtered away from the limited capacity system. Unattended messages are not analyzed for meaning but they may be stored in sensory memory for a maximum time in the "order of seconds". If attention is switched to the temporary store within this period then un-attended messages may be retrieved, but the switching operation is said to take "a time which is not negligible compared with the minimum time spent on any one class" of events. If attention cannot be switched rapidly between ears during a dichotic presentation then the listener would associate the items presented together to one ear, rather than listening to the item on one ear, switching to the opposite ear and listening to the echoic trace of the item paired with the first item, and so on, associating items by their temporal characteristics. The strategy of switching between ears during the presentation is clearly inefficient if the switching procedure takes a long time relative to the rate of presentation. With slow rates of presentation, however, switching between the items of a pair may be possible, and this feature of Broadbent's model was tested by Bryden (1962). At fast rates of presentation (2 pairs of items per second) an ear-order mode of recall was evident, but when the presentation is slowed down (1 pair of items every 2 seconds) subjects retrieved items on the basis of the temporal order of occurrence. The slower rate of presentation allowed time to switch between ears and to rehearse pairs of items together during the inter-item interval. The time taken to switch attention between the ears was the subject of an experiment reported by Moray (1960) which suggests that switching may not take as much time as Broadbent supposed. Moray argued that the dichotic listening task did not give a fair test of subjects' ability to switch between ears because when they did switch after analysis of an attended word there was no signal on the secondary channel and so they must attend to the echoic memory trace. Being a memory trace this word is more likely to be imperfect than the primary message word, and hence performance with the switching strategy will be inefficient. If the subject is aware of this constraint then switching may be avoided during the presentation. As a further test of switching ability Moray presented lists to both ears, with items temporally inter-leaved, for instance:

Left Ear:	5		9		1	
Right Ear:		4		3		8

Subjects were precued to use one of two strategies on different trials, and when instructed to use ear-order recall a total of 18·8% recall errors were committed, whereas with the temporal order of report there were 22·5% recall errors. This may suggest that subjects are able to switch rapidly between ears, for it makes no difference to them whether or not they are required to switch between ears during the presentation. However, there is an alternative explanation of this result, which postulates a third listening strategy, and which can be accommodated by Broadbent's model. When subjects were cued to recall the items in their temporal order of occurrence, and heard simultaneous pairs of items (i.e. the usual dichotic listening situation), then they produced a total of 33·2% recall errors. This difference between simultaneous and alternating presentations could be due to decay of the echoic trace of the secondary message when a switching strategy was employed, or it could be due to a different organizational strategy. With simultaneous stimuli rapid switching may not be practicable, and given instructions to recall in the temporal order the subject may organize his order of output in this order following an ear-by-ear order of acquisition. Moray suggested that with the alternating presentation subjects may not have been switching attention between ears at all, but instead they may have been adopting a strategy of listening to both ears without differentiating between them. When the items alternate the listener may not alternate his direction of attention with the stimuli, but attempt to pass all stimuli along the same channel. In the dichotic listening experiments subjects are encouraged to consider the two ears as separate information channels, and sometimes to focus their attention on one channel rather than the other. Outside the laboratory the two ears still provide us with slightly different information, but the semantic content from each ear is treated as being functionally identical. Information from the two ears is passed along the same channel, a strategy of listening which has been described as multiplexing (Green, 1964; Lindsay, 1970). The multiplexing strategy in Moray's alternating stimuli condition would necessitate no switching between ears, the digits being listened to successively and differences between the ears being ignored. With simultaneous digits the multiplexing strategy would be inappropriate because it would lead to mutual masking between the two items presented at the same time. In this condition selective attention is necessary to discriminate between completing inputs. Only when one ear is given no input would the multiplexing strategy be an efficient handling device. The employment of this strategy would allow Broadbent's model to explain Moray's finding of efficient temporal recall of alternating lists, but the other data indicate that switching rather than multiplexing was present. In one condition subjects were given binaural presentations, for instance:

| Left Ear: | 5 | 9 | 1 | 4 | 3 | 8 |
| Right Ear: | 5 | 9 | 1 | 4 | 3 | 8 |

This would lead to a similar experience as would alternating stimuli and a multiplexing strategy, for instance:

Left Ear:	5		1		3	
						heard as: 591438
Right Ear:		9		4		8

The binaural presentation adds redundant information, and if a multiplexing strategy is used to listen to the alternating presentation then it should make no difference whether binaural or alternating presentations are used. However, free recall of a binaural presentation resulted in a 5% error rate where as free recall of an alternating presentation resulted in a 12·7% error rate. The problem for Broadbent's model remains, and it appears that listeners are able to switch rapidly from one ear to the other. When they do switch ears during the lists more errors are committed than when listening to a binaural presentation where no switching is necessary.

When listeners are made to switch their attention between ears when performing the task then the amount of attention available for encoding is inversely related to the number of times which attention is switched. Mewhort, Thio, and Birkenmeyer (1971) presented four pairs of letters in a dichotic listening experiment, and subjects shadowed one message but the "message" was not always confined to one ear. The way in which the task was defined to the subjects determined whether there were 0, 1, 2, or 3 switches of attention between the ears. With a presentation of the type:

Left ear:	J	S	B	L
Right Ear:	M	A	F	K

and attention directed initially to the left ear, then with no switches the subject would shadow "J,S,B,L", with one switch, "J,S,F,K", with two switches "J,A,F,L", and with three switches "J,A,B,K". In each trial a schematic diagram indicated to the subject when he should switch. After the shadowing task the subjects recalled the items which they had not shadowed. The probability of recall decreased as the number of switches during shadowing was increased, and Mewhort *et al.* concluded that switching attention is an operation which consumes information processing capacity, and that given that we have a fixed amount of capacity available then switching reduces the amount of capacity which can be allocated to the encoding of the non-shadowed letters. When subjects are not required to switch their attention between ears then more attention may be given to the task of encoding the secondary message, or increasing the trace strength of the to-be-remembered letters. Switching consumes capacity, and if Moray's subjects were switching with alternating presentations rather than multiplexing then we would expect lower recall than with binaural stimuli because more capacity would be residual in the binaural listening trials. However, a further problem with this interpretation was raised by Broadbent and Gregory (1961) who pointed to the fact that Moray had pre-cued his subjects as to which recall order was required (ear-by-ear or temporal). If the listener knows in advance that he will be required to organize recall in one way or the other then he may be expected to adopt a listening strategy to suit the required order of report. Instructions for a temporal order of report may lead to a multiplexing strategy, and instructions for ear-by-ear report may lead to focused attention first on one ear and then the other. However, if the subject does not know in advance which order of report will be required less efficient acquisition strategies may be selected. If a multiplexing strategy is employed, and then ear-by-ear report requested more organization would be required than if a focused attention strategy had been used. So, if the subject has the choice between strategies he should perform better when he knows which strategy is most appropriate to the requirements of recall. Broadbent and Gregory found little difference between pre-cueing and post-cueing however, suggesting that the same acquisition strategy is used with alternating presentations whatever order of report is required, and that strategy is one of simultaneous selection of words from both ears.

Yntema and Trask (1963) suggested that simultaneous dichotic messages do not pass through a limited channel when being processed into memory, and are selected simultaneously, as opposed to the Broadbent view of single channel selection. Subjects are said to attend to both messages at the same time, by this model, and the ear-order grouping preference occurs in the retrieval stage. Items may be retrieved with the aid of identification "tags" which are affixed to them during input: in the dichotic listening paradigm all items presented to the subject's left ear would be tagged as such. These items might be said to be associated with each other, whereby retrieval of one item would cue the retrieval of other items presented in that "set". There is now strong evidence of persistent memory for the modality of presentation of words (e.g. Hintzman *et al.*, 1972; Cole *et al.*, 1974), and modality of presentation may be considered as one of the attributes of that which is remembered. We are returned to the words of Bower (1970) in that we do not remember the very specific information which is required for recall, but the whole experience of processing, and this certainly includes the sound of the voice which was heard, or the type-face of the display. Retrieving is easier if we can recall the social context of the message as it was presented. Blocked presentations of many trials in memory experiments show a decline in performance over trials, and this has been said to be due to a build-up of proactive interference. This may be another way of describing the habituation of discriminating features. The first list in the experiment is remembered well because of that very specific feature — it is remembered *as* the first list, as a new experience. Later lists suffer a recall decrement because retrieval cannot be made on the basis of these cues. The attributes of social context are no longer distinctive, and the only basis for differentiating one list from another is the very specific information intended to be conveyed by the experimenter. The ear of presentation in the dichotic listening task is an attribute upon which recall may be based, just as time of occurrence must be, and Yntema and Trask maintain that orders of reporting in a serial manner items which are presented simultaneously are a result of associating and retrieving items by these attributes. The relative importance of different attributes was demonstrated by their experiment which tested recall of dichotic lists with one of three imposed orders of report. Subjects heard mingled lists of digits and common words which had two, one or no crossings of semantic groups across ears:

Left ear: Word-Word-Word   Word-Digit-Digit   Word-Digit-Word
Right ear: Digit-Digit-Digit   Digit-Word-Word   Digit-Word-Digit
         (no crossing)   (1 crossing)   (2 crossings)

Following each presentation the subjects recalled words in ear-order (i.e. all left-ear items, or right-ear items, first), or in temporal order (i.e. recall items by temporal pairs), or by semantic category (i.e. all words first or all digits first). Subjects were pre-cued as to which order of report was required with each presentation. With these dichotic lists subjects found recall easiest when they organized retrieval on the basis of category membership (words, or digits), regardless of the number of crossings necessary for this order of report. However, the number of switches between the messages presented to each ear was an influential factor, and increasing the number of crossings decreased the probability of recall. If recall consists of a search through memory to find the items with the appropriate tags, following simultaneous entry of all items into memory, then the superiority of semantic category recall is due to category tags being the most salient. Efficient recall with the no-crossings array may be due to a search which is organized on the basis of two attributes (ear of arrival, and category membership) being more efficient than a search organized by one attribute. This is Yntema and Trask's redundancy hypothesis, and has been shown to be inadequate for situations where particularly strong attributes are present, as in the case of the bisensory split-span (Hede, 1973). Temporal order of recall of lists in which members of categories were presented simultaneously, thus providing two attributes for the search, was compared with temporal recall of lists in which categories alternated across ears. If the redundancy principle had held then presenting two instances of a category simultaneously would have resulted in more effective temporal recall than presenting two instances successively in different messages. Hede found no difference for temporal recall of these two arrangements when one message was presented visually and the other message aurally. Hede also found that modality recall was as efficient as temporal recall for a no-crossing array, perhaps suggesting that the rapid switching of attention between ear and eye, which is necessary for temporal recall, is possible between ear and eye. The inefficiency of this order of report for dichotic listening suggests that switching between ears is more difficult. However, that rapid switching between the ears is possible is a conclusion from an experiment reported by Gray and Wedderburn (1960), who presented three pairs of items of the following type:

| Left ear: | MICE | 6 | CHEESE |
| Right ear: | 3 | EAT | 4 |

In this case subjects were just as likely to report all items on one ear first (ear-order) as they were the words with high transition probabilities (category recall). This result is a function of organization strategies during retrieval rather than listening, however, and this has been demonstrated by Whitmore (1972) who presented a dichotic series of words such that listening to pairs of items would have produced a meaningful sequence, for instance:

| Left ear: | he | not | his |
| Right ear: | will | change | mind |

When not given specific instructions to listen to word pairs together the ear-order of report was used. Rapid switching during listening was possible, but not preferred. As Fechner (1889) has noted, rapid oscillation of attention results in a "strain". The data from these experiments do not entirely support Yntema and Trask's view that dichotic items are tagged during listening according to their meaning or ear of arrival, because subjects make best use of the meaningfulness of items when they are not presented simultaneously. Broadbent and Gregory (1964b) suggest that selection of a category is a process similar to that of selecting an ear, in that selection or resetting of selection parameters is a process which takes time and is therefore avoided with fast presentations.

An alternative to the Broadbent and the Yntema and Trask accounts of strategies of report has been provided by Mewhort (1973) in a model in which attentional selectivity and retrieval tags are incorporated. Mewhort tested the search model of order effects by arguing that if ear-by-ear report is preferred with fast presentation rates, and temporal order of report with slow rates (as is the case), and if these orders of report are dictated by the most relevant retrieval tags available, then the rate of presentation may be varied to assess the importance of different types of retrieval tags. At slow rates, when subjects prefer the temporal order of report, temporal tags are said to be more salient than spatial location tags. So, the subject should also retain more information about the temporal aspects of the presentation. Conversely, at fast rates when ear-by-ear reports are preferred and spatial location tags are more salient, then information about the spatial aspects of the display should be available. The presence of these types of information was tested by presenting four pairs of items at one of two rates, fast (2 pairs per second) and slow (1 pair per second), followed by an absolute judgement task. The subject was shown one of the eight items he had just heard, and asked to indicate its spatial position (left or right ear), and timing (1st, 2nd, 3rd, or 4th pair). The search model predicts more accurate positioning with fast rates, and more accurate timing with slow rates, but Mewhort found that timing was reported more accurately at both rates of presentation despite the greater number of alternatives. The salience of search tags was not changed by altering the rate of presentation, which is known to change reporting preferences, and this result fails to confirm the search model. The extension of Broadbent's attentional model, on points of the locus of the attention filter and the time required to switch attention, allows a role for Yntema and Trask's retrieval tags. In this hybrid model Mewhort suggests that the tagging of items, as they enter categorical memory, is a necessary aid to the organization of the sequential response, and that a major function of attention is to tag items. Attention is necessary for the organization of parallel inputs into a form which permits sequential rehearsal and response. In this sense the time necessary for a switch in attention is less important than the capacity necessary for a switch. That sequence of tagging and categorical processing will be used which imposes the least load upon the available capacity. This model accounts for Mewhort's own data by assuming that temporal tagging is necessary for the organization of sequential rehearsal. It seems likely that a tag or attribute, which is information about how a word is processed in relation to other items, is not actively acquired but is nevertheless used to organize the response sequentially. Only when a rhythmic, sequential structure is imposed upon information to be remembered can any stable memory be consolidated in Neisser's (1967) model. The temporal attributes acquired during categorization may be used to impose structure and as a basis for the organization of retrieval.

William James (1890) asserted that "an object once attended to will remain in the memory, whereas one inattentively allowed to pass will leave no traces", and empirical evidence requires only slight modifications to this statement before it can stand as a conclusion to the present discussion. Whereas an attended message may be remembered over relatively long intervals and be subject to interpretation and misinterpretation, an unattended message is represented only by a pre-categorical trace which has a relatively short life because its function is as a buffer, and to hold the message until attention is directed towards it. The intricate relationship between the processes of attending and remembering make these phenomena impossible to investigate in isolation of each other. We cannot test a subject's memory span without asking him, implicitly at least, to attend to the presentation. Even then we are uncertain as to which features of the presentation will be attended to until the pattern of recall is produced. Items which are recalled may be concluded to be those which were attended to during presentation, for attention is necessary for entry to categorical memory. Similarly, we cannot investigate attentional processes without the subject relying upon information in his memory in preparation for the response. It is the flexibility of attention which makes interpretation so difficult. The attention necessary for processing is dependent upon the nature of the material to be processed and upon its presentation characteristics. If the least amount of capacity is used by the subject in switching his attention between features of a display then this strategy will be used in preference to one of continuous attention to one channel which might demand more capacity. The direction of attention is a process which is under the control of the individual, as James indicated when he said that "our experience is determined by what we choose to attend to", and determining which of a large number of choices has been made in no mean task for the experimenter. It is the flexibility of attention which has been characteristic of the studies discussed in this chapter and which is the subject of the next.

CHAPTER 5

THE ATTENTION PROCESS

Of the two main functions of attention mentioned previously, information selection from the environment and information retrieval from memory, the function which will be developed in the present discussion concerns the process by which we admit only part of the available information to consciousness and exclude the remainder. There are so many possible perceptions, or possible perceptual hypothesis (Gregory, 1970), of the stimuli reaching us, that a stable world can result only from the maintenance of one set of hypotheses. It is the purpose of the attention process to admit to consciousness only one perceptual hypothesis at any one time. Consider Fig. 5.1, which is the well-known Necker cube. There are several object-hypotheses available for this figure, and two of them

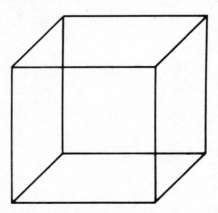

Fig. 5.1. The Necker cube. Is the lower left-hand point at the "front" of the figure or at the "back"? Can you hold both perceptual hypotheses simultaneously?

produce three-dimensional perceptions. However, these two perceptions do not exist for us simultaneously, but they alternate spontaneously. First we perceive one configuration, and then the other, with the figure alternating problematically. The Necker cube is not a unique psychological joke, but is only a particular example of the ambiguity in our environments. When we look across the room to the window do we see the world outside or a picture painted on the wall, a picture of the world outside as it might be? The surrealists have used this theme brilliantly, but these alternatives are equally viable. Continued sampling of the scene from a variety of angles and a knowledge of the structure and contents of most rooms, will lead to only one hypothesis, but the process of hypothesis formation can be fooled, as Ames demonstrated so convincingly with his distorted room. Now, suppose that alternative hypotheses offer themselves spontaneously and frequently, as they do with the Necker cube, then the consequences for behaviour would include a diagnosis of schizophrenia. A failure of selection attention has been suggested by McGhie and Chapman (1961) as a cause of schizophrenia. Consider the following statement from a diagnosed schizophrenic:

"I have noticed a lot recently that I seem to get a little mixed up about where sounds are coming from. Often I have to check up if someone speaks to me and several times I thought someone was shouting through the window when it was really the wireless at the front of the house."

and from another schizophrenic:

"I've had difficulty in tracing where sounds are coming from although I am not deaf. If the wireless is on, for example, I know the wireless is there but sometimes I feel that the sounds are coming from behind my back."

(from McGhie and Chapman, 1961)

In these cases alternate hypotheses about the stimuli received are held to be responsible for the disturbance in the organization of the drive-related behaviour. It is necessary to inhibit the admission to consciousness of alternative hypotheses about the environment in which we need to operate, and this stability of perception is achieved by attending to only one hypothesis at a time and rejecting all others. This is not to say that the process of hypothesis information is always preattentive. We often need to stop and think about a stimulus before achieving a perceptual hypothesis, as with a Rorschach ink spot for instance. In this case particular perceptual hypotheses about sections of the stimulus would be attended to before a whole configuration offered itself. Once an hypothesis about the stimulus is formed then it may be difficult to ignore it however. An hypothesis about the whole is achieved by attending to components of the stimulus, and this technique of feature analysis is evident in the interpretation of handwriting. Is the word in Fig. 5.2 meant to be "day" or is it "clay"? Context might have given a hint, but here there is none and so the two

clay

Fig. 5.2. Day or Clay?

perceptions alternate with different combinations of features dominating and then being dominated. Attention to one combination precludes attention to another.

In addition to the inhibition of simultaneous hypotheses about one configuration of stimuli, as in Fig. 5.2, attention also serves to determine which configurations should be processed. Whilst engrossed in a novel the reader is unlikely to be sampling continuously stimuli from his surroundings, unless for some specific purpose. We have the ability to attend to one source of stimulation to the exclusion of others, and this has obvious biological advantages. Unless we are able to attend exclusively to one object or one task, at the expense of other objects and tasks, the performance will suffer. We need to attend to features of whatever stimulus is available, and we need to attend to our own responses and their effects. Failure to attend results in incompetence in the performance of a learnt skill, or the desired skill will not be acquired.

After the descriptions of the systematic psychologists of the last century little work was devoted to the study of attention and other "mental" processes. The process of attention was a vitally important issue to James, and Titchener considered attention to play a central role in all behaviour. The Behaviourists abolished the study of such notions as attention and consciousness in their search for input-output rules, and it was not until the 1950s that interest was revived with investigations to find the bases on which attention could be directed and maintained. Attempts to isolate the discriminating features of a source of information which are used to direct attention to it stemmed largely, as with a great deal of research in experimental psychology, from the need to handle the increasingly complex environments which technology is providing for us. A few hundred years ago the accuracy achieved by a man-machine system was restricted by machines of variable quality. An arrow was accurate, even for highly skilled archers, over a very short range in comparison with modern weapon systems which can be designed to be accurate over colossal distances, provided that they are operated appropriately. There is now more room for operator-error than for machine-error, and this has brought a great need to understand how we process the information available to us and execute our responses. Without this understanding we cannot hope to design the machines around the limitations of our ability to process information. The machines can execute our commands efficiently, and can provide us with a vast amount of data to aid the decision process on which those commands are based. And hence the revival of interest in the process of attention: the operator has so much information available he needs to be given certain cues as to which information is important and must be attended to, and which information may be ignored safely. The identity of these selection cues has been established by a number of experiments, and it was upon these experiments that Broadbent (1958) based his filter model of attention.

Bases of Selectivity

Four early experiments are relevant to the issue of which features the relevant message must have (and all other messages not have) to enable focussing of attention. Broadbent (1954) found that when two auditory messages were presented simultaneously they could be separated by the listener and attended selectively on the basis of spatial location. Two messages coming from different directions whether real (via loudspeakers) or apparent (via earphones) could be distinguished, and Moray, Bates and Barnett (1965) extended this finding to the case of four messages. The efficacy of localization as a cue for selectivity was also demonstrated by Egan, Carterette, and Thwing (1954) who observed selectivity when two messages differed in intensity. Although selectivity was easier when two messages were presented to opposite ears, attention could be focused on the required message if it was presented to the same ear as an unwanted message but was louder. Treisman (1964b) similarly found that selectivity was enhanced by presenting the two messages with different voices, a male and a female reading the messages.

We may conclude from these experiments that selection between messages can be made on the basis of some physical cue which differentiates between them. If the messages are presented from different locations, or spoken at different intensities, or spoken by different voices, then we are able to attend selectively to one message and ignore the others. Selection of messages on the basis of a physical cue is principle which was also derived from studies of immediate visual memory conducted by Sperling and others. In that series of experiments objects were presented with displays of letters or digits for very brief durations, and were subsequently cued by a tone to recall part of the display. This partial report procedure allowed the recall of proportionately more information than the procedure whereby recall of the whole display is required. The advantage is said to be due to the readout of information from a precategorical visual store in which items are available for a very short time. Now, whereas information could be selected from this visual store on the basis of physical characteristics, with partial report of the items of one row, or one size, or one colour, the selection cue was ineffective if, for instance, all of the digits were required from a mixed display of letters and digits. The visual store retains the physical characteristics of the display, and is prior to the categorization process, so selection on the basis of one or other category of items is not possible. If the analogy holds then we may conclude that the selection of signals in a dichotic listening experiment is also effected prior to the classification of the words which constitute the message. This is the basis upon which attention may be directed but messages are not attended to because they have certain physical characteristics rather than any particular meaning. If we are within earshot of two conversations then we can choose to listen to one or other of them, or switch between the two if both are interesting or relevant. The physical characteristics of the two sets of speakers provide information on which we maintain the direction of attention, and select the messages for categorical analysis.

To explain the findings that there is no retention of the semantic content of a message which did not receive attention (Cherry, 1953), and that attention could be focussed on a message if it was differentiated physically from other messages, Broadbent (1958) formulated his filter theory of attention. Broadbent considered that each incoming message is first separated from other messages by analysis of their physical characteristics. This allows us to be aware of the physical characteristics of each message reaching the receptors whether or not we attend to it, and this assumption was confirmed by Lawson (1966) who found that pure tones which were embedded in an unattended message were perceived as well as those embedded in an attended message. The next stage of processsing in this model is detailed word analysis, but due to the limited capacity of the word analyzing mechanism only one input channel is allowed to reach this stage, and this is the message which has been selected on the basis of pre-selected physical characteristics. One and only one message can be analyzed at a time, and the others are said to be filtered away. When dichotic messages are presented one is not attended to, it is rejected, and not analyzed for meaning.

This model of attention has been rejected following empirical demonstrations of the semantic content of an unattended message affecting performance under certain circumstances. If behaviour is affected by the meaning of an unattended message then that message cannot be rejected altogether, as Broadbent suggested, and this implies that either more than one message may be attended to simultaneously, or that attention is not necessary for word analysis. Moray (1959) found that subjects occasionally responded to their own names when they were presented as part of the unattended message. An instruction in the non-shadowed message was more likely to be followed if preceeded by the subject's name. Moray compared "all right, you may stop now", with, for example, "John Smith, you may stop now". These instructions were always obeyed when in the attended message, but not in the unattended message except when the subject's name was presented. The subject shadowed his own name on 33% of occasions when it was presented in the to-be-ignored message. This result is intuitively consistent with everyday experience: if one's own name is called out in a noisy crowded room then our attention is called even though we may have been listening carefully to someone else. The moral is that if you are going to talk about someone who is in the same room as you then you should mention her name after the gossip and not before. However, the problem for Broadbent's model is that semantic information in the unattended message is occasionally acted upon, whereas it should have been rejected as soon as the physical characteristics analyzer indicated that it was not presented to the attended message.

The potency of the listener's own name has been shown in two other experiments. Oswald, Taylor, and Treisman (1960) played recordings of names to sleeping subjects who had been instructed previously to clench a fist whenever they heard their own name, and whenever they heard another critical name. More clenching responses were observed to the critical names than to irrelevant names, and the subject's own name elicited most responses of all. This result again accords with experience, and with the logic of biological function. It is important that we should be aroused by someone calling our name for the successful reception of the ensuing communication. Similarly, it was reported by Howarth and Ellis (1961) that when attempting to recognize names presented with a low signal-to-noise ratio subjects had a lower recognition threshold for their own name than for other names. Subjects' own names were recognized on 77% of occasions, and other names were recognized on 50% of occasions. The listener's own name is a very effective stimulus whether it is not attended to, whether it is presented whilst the listener is asleep (and hence not attending), or whether presented in adverse listening conditions. The first two of these results have some interesting implications for the role of attention in word recognition, for semantically important words appear to be analyzed prior to attention being directed towards them. Important words might be thought to be given priority for entry into a single-channel word analyzer, but this leads us to wonder how important words are designated as being important *before* they are analyzed for meaning. The solution which Deutsch and Deutsch (1963) came to was that attention is not necessary for word analysis, and that attention is directed to any words which are important after pre-attentive recognition. If this is the case then we must argue that any words presented to us are analyzed whether we attend to them or not, and as we shall see later, there is a great quantity of conflicting data on this issue.

However, in the context of the present discussion it is sufficient to conclude that the listener's own name can elicit a response when it is not attended to and should, according to Broadbent (1958), be rejected without analysis for meaning.

Treisman (1960) also found an effect which was dependent upon the meaning of the unattended message in an experiment in which subjects shadowed prose presented to one ear whilst ignoring prose presented to the other ear. When the irrelevant prose was contextually probable following presentation of the relevant message, then the subject occasionally repeated one or two words from the message he was meant to ignore. Treisman engineered this by switching messages across ears at some arbitrary point, with the irrelevant prose suddenly being presented to the ear which was being attended:

Attended Ear: "... sitting at a mahogany/three possibilities ..."
Unattended Ear: "... let us look at these/table with her head ..."

In this particular case the subject might have uttered:

"... sitting at a mahogany table possibilities ..."

With low orders of approximation to English (i.e. almost randomly selected words) fewer shadowing intrusions were made when the messages were switched between ears. The significance of this result is that if selection for analysis had been made on the basis of physical characteristics alone (e.g. "attend to your right ear and ignore the left"), then contextual information should have been ineffective in producing a change in the direction of attention, and subjects should have been able to shadow all the words presented to one ear regardless of their transition probabilities.

Treisman (1964b) has also reported that the semantic content of two messages can be a useful cue for separation when other cues are absent. Two messages were presented binaurally and the subject was required to shadow one of them, which was always a novel read by a female speaker. The other message consisted of a passage of either the same novel or of a biochemical discussion, or was spoken in an unknown foreign language. The unattended novel was either read by the same speaker or a new speaker. This experiment provides a measure of the effectiveness of semantic cues in the absence of physical cues of separation, and of the effectiveness of physical cues in the absence of semantic cues. The results are presented in Table 5.1, with the dependent measure always the efficiency of shadowing the attended message.

The effect of presenting the distracting message in a different voice, and hence providing a physical cue for selectivity, was to increase the shadow-

Table 5.1. The effect upon shadowing an attended prose message of various unattended messages. Both messages were presented to both ears. From Treisman (1964b)

	Shadowing efficiency	Intrusions from UM
Unattended message (UM)		
different voice, same novel	74%	1%
same voice, same novel	31%	20%
same voice, biochemistry	40%	12%
same voice, unknown language	55%	1%

ing efficiency by some 40%. However, when there was no physical cue for selectivity, changing the semantic content of the distracting material increased the shadowing efficiency by almost 10%. Although the improvement is small it is consistent for other types of material. An unknown foreign language spoken by the same female was also rejected more successfully than another passage from the novel. The semantic content of competing messages can be used to aid discrimination between them, but selection on this basis is less efficient than selection to the basis of such physical features as spatial location and voice of speaker.

The initial formulation of the filter theory of attention is shown to be inadequate by these experiments which indicate that the semantic content of unattended messages is not ignored altogether, but may effect behaviour in some circumstances.

Attention Control and the Capacity Model

A word of caution is appropriate at this point in the interpretation of results from experiments which employ the shadowing technique to control the direction of attention. Shadowing undoubtedly does force the subject to listen to the required message, otherwise he would not be able to repeat it, but if we are to obtain a measure of the breadth of attention then we need a technique which does not focus attention abnormally. The shadowing studies may provide a demonstration of the ability of subjects to report their experiences whilst attending closely to one aspect of their environment, but it is possible that the shadowing technique itself is responsible for producing a particular distribution of attention which is not necessarily representative of volitional activity. The argument is best viewed from the viewpoint of the capacity model of attention which is based on the shared-capacity notions of Moray (1967), and which has been outlined by Underwood and Moray (1971) and Kahneman (1973). This model considers that a subject has a fixed amount of capacity available for distribution according to whatever strategy he chooses. The distribution of capacity for processing a particular set of stimuli is said to lead to the experience of attention. If a large proportion of the available capacity is allocated to one source of stimuli then the subject is said to be attending to that source. This does not mean that other stimuli cannot be processed, for if the total amount of available capacity is not consumed by the primary task then secondary tasks may be performed simultaneously with the first. Thus we are able to hold a conversation (primary task) whilst walking down the street (secondary task) because the secondary task consumes so little processing capacity that the capacity limit is not exceeded. The conversation consumes the bulk of the available capacity, and is said to be attended to whilst other activities may be described as automatized. Automatization may logically follow the elimination of the need for capacity to be allocated to perception, response organization, response execution, or response monitoring, in the production of sequential responses dependent upon a changing environment.

Whereas this description of behaviour allows only one stimulus to be attended to at any one time it does not prohibit the completion of simultaneous tasks. Certain activities do not require continuous monitoring (attention) for their performance, and in the context of the present discussion the problem is whether attention is required for word recognition. However, to return to our criticism of shadowing, the capacity model argues that the performance of the shadowing activity itself consumes processing capacity which might otherwise have been allocated to the analysis of the secondary message. The distributions of processing capacity in shadowing and non-shadowing situations are simplified in Fig. 5.3. When a subject shadows one message of a dichotic presentation the capacity remaining for analysis of the second message may be reduced, so rendering complete recognition of all secondary inputs impossible. If this view of the distribution of selective attention is valid then the shadowing experiments do not produce false results in the sense that they do not describe behaviour in particular situations, but they do not represent the attention process as we know it outside the laboratory. They do indicate the extent

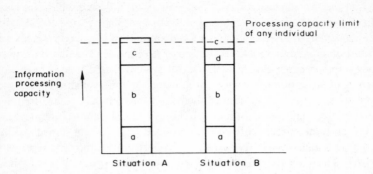

Fig. 5.3. The allocation of processing capacity during dichotic listening in two experimental situations. *a*. Capacity required for ongoing processes such as separation of the two messages. *b*. Capacity required for analysis of the attended message. *c*. Capacity required for analysis of the secondary message. *d*. Capacity required for shadowing response (output and monitoring).

to which subjects are able to respond to secondary messages when involved in a very engaging primary task. If attention is an all-or-none process then the use of shadowing or any other attention control task may be justified, but if processing capacity may be distributed then shadowing may be biasing this distribution. If we are concerned to know how much of a secondary message may be analyzed when totally engaged on a primary task, then shadowing is useful, but not if we want to know how many messages can be analyzed at the same time. These are different questions, and different procedures are applicable to them.

A demonstration of the effect of the shadowing response upon the effectiveness of the secondary message was reported by Underwood and Moray (1971). Subjects listened to dichotic lists of letters, and responded whenever they heard digits in either the attended or the unattended message. When shadowing the attended message they detected approximately 69% of the attended digits, and 13% of the unattended digits. In another condition subjects were instructed to attend selectively to one message, but again to respond to any digit. When monitoring rather than shadowing subjects detected 90% of attended digits and 48% of unattended digits. The increase in detection of unattended digits cannot be attributed to less attention being allocated to analysis of the primary message because digits in this message were also detected more successfully. The difference between 13% and 48% for performance on the digit detection task is attributed to processing capacity being allocated to the shadowing task in the former case. The question also arises of why the detection of attended targets should rise when subjects monitor rather than shadow, for the main reason for using shadowing is that it directs attention to the specified message. The deficit should not be due to an attentional difference between the two tasks therefore, and it seems that when shadowing the subject's own voice masks the stimuli to a certain extent, and makes the messages more difficult to hear.

If shadowing consumes capacity then in situations where it consumes less capacity more of the unattended message should be responded to. Underwood (1974a) tested one highly practised subject with material similar to that used by Underwood and Moray (1971). This subject detected approximately 96% of the attended digits and 67% of the unattended digits. Shadowing was so easy for the practised subject that many more digits were detected than by unpractised subjects. The improvement of the practised subject over unpractised subjects who listened selectively to the lists indicates that practice also influences such processes as monitoring the attention sharing process. Separating the two messages does take up capacity (Taylor, Lindsay, and Forbes, 1967) and so practice with dichotic inputs should result in a need for less capacity in order to separate them. Shadowing does not always render analysis of the secondary message impossible, but in cases where it does not it may be difficult to determine which listening strategy the subject is employing, but this is a problem general to the whole field of attention research. As yet we are incapable of distinguishing between subjects who attend continuously to one message and perceive all of the second message to a certain extent, and subjects who switch attention rapidly from one message to the other perceiving none of the message to which they are not attending at that time. With unpractised shadowers rapid switching of attention results in high error rates in shadowing performance, but with the highly practised shadower (who was Neville Moray, a proponent of switching strategies!) high error rates may have been avoided by switching quickly and for short periods at non-critical instants during the presentation of the primary message.

Shadowing a speech message does not consume all of the available capacity of course, otherwise nothing of the secondary message would gain a response. Salter (1973) has shown that instructions to shadow one message of a dichotic presentation but also to report as many words from the other message leads to more secondary words being repeated than primary words lost. There is a net gain of words repeated indicating the availability of spare capacity when the subject shadows one message. There is even more spare capacity when the subject simply listens to one message.

Perceptual Selection and Response Selection

Bearing in mind this criticism of the principal attention control method we may continue to consider the extent to which unattended messages are processed. The Broadbent filter model was rejected by experiments showing that semantic information in the unattended message can occasionally be effective. To account for the results, which suggest that categorical analysis of all messages may take place, Treisman (1960) offered a modified version of the filter theory. Treisman suggested that unattended messages are not filtered off altogether, but are "attenuated". A simplified version of an attenuator would act to reduce the signal-to-noise ratio of each rejected message, so that information would still be available, but in a degraded form. This point has subsequently been clarified, and it appears that Treisman intended that the "information content" of the unattended messages be attenuated rather than their loudness (see Neisser, 1967, p. 212). Acting upon incomplete information the word analyzing mechanism would not recognize all of the unattended message, but even with reduced information certain important words or highly probable words may be recognized and responded to. Hence, the listener's own name, and contextually probable words in the unattended message contain sufficient information for recognition.

There are two sources of information which influence the recognition of words, whether they are seen or heard, for both sensory information and contextual information affect recognition. When a certain amount of information has been accumulated the dictionary unit (Treisman, 1960) or logogen (Morton, 1969) fires, and a recognition response may be available. The activation of a logogen corresponds to the subjective recognition of a word-meaning and for every word-meaning in memory there is some stimulus which can activate the corresponding logogen. External sources of stimulation such as the stimulus presented for recognition, and previously presented stimuli will limit the number of stimuli which will be perceived. Given the input "the driver changed gear and turned the . . . " we would be more likely to hear "corner" than "milk", even if the two words were equally distinguishable. The point has been demonstrated empirically by Tulving and Gold (1963), who first showed subjects a number of words to establish the context of a visually presented stimulus which they were to identify. For instance, "more money buys fewer products during times of . . . " was followed by the test stimulus "inflation" or the stimulus "rasp-berry". Shorter exposure durations were required for the identification of congruous words than incongruous, as indicated in Fig. 5.4, and the great-er the amount of context the greater the effect upon recognition whether the context was appropriate or inappropriate. Similarly, identical stimuli may lead to different perceptions given different contextual information.

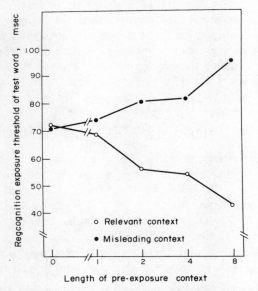

Fig. 5.4. Visual duration threshold as a function of length of context for congruous and misleading contexts. (From Tulving and Gold, 1963.)

The interpretation of the input "they are boring professors" can be biassed by previously presented contextual information which indicates whom "they" are. Recognition thresholds are lowered by the presentation of both stimulus information to the senses and contextual information to be stored in memory. Certain important words may have permanently lowered thresholds, and their corresponding logogens would require less sensory and contextual information before they are activated. One's own name may therefore be recognized more often than other names because it has a lower recognition threshold. Whereas this model does get away from the problem of how an unanalyzed word is classified as being important it does require a certain amount of preprocessing of inputs by the nervous system in order that very different stimuli are perceived as being the same pattern. However, more probable words are more likely to be recognized than less probable words given similar stimulus conditions, and Treisman incorporates the feature of recognition units and their bias in her model of the attention process. Unattended messages are attenuated, and so less information about unattended words affects the logogen system. But because sensory information is not the only input to the logogen system unattended words may receive responses. If sufficient contextual information has been gathered then recognition will proceed. Hence, when the input to the primary ear is "sitting at a mahogany three possibilities ..." and the word "table" is presented to the secondary ear at the same time as "three" then the logogen corresponding to "table" is excited, the response is available and the subject shadows part of the unattended message. Selection is still said to be made on the basis of physical characteristics, but whereas Broadbent considered that one message is analyzed and all others rejected completely, Treisman argues that other messages are attenuated but may be recognized if sufficient information about them penetrates the attenuation barrier.

Bloomfield (1972) has challenged the view that only physical cues are used for message selection in dichotic listening. and has argued that contextual cues also determine the direction of attention. Subjects in his experiment heard lists of high association word pairs in each ear:

Left Ear: "... you me dog cat top   bottom light dark ..."
Right Ear: "... dry wet girl boy bread butter king queen ..."

and subjects shadowed a list presented to one or other ear. Bloomfield observed shadowing accuracy given unattended words of high and low contextual probability with attended words:

Left Ear: ". . . you me dog boy top . . ."
Right Ear: ". . . dry wet girl cat breat . . ."

In this example "boy" and "cat" are associated with the previous words in the opposite ears, whereas the word in the same ear has a low association value: the pair "dog-boy" has a lower association between items than "dog-cat". When the unattended word was associated more with the previous attended word than was its accompanying attended word the subjects heard and shadowed the unattended word on 37% of occasions. When the attended pair had a high association value the switching rate was only 7%. This result is similar to Treisman's observation of intrusions from the unattended message when that message was contextually more probable than the accompanying attended message.

In a second experiment Bloomfield substituted the word "tap" for a number of unattended words, and subjects were instructed to shadow the attended message, but to tap on the table should they hear the instruction in the other message. When subjects shadowed the attended message word correctly they never responded to the "tap" instruction if the attended word had a low probability, but responded on 27% of occasions when the attended word was probable. This result suggested to Bloomfield that subjects were selecting which ear they should attend to on the basis of both physical and semantic cues, because "the relatively low probability of the instruction to tap will mean that it does not effectively compete with low probability items in the shadowed message and channel selection will be determined on the basis of spatial origin alone" (ibid., p. 465). Bloomfield does not account for the increased likelihood of tapping when a high probability word is shadowed. Underwood (1973c) pointed out that these data are best accounted for by the capacity model of attention. Words which are highly probable require less processing capacity for their identification than do contextually improbable words: less sensory information is necessary because the recognition threshold is lowered by the accumulation of contextual information. Only when highly probable words were presented did Bloomfield find evidence of analysis of the unattended message, and it is when highly probable words are presented that the capacity model predicts that processing capacity will be available for analysis of the unattended message. However, the attenuation model fails to account for Bloomfield's result in that under some circumstances a low probability unattended word is heard, and under others it is not. The attenuation model cannot account for this variation, for a given word with a given contextual probability should have a recognition threshold which is independent of an unrelated word which is attended to.

Neisser (1967) has also offered an alternative view of Broadbent's filter model, in which unattended messages are not actively rejected, but are not processed beyond a certain level of analysis. Perception, to Neisser, is a process of analysis-by-synthesis or reconstruction, and with dichotic inputs one message is reconstructed and the other is not. The second message is not rejected but it fails to be selected because we can only analyze one message at a time. Unattended messages are said to be analyzed by "pre-attentive process", which perform analyses of physical characteristics and may detect simple units such as the listener's own name. Preattentive processes also provide information for activities which are automatized. We may walk down the street without bumping into a tree, and although we may not remember noticing the tree it must have been seen to be avoided. Regular features of the environment, which fit into our conception of the world, do not need to be focused upon in order for us to operate in the environment. When the unexpected appears attention is summoned and the input is processed at the level of awareness. We have the ability to selectively process those parts of the available stimuli which are of interest to us, and in focusing upon them they are perceived with what Titchener (1908) described as a particular vividness. Other stimuli are not rejected as such, but they do not gain the benefit of perceptual synthesis. By attending to one speech message the listener covertly reconstructs it for himself, and that message may then be assimilated into his active verbal memory. Unattended messages may only attract attention when they are important to the listener, or are contextually probable and may therefore override physical location cues. Otherwise unattended messages reside only in echoic memory, and then for only a relatively short period.

The attractions of Neisser's model are firstly that it incorporates the notion of vividness and hence accords with subjective experience (something which the other models may be stretched to do), and secondly that it points out the functional similarity between the Broadbent-Treisman perceptual selection models and the Deutsch-Norman response selection models.

The late-selection, or response selection, theories of Deutsch and Deutsch (1963), Norman (1968), and Keele (1973) differ from the early-selection theories principally in the extent to which unattended messages are said to be analyzed for meaning. Whereas the early-selection theories argue that unattended messages are attenuated or filtered prior to categorical analysis because of the limited capacity of the word analyzing mechanism, the late-selection theories argue that all incoming messages are analyzed for semantic content but that only one of them gains attention because of the limited capacity of the response organization process. For one set of theories attention is necessary for word analysis and for the other set attention is necessary for response organization. Norman (1968) suggests that attention controls the entry of information from primary memory into secondary memory, in a system in which representations may be activated temporarily or permanently. All inputs temporarily activate their representations or logogens, but only selected representations are extensively analyzed. Unattended messages are analyzed for word meanings, but there can be no integration of these words into meaningful structures.

These models are empirically indistinguishable on account of the indeterminable number of locations of selectivity. Even with the simplest of cognitive models, with the sensory input first being stored in immediate (sensory) memory, and then categorical memory, from which it may be retrieved and integrated into a response, there are numerous opportunities and necessities for selective admission from one process to the next. Information in categorical memory may be elaborated in many different ways, and with limited time one elaboration will be selected or biassed in favour of others. Retrieval from memory is also selective, and this is a major source of forgetting. Not even all retrieved items will be offered in response of course, and the individual's own decision criteria will be one source of variance, but the output analysis would be simple if items were stored on the basis of one attribute as verbal learning theory once believed. As it is, events are remembered rather than items, and the word presented to the subject is only a part of the event. Any of the attributes of the event may be used as retrieval cues, and here we have another source of selectivity.

This point may be demonstrated by use of a series of experiments which attempted to distinguish between the early and late selection theories of attention. Treisman and Geffen (1967) tested for the immediate recognition of words in both messages, with the attenuation model predicting no response to the unattended message and the response selection model predicting equal analysis and response to both messages. This experiment eliminated the delayed test procedure which found no memory for unattended words when the test was made more than a few seconds after presentation (Cherry, 1953; Moray, 1959; Mowbray, 1964). Treisman and Geffen designated certain words in prose passages as "targets" (e.g. digits, colours, parts of the face, with examples of targets in these categories being "three", "blue", "eye"). Subjects were required to respond to any target words as soon as they heard them, by tapping on the table. One of the dichotically presented prose messages was shadowed, to give a measure of the direction of attention. When target words were a part of the attended message they were responded to on 87% of occasions, but when they were a part of the unattended message only 8% were detected. Treisman's conclusion was that words in the unattended message had been attenuated and had failed to excite their stored representations, otherwise they would have gained a tapping-response as often as did attended words. Interestingly, the context of the prose influenced the detection of target words according to whether they were in the unattended or attended message. Target words which were out of context with the attended message were detected much less often than contextually probable words, but context had a smaller effect upon the response to unattended words. However, we would not expect an effect of contextual probability for unattended words if these words are not analyzed beyond their specific meanings without integration into an underlying sentential meaning, as described by Norman (1968). The effect of context cannot be considered a crucial test between the two sets of theories, and Deutsch and Deutsch (1967) also rejected the target detection data as being inconclusive. Awareness of the content of the message is viewed by their model as a response in itself: to direct attention to a stimulus is to respond to it, and it is in this sense that the limitation is in the number of messages to which we are able to respond. Perception is indistinguishable from response if responses are viewed in this broad, non-behaviouristic sense, and this functional similarity defies empirical separation. If attention serves to present a stimulus to conscious awareness after preliminary or preattentive processing then a different view of the problem involves the consideration of the extent to which word analysis may proceed prior to consciousness. However, the reinterpretation of Treisman and Geffen's data offered by Deutsch and Deutsch was that the experimental design did not permit parallel processing of the responses to the two messages. Having the subjects shadow one message precluded any overt response to the other message because of the limited capacity available for the organization of the response. We have already seen that when the subjects produce no continuous overt response during the presentation of the messages they are able to respond to more of the secondary message than when shadowing (Underwood and Moray, 1971; Underwood, 1972, 1973a). Whereas this result does not support the early-selection models it does not give unequivocal support to the late-selection models either, for the elimination of the necessity to organize independent responses did not lead to equal analysis of attended and unattended messages. The Deutsch and Deutsch interpretation of Treisman and Geffen's result is not entirely satisfactory, for Lawson (1966) had reported that if subjects shadowed one message of a dichotic presentation, with instructions to respond to tones superimposed on either message, then they did respond to tones in the unattended ear. Late-selection theories of limited response processing would predict that responses to two channels are not possible except where both messages are "important".

Treisman and Riley (1969) extended the case of detection of physically different target items to targets which contain semantic information. They presented lists of dichotic digits, and the task for the subject was to shadow one list and respond to target items, which were letters. Each list contained sixteen pairs of items, and one item in each list was a letter. Letters were either spoken by the same person who recorded the lists (a male speaker), or by a different person (a female). Targets which differed from the list on one dimension (letters against digits) were detected on 70% of occasions when they were attended to, and on 39% of occasions when they were in the message which was not shadowed. Targets which differed from the list on two dimensions (female-voice letters against male-voice digits) were "always" (99% of occasions) detected regardless of whether or not attention was directed toward them on presentation. The late-selection theories predict no difference in the rates of detection due to physical characteristics since this should not affect response organization:

these theories do not postulate any specific physical characteristics analyzer upon which selectivity may be based. This result is in line with predictions made by early-selection theories however, which consider that if different voices are used for the two messages then different analyzers may be employed simultaneously. Treisman (1969) accounted for the numerous reports of parallel processing of stimuli by proposing that if stimuli are processed by different analyzers then they may be perceived simultaneously, but that if two stimuli vary along the same dimensions then processing must be serial. So, if a dichotic pair of words must be analyzed for meaning they are analyzed successively, but if the pair also vary in their physical characteristics from the rest of the list then simultaneous analysis will proceed. When a single item is spoken in a different voice to the test of the list it may be detected as a target entirely on the basis of its physical characteristics, and its semantic content decoded when attention is directed to its echoic representation. Subjects can listen for a letter in one channel, a different voice in another channel, and presumably a change in intensity in a third channel. These processes engage different analyzers which may operate simultaneously.

An alternative explanation which might be suggested by late-selection theorists is that any stimulus which is different from its fellows, or unexpected, will demand attention on the grounds of importance. We almost always notice when something in our environment is different even though we cannot always say exactly what has been changed. The ability to detect changes in our input has obvious evolutionary advantages, and "stimulus change" could be argued as a case for analysis in a similar manner to analysis of certain other important signals which have a reduced perceptual or response threshold.

Effects of Unattended Messages

Selective listening and looking

The direct method of testing between the early-selection and late-selection theories of attention is to present unattended material and to test the listener's reception of that material whilst attention is directed away from it. This method, used extensively by Treisman, has not proven itself to be fruitful because a low rate of response to an unattended message may be interpreted in support of either theory of selection. Poor performance may result from serial ordering of analysis or of response organization and execution. A further logical problem is that perceptual analysis may be considered to be identical with response organization: we may order our perceptions or categorizations as we intend to represent and reproduce them. In such a case there is no distinction between selection of perceptions and selection of responses.

An alternative method of describing the effects of focused attention is to demonstrate the effects upon behaviour in general of material which is not attended to, and upon the perception of a response to the attended message in particular. An advantage of this method is that at no time is the subject informed that he must respond to the secondary message: there is no advantage to the listener in attempting to attend to anything other than the primary message. Indeed, in some circumstances it is to his advantage to attempt to reject the secondary message to avoid interference effects. Moray (1959) got around the problem of subjects listening to the unattended message by instructing them to make as few shadowing errors as possible, and not informing them of the purpose of the second message. Subjects reported that "they thought that this was just an attempt by the experimenter to distract them", but they still heard instructions prefixed by their own names on 33% of occasions. The importance of a set to expect certain messages is indicated by Moray's result that on informing subjects that they would hear an instruction to change ears they heard the instruction on 80% of occasions when it was prefixed by their own names and in the unattended message.

Treisman (1964b) and Underwood and Moray (1971) have demonstrated interference effects from unattended messages upon the response to attended message by comparisons between performance under dichotic and monaural listening conditions. The presence of an unattended message was found to reduce shadowing efficiency only slightly when prose was presented to both ears, but presentation of two irrelevant messages on separate channels caused considerably more interference than one irrelevant message (Treisman, 1964b). Three separate messages were heard by presenting two of them to separate ears, and the third message to both ears. This third message is then localized as coming from somewhere in the middle of one's head, and quite distinct from the other two. Subjects are able to attend selectively with this trichotic arrangement, although not so efficiently as with one or with two messages, and the result is an important one for peripheral gating theories of attention. Hernandez-Peon, Scheerer and Jouvet (1956) found that evoked responses measured at the cochlear decreased when attention was directed away from the auditory modality by the presentation of a visual stimulus. This might be taken to suggest that attention serves to attenuate the information passed from the sense receptors to the cortex, but Treisman's result denies this possibility. To reject one message the listener must also listen to another message arriving at the same ear. Hence the total input to that ear cannot be attenuated. Attention does not operate at the level of the sense receptors in this case, but it may do in other situations of course.

The presence of an irrelevant message was found to affect the detection of occasional digits in lists of letters whether subjects shadowed or listened selectively (Underwood and Moray, 1971), but when the digits were spoken in a different voice from the letters an advantage was found for dichotic presentations. The presence of a background voice at the same time as the letter served to emphasize the change in pitch.

Physiological effects of unattended words have been observed by first associating a word with an electric shock, and then observing galvanic skin responses (GSR) on presentation of the shock-associated word in the unattended message. Moray (1969) first presented subjects with prose passages which contained the word "country". Each time the subjects heard this word they received a shock to their hands, and after a few trials a GSR was obtained the word. Subjects then shadowed one prose passage and were told to ignore a second passage which was heard simultaneously. The word "country" was presented in both the shadowed and unattended message and GSR measures recording at the time of presentation of this shock-associated stimulus. Whereas all subjects have a significant GSR when the word was heard in the attended message, only one quarter of them responded when it was in the unattended message. A physiological effect of unattended words would not necessarily imply that these words were processed to the level of awareness, for these responses may be observed with subjects who are asleep (Oswald, Taylor, and Treisman, 1960). Indeed, Moray states that his subjects did not hear the shock-associated words even when they responded to them, but discriminative responses do indicate processing to a certain level, and as yet the possibility of pre-attentive semantic analysis cannot be ruled out.

An extension of this experiment has been reported by Corteen and Wood (1972), who investigated galvanic skin responses to words from the same semantic category as those previously shock-associated. During the pre-test session subjects listened to a list of twelve words which was repeated a number of times. Three of the twelve words were names of cities, and were shock-associated during the pre-test session. Dichotic passages of prose were then presented, and subjects shadowed the prose heard in one ear. In the unattended prose twelve test words were embedded which were the three shock-associated city names, three new city names not previously presented, three of the non-shocked nouns from the pre-test list, and three new nouns, as a control measure. The GSRs to each of these words were observed with relation to an arbitrary criterion of response intensity and latency. The new nouns, neither shock-associated nor from the shock-associated list, gave a galvanic skin response on 8·7% of occasions, and this serves as the base rate of response. The city names which had previously been shock-associated, but which were now in the unattended message, gave a criterion response on 37·7% of occasions, indicating that the direction of attention does not restrict entry to the logogen system. City names which had not been associated with electric shocks also elicited a high proportion of GSRs, a response being given on 22·8% of occasions. This semantic generalization effect demonstrates that subjects are not responding to particular phonemic patterns, but to the meaning of these patterns. Nouns from the pre-test list elicited responses on 12·3% of occasions. There were no interruptions with the shadowing of the attended list during the presentation of test items, over the general shadowing error rate, and subjects claimed to be unable to remember any of the words in the passage which they were told to ignore.

The interesting feature of Corteen and Wood's experiment is that a certain amount of semantic generalization evidently occurred from shock-associated city names to other city names. This eliminates the possibility that GSRs were being obtained following an acoustical analysis of the unattended message. In Moray's experiment it could have been the phonemic features of the word "country" which elicited the conditioned response, but in this case the semantic features of the stimulus appear to be critical. A further feature of interest is the absence of an effect upon the shadowing of the attended message, indicating that subjects were not aware of the presence of the shock-associated stimulus to which they were responding.

However, before this result is described as offering unqualified support for late-selection theories in that word recognition is demonstrated without awareness, it must be pointed out that the shock-associated words produced responses on a little more than a third of the times they were presented. Loftus (1974) has provided a similar cautionary note concerning the fallacious statement that Moray (1959) found that the subject's own name "virtually always breaks through the attentional barrier". Corteen and Wood found that unattended words *sometimes* elicit autonomic responses, and this is as perplexing to the late-selection theories as it is to early-selection theories. The Deutsch-Norman models might account for the relatively few number of responses to unattended words by suggesting that instructions to ignore all but the shadowed message would act to inhibit elaboration processing of the unattended message. The passage which contained the shock-associated words would be regarded as irrelevant even though it would be unselectively rendered to a preliminary analysis. This minimal analysis for recognition could reduce the possibilities of any further covert response, but the semantic generalization data indicate that the unattended words were not analyzed for word meaning alone. Early-selection theories can explain the 37·7% of responses to shock-associated words by the attenuation principle, whereby imperfect sensory information activates the word-recognition units which have lowered thresholds. The logogen units would have lowered thresholds in this case because of their previous association with a subjectively important stimulus (an electric shock) within the context of the experimental situation. Awareness of an active logogen was not apparent in this experiment, but this is not critical for early-selection models: conscious awareness may occur after selection between inputs and preliminary analysis of the contents of one message. If this view of the early-selection theories is taken then they again tend to resemble the late-selection theories. The semantic generalization effect would then be attributed to the lowering of the thresholds of all words in the same category as the important words, that category becoming apparent as the subject is repeatedly shocked whenever an instance of the category is presented.

The capacity model may also account for Corteen and Wood's result by assuming that the recognition thresholds of important words would be sufficiently low to allow activation by the sensory analysis given by the available capacity. A certain minimal amount of capacity would be allocated to the unattended message even though it was indicated as being a distractor because it is maladaptive to ignore totally everything but that to which one attends. This capacity would be sufficient for the analysis of words with reduced or permanantly low thresholds. Conscious awareness is reserved for those messages which are considered to be the most important at that time. The subject could obviously choose to be aware of the contents of the secondary message, but analysis and shadowing of the primary message would then deteriorate. Consciousness is seen by Shallice (1972) to reduce ambiguity of perception by inhibiting the influence of other perceptions upon behaviour. Behaviour can then only take account of any one perception at any one time.

Corteen and Wood used shadowing accuracy (errors and omissions) as a measure of the effect upon conscious activity of the presence of a conditioned stimulus in the unattended message. A more sensitive measure would have been shadowing latency — the time between presentation of a word and its output by the subject — and this is the measure used by Lewis (1970). Subjects in this experiment shadowed lists of eleven unrelated words which were presented to one ear, and were told to ignore simultaneous words in the other ear. The unattended word was either unrelated to the other half of that dichotic pair, or was a synonym of its partner, or an antonym, or had a high sequential dependency (e.g. bookcase). The mean shadowing latency was 699 msec when the unattended word was unrelated in meaning to the shadowed word. For accompanying synonyms and sequentially dependent pairs shadowing latencies were increased to 726 msec and 719 msec respectively, but for antonyms the mean latency was reduced to 643 msec. Although the meaning of the unattended words was influencing behaviour subjects were unable to recall any of the unattended message at the end of each trial. This result poses a problem for early-selection models of attention, for the semantic content of an irrelevant message should have no effect upon shadowing. However, if unattended messages are attenuated and only reduced information accumulates in the logogen then some effect might be predicted by these models. An attenuated word may, as we have seen, activate a logogen, and we only have to reject the idea of a recognition response threshold and replace it with a recognition awareness threshold to accommodate Lewis's data. The accumulation of information by the logogen may not produce an all-or-none response, being dependent upon whether or not the threshold is exceeded, but any information, however little, may produce excitation which corresponds to a degree of recognition. If a great deal of information is accumulated then the logogen might become so activated as to reach awareness, otherwise awareness is restricted to those perceptions being attended to intentionally. The problem is then one of accounting for the synonym-antonym difference. Synonyms increased shadowing latencies in comparison with unrelated words, and antonyms decreased shadowing latencies. Coltheart (personal communication) has suggested an explanation for this difference which is based upon possible sampling errors in the selection of words for the experiment. If one takes a word with given frequency and length characteristics (e.g. "black"), and then attempts to generate a synonym and an antonym the trend is for the synonym (e.g. "sooty") to have a lower frequency of occurrence than the antonym (e.g. "white"). If this trend held for the stimuli used by Lewis then we would expect the synonyms to cause more processing difficulty than would the antonyms. By the capacity model, the word accompanying a synonym would be processed at a time when less capacity was available because relatively more capacity would be required for the analysis of a low frequency word than for a high frequency word. Lewis's result may then stem from antonyms having a higher frequency and requiring less capacity for analysis than the low-frequency synonyms.

Subjects may have been unable to recall any of the unattended words because either they were never aware of them, recognition or partial recognition proceeding without conscious direction, or recognized words from the unattended message may have been forgotten rapidly and efficiently. The cue for forgetting may have been the ear of arrival, which was described to the subjects as to be ignored. Mandler and Worden (1973) have demonstrated the feasibility of the rapid forgetting hypothesis by an experiment in which subjects processed words semantically (declaring whether each word in a list was a noun or a verb) but if distracted immediately by a secondary task then recall and recognition were reduced considerably. Momentary awareness of semantic processing followed by rapid forgetting is a phenomenon well-known to typists, and to shadowers, but it is questionable whether or not this is the fate of unattended inputs. All tests of retrieval of unattended inputs indicate the brief retention of acoustic characteristics, but no awareness of semantic characteristics until after attention is redirected (e.g. Murray and Hitchcock, 1969; Norman,

1969b; Glucksberg and Cowen, 1970; but see the discussion in the previous chapter).

Treisman, Squire and Green (1974) have confirmed in part the effect reported by Lewis, finding that a word in the unattended message can effect the latency of shadowing a related word. However, the effect was observable only for word pairs at the beginning of the presentation, when attentional selectivity was broad. The effect may operate only when the irrelevant words are not fully unattended. A comparable effect is also demonstrated with briefly shown visual stimuli (Underwood, 1976a). When subjects attend to a simple picture-naming task simultaneously presented words affect the naming latency according to the semantic association between picture and word. In the first experiment subjects were not informed as to which side of fixation the picture would appear: on half the trials the picture appeared to the left of the fixation point in the tachistoscope, and on half of the trials it appeared on the right. The word always appeared on the opposite side of fixation to the picture. The irrelevant words were from one of three categories on each trial, and in a control condition no word was presented. When the word corresponded to the required naming response (e.g. with a picture of a cat, the word CAT was shown), it had no effect upon latency, inhibitory or facilitatory, in comparison with the no-word condition. A word related to the picture increased the naming latency (e.g. a cat, with the word CREAM), but a word unrelated to the picture caused more interference still. It appears that all stimuli available within the visual field received some processing, but that high association between simultaneously presented stimuli facilitated processing in comparison with those trials where the stimuli were unrelated. This interpretation is complicated by a second experiment in which subjects were pre-cued as to the location of the picture. Selectivity might therefore be expected to be narrow in this situation, and irrelevant words ignored successfully. Indeed, the naming responses in this experiment were faster than in the comparable conditions of the previous experiment, suggesting that the pre-cue was affecting the acquisition strategy employed. There was no effect here of presenting unrelated words or word-like strings of letters, but related words still retarded the naming response by a small though consistent fraction. In states of narrowed attentional selectivity it may be the case that irrelevant words have their recognition thresholds lowered by the context of the attended stimulus, but that unrelated words (which do not gain the benefit of this contextual   information) do not activate their lexical representations. Logogen activation of any irrelevant word may disrupt post-recognition processing of the attended stimulus, but it is the recognition of the attended stimulus which initiates the interference cycle. When selectivity is broad and capacity allocated to a number of stimulus sources then processing of a task-irrelevant stimulus may reduce the amount of capacity available for processing of the attended stimulus. When attention is directed to one aspect of the stimulus array words in other parts of the stimulus array may be recognized if the activation thresholds of their logogens can be lowered by the attended stimuli. The reading of individual words may be an automatic process, but when attention is directed elsewhere then additional cues are necessary before recognition can be successful.

Reading, however, is an activity in which attention to the pointed stimulus is not broadly distributed. Skilled readers pick up information about the meaning of the text from many sources without necessarily being aware of the phenomena. The influence of contextual information during reading has been demonstrated by Marcel (1974), who found that faster readers were more affected by contextual constraints than were slower readers. It seems that slower readers need to extract more visual information during word recognition, rather than relying upon the context provided by previously recognised words. The use of contextual information is a generally available strategy, and "sophisticated guessing" is a tuition feature of many speed-reading courses. Contextual information is influential whatever strategy is employed, however, as indicated by the demonstrations of spreading excitation in the semantic network (e.g. Meyer and Schvaneveldt, 1971; Loftus, 1973; Conrad, 1974), and of pre-attentive lexical access (e.g. Bradshaw, 1974; Underwood, 1976a,b). Willows and MacKinnon (1973) found that reading speed was not affected by to-be-ignored lines of text printed between the lines of attended text, but the semantically related irrelevant text did cause interference with a comprehension exercise presented after reading. The words presented between the lines were not recalled, but they did increase the number of comprehension errors committed, sometimes being offered incorrectly in response to the content questions. In skilled reading we extract lexical meaning from words in the text independently of the direction of attention, even though we may not be aware of the specific lexical meanings of the unattended words. These words contribute to the assimilation of the general meaning of the text, but the Underwood (1976a) experiment suggests that unattended words only contribute when attention is selective if the words are related to the attended words. Unrelated words demand some attention before they can aid the extraction of meaning from text.

Another perplexing set of findings, for early-selection theories at least, has been described by MacKay (1973). His experiments were designed to test a specific theory of the analysis of semantic components in language which postulates two levels of analysis of linguistic information which correspond to two memory systems. At one level information is processed for lexical content or semantic components of individual words, and for surface structure content. To analyze the deep structure of a string of words the second level of analysis and storage is required, and attention is necessary for this analysis. Analysis at the first level may be applied to attended or unattended inputs. This model has certain similarities with the Deutsch-Norman late-selection models in that word analysis may proceed without attention, but here attention is necessary for the assimilation of individual words meanings into the overall meaning of the communication. To test these ideas MacKay presented ambiguous sentences to one ear and had his subjects attend by requiring them to shadow in some cases and write them in others. At critical points in these sentences MacKay presented disambiguating words to the unattended ear, which subjects were instructed to ignore. The dependent measure was the extent to which the words in the unattended message affected the interpretation of the attended sentences, and so the first step was to establish the response bias to each ambiguous sentence in the absence of the unattended words. Lexical ambiguity was influenced by a critical word in the unattended message causing a 4·2% shift in the number of interpretations in the direction of the meaning of the unattended word. For instance, when attending to the sentence "They threw stones toward the bank yesterday" subjects were presented with the word "river" or the word "money" at the same time as hearing "bank". After completion of shadowing or writing they then had to say whether the sentence meant "They threw stones toward the side of the river yesterday" or "They threw stones toward the savings and loan association yesterday". Presentation of "river" biassed the interpretation of the sentence to ". . . the side of the river . . . " However, if the attended message had deep structure ambiguity as with the sentence

"They knew that flying planes could be dangerous", then the effect of an unattended phrase with one of the alternative biases (e.g. "growling lions") is minimal. The unattended message is effective only when it disambiguates the lexical or surface structure of the attended message. On this evidence we must reject the early-selection theories of attention unless we can argue that the critical attended words served to lower the recognition threshold of the related words in the unattended message. If the unattended words are attentuated but not rejected entirely then they might be expected to affect the interpretation of an ambiguous message, and if the late-selection models are correct in asserting that all unattended words are analyzed then it is surprising that an effect greater than a 4·2% bias shift was not observed. An additional problem is that the isolated unattended words in MacKay's experiment may have caused involuntary shifts of attention to the non-shadowed ear. (This criticism also holds for Lewis's experiment.) It is one of the assumptions of Moray's (1969) model of attention that a change of activity in an unattended channel will result in attention being called to that channel for at least a short time, and Mowbray (1964) found an 80%-90% disruption of shadowing when he presented individual words in the unattended message. Although Mowbray's subjects knew that they were required to recall the unattended words it is not unreasonable to suppose that subjects might have switched attention to the non-shadowed message in the MacKay and Lewis experiments. The absence of an effect with an ambiguous deep structure may then be due to the nature of the disambiguating message. The information necessary for interpretation needs to be collected rapidly, because attention cannot remain on the non-shadowed message for a very long time. If the unattended message lasts for more than a few hundred msec then the necessary information may not be collected. With deep structure ambiguity the examples which Mac-Kay provides of disambiguating information all contain unattended messages of length two words, which may be too long for assimilation with a rapid switching strategy.

There is an accumulation of evidence to suggest that the semantic attributes of unattended words can affect performance which is based upon attended information heard at the same time. Furthermore, these un-attended words do not appear to be processed at the level of awareness more generally associated with word recognition. It appears that the logogen units involved in the recognition of spoken words may be activated whether or not attention is directed towards those words. Activity of a logogen will influence concurrent performance, possibly by interference with the activity of other logogens. The capacity model views the direction of attention as the direction to which the bulk of processing capacity is allocated. We can choose to direct most capacity to one task; in which case we would gain a great deal of information from that source, or perform the activity accurately. Alternatively we can choose to distribute capacity between tasks, performing a number of activities less well than any of them alone, or gaining information from a number of sources. From the dichotic listening experiments one conclusion is apparent, and that is that we can be aware, or conscious, of only one stream of analysis at any time. Other words may be recognized or partially recognized, but we can only be aware of and respond to one analysis. Unattended words may be analyzed, but they cannot initiate voluntary activity. Capacity has the role in this model of determining the extent to which analysis of a word may proceed. The activation of a logogen does not imply comprehensive analysis and assimilation into ongoing activity, for this elaboration coding requires attention and by this we mean more processing capacity. A word which activates a logogen which does not receive capacity may not be related to the items in consciousness and may not reach awareness. This view of consciousness is not dissimilar to that of Neisser (1963), in which a number of activities are permitted simultaneously, with only one main sequence of thought which may be affected by other activities. There is a limit to the number of sequences of which we are conscious because our behaviour is "drive-organized", and without the restricted number of perceptions we would have conflicting information upon which to act.

Subliminal stimuli

Stimuli may activate their logogens without necessarily exceeding the threshold of awareness. This threshold varies as a function of the importance of that word to the individual (e.g. the listener's own name will have a low threshold), and as a function of the direction of attention. A word presented in a message which has been allocated a large proportion of the available capacity will readily enter awareness as a matter of strategy. A weakly presented stimulus may also affect behaviour regardless of the direction of attention, as indicated by the subliminal perception studies.

A stimulus which we are not necessarily expecting but which is certainly not being rejected actively may have a considerable effect upon perception. Dunlap (1900) found the Muller-Lyer illusion to be effective even when the fins were too faint to be seen and were not reported as being seen, and Smith and Henriksson (1955) found that a square was judged to resemble a trapezoid when an imperceptible array of fins was shown immediately before the square. Although the square in Fig. 5.5(A) has the same objective characteristics as that in Fig. 5.5(B) it does not appear so.

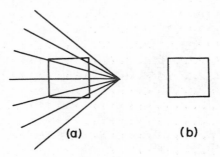

Fig. 5.5. An illusory trapezoid. The squares in (A) and (B) have the same dimensions. The effect can be obtained if the fins in (A) are presented subliminally (Smith and Henriksson, 1955.)

By presenting the fins at a duration below that required for phenomenal awareness a straight forward square (B) can be made to appear as a trapezoid (A). Subliminal verbal material has also been shown to affect concurrent performance. Zuckerman (1960) used a Thematic Apperception Test, whereby subjects were shown a picture and were asked to write a story about the scene portrayed. Zuckerman superimposed a subliminal message over the pictures, instructing the viewer to either "DON'T WRITE" or "WRITE MORE". These messages led to shorter or longer messages respectively, although when these instructions were presented supraliminally they had no effect upon the response to the T.A.T. picture. Smith, Spence and Klein (1959) showed a similar effect in an experiment involving the perception of emotion expressed by human faces. Quite expressionless faces were presented, but superimposed were the subliminal messages, either "HAPPY" or "ANGRY", and the emotions tended to be perceived according to these messages.

Also related to the issue of whether unattended messages are recognized, and whether they reach awareness, are the perceptual defence experiments. Recognition awareness thresholds are raised for words which are unpleasant for certain subjects, although galvanic skin responses to such words may be observed at exposures too short for verbal response (McGinnies, 1949). Autonomic responses before volitional response may indicate the presence of two stages of recognition whereby a logogen may be activated at a level insufficient to enter awareness but sufficient to influence behaviour. Alternatively the perceptual defence effect may be due to the conservative strategies adopted by subjects. With neutral words a subject may be prepared to respond before he is sure of the identity of a stimulus, but having partially recognized what may be a taboo word he may be reluctant to respond until he has had a longer look and is certain of the identity of the stimulus. A demonstration of this response conservatism was reported by Boulos (1963), who presented subjects with three letters of words which contained four. The task was to utter the first word that came to mind which was suggested by the incomplete word. Some of these incomplete words had a number of solutions, at least one of which was unpleasant or emotional (e.g. the stimuli were "sh t", "f rt" etc.), and the completion latencies of these words was often very much longer than that for non-emotional words. Subjects evidently had difficulty in finding alternatives to the obvious and freely available emotional solutions which they were reluctant to offer. Apart from response conservatism when words are present in consciousness there remains the possibility that the recognition or partial recognition which caused the GSR and interference in perceptual defence and selective attention experiments is not available to awareness. Emotional words may have higher awareness thresholds than non-emotional words as well as higher volitional response thresholds. As shown by Lazarus and McCleary (1951) recognition does not imply awareness, however, and hence the feasibility of the two-process model is established. In an elegant demonstration of the subception effect they found that shock-associated nonsense syllables could elicit galvanic skin responses whether or not they were presented too briefly for awareness. In view of this result we should not be surprised with Corteen and Wood's report of GSR's elicited by unattended words in a shadowing task.

In the perceptual defence and subception experiments information presented below the exposure duration or intensity required for awareness is observed to affect autonomic activity, and concurrent conscious perception. The recognition threshold may have been reached, but not the awareness threshold. This multiple threshold view of information processing escapes the apparent paradox of postulating that the perceptual system is able to recognize an item and then decide whether it should be perceived or not (see Eriksen and Browne, 1956). Recognition thresholds which vary for different types of material may also account for the problematic finding of the word-superiority effect, reported by Reicher (1969) and Wheeler (1970). In this experiment the subject's task was to decide which of two letters he saw in a tachistoscope. For example, the letter "D" might be shown briefly, and then the subject is required to say whether the letter was a "D" or a "K". The crucial point about this experiment is in the second condition where the target letter forms part of a word. For example, "WORD" might be shown, and again the subject decided whether the letter in the predefined position (the last letter) is a "D" or a "K". Note that the three additional letters are redundant, because "WORK" is just as valid a unit as "WORD". However, when the target letter was a part of a meaningful unit then it was recognized easier than when it was presented in isolation. When the order of the three redundant words was randomized then the target letter was as difficult to recognize as when it was alone, and so we can assume that it was the meaning of the total presentation that facilitated recognition of a component of the presentation. The problem here is in determining how meaning can help the perception of a stimulus, when meaning is derived from the perception. If we have two stages of perception then the Reicher-Wheeler result is no longer paradoxical, for the complete word could activate its logogen at a lower exposure duration than could a single letter. Information about the meaning of a word is available prior to the word being available to awareness. Knowledge about the meaning of a word can aid recognition of individual features by restricting the number of possible alternative configurations. Individual letters obviously contribute to the total pattern, but complete identification of a letter may not be necessary for recognition of the word, and once the word is recognized then individual features may be derived. The features of a target letter may be recognized with the aid of stimulus and contextual information in one situation, but with stimulus information alone in the other situation.

The Stroop effect

The availability of meaningful information prior to awareness of the physical features which combine to convey that information is one explanation of the Reicher-Wheeler effect, and is consistent with the general hypothesis supported here. A startling demonstration of the availability of unwanted meaningful information is the Stroop effect. The subject's task here is to identify a series of colours, and name them one after the other. This is straightforward enough, but Stroop (1935) presented the test colour as words and these words were the names of other colours. This is the effect demonstrated on the front cover, the task being to name quickly the colour of the ink used to print the words and ignore the words, which happen to be colour names. The task is by no means impossible, but erroneous responses are common, and the reader may find himself exaggerating the response. The naming task here may be said to require more processing capacity than when the ink does not spell out conflicting solutions. Stroop found that the determination of the colour was inhibited considerably when the word was the name of another colour, even though the word itself was irrelevant to the task. When subjects were required to read the names of these same stimuli, and ignore the colours of ink in which they were printed, then there was negligible interference in comparison with a test in which all words were printed in black ink. It is very difficult to select physical information in this task and at the same time ignore conflicting semantic information, a curious phenomenon in comparison with the effects of selection on the basis of physical cues and not semantic cues, which appear from investigations of the extraction of information from visual and auditory presentations (Broadbent, 1958; Sperling, 1960; Morton, Crowder and Prussin, 1971; Darwin, Turvey and Crowder, 1972). A weak version of the Stroop effect is presented in Table 5.2, in which the task is to count the number of physical items in each line, ignoring the identity of the items. In SET C the digits in each line conflict with the number of digits, causing a slight interference effect, and in SET B there is no conflict. Using similar stimuli to these I found no difference between the times to name the number of asterisks in each line and the number of

Table 5.2. Is it easier to count the number of items per line in Set A, B or C? Ignore the type of items on each line, and concentrate on counting the number of items as quickly as possible.

Set A	Set B	Set C
****	4444	888888
********	1	3333
**	666666	4
******	55555	99999
*	999999999	77
*****	22	6666666
*********	7777777	555555555
***	333	22222222
*******	88888888	999
****	333	3333333
********	7777777	111
*****	999999999	44
******	22	1111
*	1	55555555
**	666666	33
*********	55555	666666
*******	4444	2
***	88888888	88888
********	7777777	666666666
***	333	444
*******	999999999	9999999
**	55555	7777
********	1	66666666
*****	666666	22222
*	22	555555
******	88888888	8
****	4444	111111111

digits when the digit was consistent with the number of digits (approximately 31 seconds for each whole set). Subjects averaged approximately 38 seconds to count when the digits conflicted with the correct response. When random digits or random letters are used then the task is no more difficult than with asterisks. With the conflicting digits (SET C) naming responses do tend to be slower than with meaningless or irrelevant information, as Stroop reported. It is difficult in the counting task, and much more difficult in the colour identification task, to ignore the meaningful information and respond solely to the physical characteristics of the stimulus. The two general explanations of this effect can be represented in the terms of the late-selection and early-selection theories of attention. The more popular explanation of the Stroop effect is that the competing covert responses of colour and colour-name interfere with each other and provide difficulty for the subject in choosing the most appropriate overt response (Klein, 1964; Keele, 1973). Both colour and word recognitions are available as responses, and the increased colour-naming latency is considered to be due to the necessary process of selecting the response. The alternative explanation is that subjects are unable to attend selectively to the colours without attending to the words in which they are printed, and that the word interferes with the process of verbally encoding the name of the colour (Treisman, 1969; Hock and Egeth, 1970). The additional process here is selection between analyzers rather than selection between responses for the analyzers, and the Stroop effect derives from an inability to reject an irrelevant analyzer. The inappropriate analysis proceeds and produces an interfering response, and the result of this analysis is available at the level of awareness in contrast with a number of the effects of irrelevant messages mentioned previously in this discussion. Treisman and Fearnley (1969) have reported that irrelevant physical information may cause interference in a naming task. They found no difference in a "same-different" judgement task between a condition in which the colour of one word (a colour name) was matched with a colour name printed in black, and a condition in which a colour name (in another colour of ink) was matched with the colour of a row of crosses. In both cases a match across attributes is required, a colour being compared with a colour name, but in the first condition the interference is from a word which names an irrelevant colour and in the second condition the interference is from an irrelevant colour of ink in which the relevant word was printed. When there was no matching across attributes (matching two colours, or two-colour names), then response latencies were somewhat faster. This result suggests that the Stroop effect is not a result of the reading response being more practised than the colour identification and therefore more difficult to ignore. Words were no more difficult to ignore than colours, and in both critical conditions subjects were unable to select the appropriate analyzers and reject the inappropriate. When matching within a class of analyzers (e.g. words), then subjects were able to reject the irrelevant class of analyzers. The late-selection theory predicts interference in both "within" and "across" conditions, the inappropriate responses being available in both conditions, but the early-selection theory predicts interference from a class of analyzers only when that class is required for part of the task. Colour names can only interfere when colour naming is a necessary part of the task, and if the "same-different" response may be made entirely on the basis of the colours of two inks, then names will cause no interference. Subjects were slower due to interference when both classes of analyzers were used to make a match, but faster when only one class of analyzer was necessary.

Hintzman, Carre, Eskridge, Owens, Shaff, and Sparks (1972) have criticized the early-selection position on the basis of a Stroop experiment in which the colour of the ink occasionally matched the colour name. In these instances the naming latency was faster than when the word conflicted with the colour, and when the word was neutral with respect to colour. Hintzman *et al.* concluded that the facilitation of naming when the word coincided with the target colour contradicted the early-selection theory, because word analysis should have interfered with the ability to encode ink colour by this theory. Both ink colour and colour name influence performance, both the word and the name of the colour contacting memory. When these two names coincide then a speeded response is observed, but either of the selection theories can account for the result. It may be impossible to reject printed names when colour names are sought either because the same class of analyzers is in use and therefore rejection of one analyzer impossible, or because both analyzers would always be used. These alternatives amount to the same result. The theories differ in that the selection of analyzers model predicts that under certain circumstances interference will not occur because the potentially interfering information is not analyzed. When the word is also the name of the colour of the ink in which it is printed both theories predict a facilitation of response because by both the word is analyzed, and by both the elimination of choice speeds the response.

Whether words are always seen as such and are affective upon behaviour, or whether they are only read when words are involved in concurrent processing, we have numerous instances here of information which is unattended or intended to be unattended but nevertheless received. Information which is received may or may not reach awareness. Attention is not necessary for the perception of certain messages, and it is not necessary for the guidance of all responses. The dichotic listening experiments have provided examples of unattended words being heard, and of unattended words which perhaps did not reach awareness but still affected concurrent activities. Experiments using subliminal stimuli have also shown changes in behaviour which the subjects were not effecting consciously. Word recognition is a process which may be completed independently of awareness, and independently of intention, as indicated by the Stroop effect.

Capacity, Awareness, and Doing Two Things At Once

Despite a mass of evidence which suggests that humans are limited in the number of tasks which they can perform simultaneously, which gives strength to the single-channel theory of information processing, we are nevertheless able to engage in two or more tasks under certain circumstances. Studies of the so-called psychological refractory period have demonstrated that we are unable to respond quickly to a signal if it arrives within a certain interval of a first signal, and the dichotic memory span experiments found a preference for ear-by-ear reporting strategies with fast presentations, which again suggested a limit to the amount of information processed at one time. Storage in a preperceptual buffer of the items arriving at the unselected ear, with processing after analysis of the selected items, is an explanation in support of early-selection theories of attention and of the single-channel view of perceptual activity. This explanation is in conflict with the data previously discussed which indicate that words may be analyzed and responded to even though they are not attended to, and the listener may have no knowledge of them. Alternative explanations based upon selection between responses when all stimuli are analyzed must account for the absence of responses to unattended target words in selective listening experiments. If all words are analyzed then any words which are important to the task should be responded to. A possible process which may inhibit the entry to awareness of all but the most important of the presented words is that of attention. Attention may serve not only to discriminate finely between stimuli and to elaborate the associations between stimuli, but also to prevent the response availability of other stimuli which would interfere with the performance of the primary task. The primary task in most attention experiments has been shadowing, a task which subjects do not find easy. The consumption of processing capacity, in unpractised subjects, by the shadowing task effectively restricts the capacity available for processing of the secondary message. Words may be recognized without being attended to, but they cannot be related to ongoing behaviour without an allocation of a certain amount of the available capacity. Capacity also reduces the recognition threshold of words by providing more sensory and contextual information. When a word is given little capacity then recognition may be incomplete, and activity of the representation of the word limited. By increasing the amount of capacity necessary for the performance of the primary task we are ensuring that entry of unattended words to awareness will be inhibited, and that processing of unattended words will not be extensive. Unattended words which do enter awareness tend to disrupt the primary task, and the more difficult the primary task is, the more important it is to suppress all other perceptions. Unattended stimuli, then, may be recognized, but they do not necessarily enter awareness. When capacity is available they may be processed to a greater extent than when the attended tasks are more demanding, and their performance consumes most or all of the available capacity. We are able to perceive and respond to stimuli without being aware of perception or response, or so it seems in retrospect. Whilst attending to a conversation or to one's thoughts we are able to drive or walk along the road successfully, and then realize that we have no awareness of the road just encountered: this is what Reed (1972) describes as the "time-gap" experience. Whether we were briefly aware of the road, the perception of which was rapidly forgotten, or whether we were never aware of it at all, is a question not yet answered by experiment. When complex skills are acquired their basic components may be said to be automatized, the components are integrated within a sequence such that choice is eliminated. We approach a junction or other hazard, and decelerate without debate. Deceleration is automatized in this situation for we release the accelerator pedal and perhaps brake without consciously considering the activity. Automatization of the components of a skill is not essential, but the skilful action may be performed more efficiently if every step is not given deliberation during the performance. Reading single words or phrases may also be an automatized skill, as LaBerge and Samuels (1974) argue. Hence we are able to read a page of text and then realize that we have not understood the global concepts discussed. The integration of meanings of individual words and phrases into the reader's schema is a process requiring attention for its direction, even though the words may be analyzed preattentively.

Kimble and Perlmuter (1970) have argued that if we attended to an activity which has become automatized then it will be performed less efficiently, as in the story of the old man who could not get to sleep because he was unable to decide whether his beard should be above or below the sheets. In their analysis of volitional behaviour attention, or consciousness is necessary for voluntary acts but when that act becomes automatized through practice "the individual devotes his attention to more demanding enterprises". By releasing capacity from the components of one skill, and permitting automatized activity the performer may relate the activity to others. When the tennis player ceases to attend closely to the position of his feet when making his stroke then processing capacity will be released for such activities as the consideration of strategies of play. Until his strokes are automatized, or at least do not demand continuous attention once initiated, then the opponent may not be beaten by conceptual activity.

The performance of two tasks simultaneously, receiving and responding to the messages, does not pose any problem for the single-channel view of attention. We know that two activities which are independent can be performed if at least one of them is automatized. In 1887 Paulham claimed to be able to recite one familiar poem orally and at the same time write out another one (see Woodworth and Schlosberg, 1954). In general there was little interference between the two emissive tasks, and Paulham could even perform a simple multiplication problem on paper at the same time as reciting a poem. Here is an example of attention switching between tasks, with automatization of the non-attended task once the response had been programmed. In this example two outputs were manipulated with apparent simultaneity, and Shaffer (1971) has reported a detailed examination of the performance of highly practised typists which indicates that functionally distinct components of the skill were being processed simultaneously. Stimulus recognition and response organization were not necessarily handled by the same process, but were at least processed simultaneously. Parallel processing meant that the subject was able to recognize one stimulus whilst still organizing the response to the previous stimulus.

Overlapping activities are a consequence of automatization, and Shaffer's skilled performers need not necessarily have been attending to either of the stages of recognition or response. In a further dual-task experiment reported by Shaffer (1973) a skilled typist was able to copy-type prose which was presented visually, and shadow different prose presented aurally. This subject made very few errors on either task: less than 1% errors of typing, and less than 5% errors of shadowing. Even though the material used was prose, with high redundancy between letters and between words, these levels of accuracy are strongly indicative of parallel processing rather than switching between tasks. However, when both messages were presented aurally, one to each ear, then the subject missed approximately 40% of each message. Similarly when the subject was required to type the auditory message and read aloud the visual text, performance dropped to approximately 60% correct transmission of each message. When the two tasks require transmission of a visual message visually, and an auditory message orally, then the two messages may be processed. If the transmission lines are crossed, however, then simultaneous processing is more difficult. A possible cause of the difficulty here is in the separation of the inputs and outputs. The modality of presentation is a useful tagging device by which the subject can keep a track of which message a particular word belonged to if attention is directed away from that word for a short time, or if the message is not receiving the necessary amount of capacity for constant monitoring. Errors will appear if the modality attribute is lost through confusion (not enough capacity available) or is inappropriate, as with dichotic inputs. When the subject was listening to one message and seeing another she was not responding to individual stimulus units, but to attributes of each message which facilitated performance, and in this case the modality of presentation was a useful cue for monitoring each word or set of words, and ensuring that they were reproduced within that modality. For transcription across modalities an additional operation was required, and there was apparently insufficient capacity to perform the transfer between modalities in this situation.

This analysis may also be applied to the result of an experiment conducted by Allport, Antonis and Reynolds (1972). They found that subjects could perform two transcription tasks when different symbolic languages were used with different input modalities, thus providing two sets of attributes to aid separation of messages. Subjects were able to shadow an aurally presented prose message and simultaneously play a previously unseen piece of music on a piano. Although the musical task was rather simple for the subjects used, there was nevertheless little interference between the tasks. This experiment again suggests that if the subject is able to separate the input-output transmission lines then two tasks may be performed together. Separation of activities would be facilitated if one of them is a highly practised skill and may therefore be performed with the minimum attention. In relation to Shaffer's experiments it would have been interesting to know whether the musicians could have played a tune presented aurally (on a silent keyboard preferably), and at the same time read aloud a prose message presented visually.

In a dual-task performance, when capacity is distributed between two activities, subjects may be aware of the detailed structure of only one activity at any instant. In the "time-gap" situation the individual is unable to recall any of the information used by the automatized activity, but he may or may not have been aware of that information at the time of presentation and use. All we have to go on is the indirect evidence that semantic processing prior to rapid and efficient forgetting is a possibility. We also have evidence of automatized semantic processing. Attention is identified with conscious activity here: when we are conscious of an event we may be said to be attending to that event. Other events may be processed and gain a response without being attended to, but if the event is to be integrated into the individual's schema then attention is required. Attention serves the organization of goal-directed behaviour by restricting the number of events under the consideration of the individual, to exclude the relevant and unfortunately often some of the relevant events. The serial nature of overt behaviour is a reflection of the serial nature of consciousness, and if our conscious perceptions were not sequential then our responses could not be organized to achieve our goals. Consciousness is necessary for the initiation and inhibition of volitional activity, whereas automatized or involuntary activity is instinctive or conditioned. When voluntary activities become skilful and automatized then they are performed outside of consciousness and need no initiation by the individual. Images (James, 1890) or plans (Miller, Galanter, and Pribram, 1960) of the intended response are unnecessary for automatized activity, and so the conscious monitoring of feedback of performance is redundant. Hence when performing two tasks, only one of which we may be aware of at any instant, we must argue that either one task is totally automatized, or alternatively that it does not require attention for the total performance. A task may be performed with occasional periods of attention during which the individual may be aware of elaboration coding, or of plans of response, or of the feedback of the effects of the response, provided that whilst the individual is not aware of the task its performance may proceed automatically.

To achieve goals which are not immediately within reach we have evolved a system of memory by which events related to those goals may be represented and correlated. To extract from memory only those events which are related to the goal in hand a process of selection is necessary which not only differentiates between relevant and irrelevant events to exclude the irrelevant, but also differentiates the representation of a stimulus from its presentation: we may be aware of the ticking of a clock, or we may be aware of thinking about the ticking of a clock once we have encoded this event. Consciousness is necessary for this encoding procedure, for we must select the attributes of an event which will help us to achieve the current goal. The evolution of refined sensory apparatus which provides us with detailed unprocessed information demands a process of selection to exclude information which is not goal-related. In the selection of pertinent information by the attention process other information is prevented from reaching consciousness, the level of awareness at which events may be related to the individual's representation of his environment, and encoded for subsequent use.

REFERENCES

Some frequently cited journals have been abbreviated to the following here:

A.J.P.	American Journal of Psychology
Acta Psych.	Acta Psychologica
B.J.P.	British Journal of Psychology
C.J.P.	Canadian Journal of Psychology
Cog. Psych.	Cognitive Psychology
J.A.S.A.	Journal of the Acoustical Society of America
J.E.P.	Journal of Experimental Psychology
J.G.P.	Journal of General Psychology
J.V.L.V.B.	Journal of Verbal Learning and Verbal Behavior
P. & P.	Perception and Psychophysics
Psych. Bull.	Psychological Bulletin
Psych. Rev.	Psychological Review
Psychon. Sci.	Psychonomic Science
Q.J.E.P.	Quarterly Journal of Experimental Psychology

AARONSON, D. (1967). Temporal factors in perception and short-term memory. *Psych. Bull., 67*, 130–144.

AARONSON, D. (1968). Temporal course of perception in an immediate recall task. *J.E.P., 76*, 129–140.

AARONSON, D., MARKOWITZ, N., and SHAPIRO, H. (1971). Perception and immediate recall of normal and "compressed" auditory sequences. *P. and P., 9*, 338–344.

ADAMS, J. A. (1967). *Human Memory.* New York: McGraw-Hill.

ALLPORT, D. A. (1973). Long-term memory for visual scenes. Paper read at joint meeting of the Experimental Psychology Society and the Netherlands Psychonomic Foundation, held in Amsterdam.

ALLPORT, D. A. (1976). On knowing the meanings of words we are unable to report. The effects of visual masking. In: S. Dornic (Ed.), *Attention and Performance VI*. New York: Academic Press.

ALLPORT, D. A., ANTONIS, B., and REYNOLDS, P. (1972). On the division of attention: A disproof of the single channel hypothesis. *Q.J.E.P., 24*, 225–235.

ANDERS, T. R. (1973). A high-speed self-terminating search of short-term memory. *J.E.P., 97*, 34–40.

ANDERSON, J. R. and BOWER, G. H. (1973). *Human Associative Memory.* Washington D.C.: Winston.

ASCH, S. R. and EBENHOLTZ, S. M. (1962). The principle of associative symmetry. *Proceedings of the American Philosophical Society, 106*, 135–165.

ATKINSON, R. C. and SHIFFRIN, R. M. (1968). Human memory: A proposed system and its control processes. In: *The Psychology of Learning and Motivation Vol. 2*, edited by K. W. Spence and J. T. Spence. London: Academic Press.

AVERBACH, E. and CORIELL, A. S. (1961). Short term memory in vision. *Bell Systems Technical Journal, 40*, 309–328.

BADDELEY, A. D. (1966a). Short-term memory for word sequences as a function of acoustic, semantic and formal similarity. *Q.J.E.P., 18*, 362–365.

BADDELEY, A. D. (1966b). The influence of acoustic and semantic similarity on long-term memory for word sequences. *Q.J.E.P., 18*, 302–309.

BADDELEY, A. D. (1970). Estimating the short-term component in free recall. *B.J.P., 61*, 13–15.

BADDELEY, A. D. (1972). Retrieval rules and semantic coding in short-term memory. *Psych. Bull., 78*, 379–385.

BADDELEY, A. D. and DALE, H. C. A. (1966). The effects of semantic similarity on retroactive interference in long- and short-term memory. *J.V.L.V.B., 5*, 417–420.

BADDELEY, A. D. and ECOB, J. R. (1973). Reaction time and short-term memory: Implications of repetition effects for the high-speed exhaustive scan hypothesis. *Q.J.E.P., 25*, 229–240.

BADDELEY, A. D. and LEVY, B. A. (1971). Semantic coding and short-term memory. *J.E.P., 89*, 132–136.

BADDELEY, A. D. and PATTERSON, K. E. (1971). The relation between short-term and long-term memory. *British Medical Bulletin, 26*, 237–242.

BANKS, W. P. (1970). Signal detection theory and human memory. *Psych. Bull., 74*, 81-99.

BARNES, J. M. and UNDERWOOD, B. J. (1959). "Fate" of first-list associations in transfer theory. *J.E.P., 58*, 97-105.

BARON, J. (1973). Phonemic stage not necessary for reading. *Q.J.E.P., 25*, 241-246.

BARTLETT, F. C. (1932). *Remembering*. London: Cambridge University Press.

BJORK, R. A. (1970). Positive forgetting: The noninterference of items intentionally forgotten. *J.V.L.V.B., 9*, 255–268.

BJORK, R. A., LaBERGE, D., and LEGRAND, R. (1968). The modification of short-term memory through instructions to forget. *Psychon. Sci., 10*, 55–56.

BLOOMFIELD, T. M. (1972). Single channel theory and dichotic listening. *Nature, 236*, 465–466.

BOAKES, R. A. and LODWICK, B. (1971). Short-term retention of sentences. *Q.J.E.P., 23*, 399–409.

BORKOWSKI, J. G., SPREEN, O., and STUTZ, J. Z. (1965). Ear preference and abstractness in dichotic listening. *Psychon. Sci., 3*, 547–548.

BOULOS, A. S. (1963). Ambiguity: A factor in the recognition of verbal stimuli. Unpublished PhD Thesis, University of London.

BOUSFIELD, W. A. (1953). The occurrence of clustering in the recall of randomly arranged associates. *J.G.P., 49*, 229–240.

BOWER, G. H. (1970). Analysis of a mnemonic device. *American Scientist, 58*, 496–510.

BOWER, G. H., CLARK, M., WINZENZ, D., and LESGOLD, A. (1969). Hierarchical retrieval schemes in recall of categorized word lists. *J.V.L.V.B., 8*, 323–343.

BOWER, G. H., LESGOLD, A., and TIEMAN, D. (1969). Grouping operations in free recall. *J.V.L.V.B., 8*, 481-493.

BOWER, G. H., and WINZENZ, D. (1969). Group structure, coding, and memory for digit series. *J.E.P. Monographs, 80* (Part 2, 2), 1–17.

BRADSHAW, J. L. (1974). Peripherally presented and unreported words may bias the perceived meaning of a centrally fixated homograph.   *(J.E.P.,), 103,* 1200–1202.

BREGMAN, A. S. (1968). Forgetting curves with semantic, phonetic, graphic and contiguity cues. *J.E.P., 78,* 539–546.

BRIGGS, G. E. (1954). Acquisition, extinction, and recovery functions in retroactive inhibition. *J.E.P., 47,* 285–293.

BROADBENT, D. E. (1954). The role of auditory localization and attention in memory span. *J.E.P., 47,* 191–196.

BROADBENT, D. E. (1958). *Perception and Communication.* London: Pergamon Press.

BROADBENT, D. E. (1970). Psychological aspects of short-term and long-term memory. *Proceedings of the Royal Society of London, Series B, 175,* 333-350.

BROADBENT, D. E. and GREGORY, M. (1961). On the recall of stimuli presented alternatively to two sense organs. *Q.J.E.P., 13,* 103–109.

BROADBENT, D. E. and GREGORY, M. (1964a). Accuracy of recognition for speech presented to the right and left ears. *Q.J.E.P., 16,* 359–360.

BROADBENT, D. E. and GREGORY, M. (1964b). Stimulus set and response set: The alternation of attention. *Q.J.E.P., 16,* 309–318.

BROWN, I. D. (1965). A comparison of two subsidiary tasks used to measure fatigue in car drivers. *Ergonomics, 8,* 467–473.

BROWN, J. (1954). The nature of set-to-learn and of intra-material interference in immediate memory. *Q.J.E.P., 6,* 141–148.

BROWN, J. (1958. Some tests of the decay theory of immediate memory. *Q.J.E.P., 10,* 12–21.

BROWN, J. (1970). Recognition and the direction of attention. *Acta Psych., 33,* 149–157.

BROWN, R. and McNEILL, D. (1966). The "tip of the tongue" phenomenon. *J.V.L.V.B., 5,* 325–337.

BRUCE, D. and CROWLEY, J. J. (1970). Acoustic similarity effects on retrieval from secondary memory. *J.V.L.V.B., 9,* 190-196.

BRUCE, D. and PAPAY, J. P. (1970). Primacy effect in single-trial free recall. *J.V.L.V.B., 9.* 473–486.

BRUCE, D. J. (1956). Effects of context upon intelligibility of heard speech. In: *Information Theory: Third London Symposium,* edited by C. Cherry. London: Butterworth.

BRYDEN, M. P. (1962). Order of report in dichotic listening. *C. J. P., 16,* 219–299.

BRYDEN, M. P. (1963). Ear preference in auditory perception. *J.E.P., 65,* 103–105.

BRYDEN, M. P. (1965). Tachistoscopic recognition, handedness, and cerebral dominance. *Neuropsychologia, 3,* 1–8.

BRYDEN, M. P. (1971). Attentional strategies and short-term memory in dichotic listening. *Cog. Psych. 2,* 99–116.

BURROWS, D. and OKADA, R. (1971). Serial position effects in high-speed memory search. *P. and P., 10,* 305–308.

BULL, R. and REID, R. L. (1975). Recall after briefing: Television versus face-to-face presentation. *Journal of Occupational Psychology, 48,* 73–78.

BUSWELL, G. T. (1922). Fundamental reading habits. *Supplementary Educational Monographs,* No. 21.

CAVANAGH, J. P. (1972). Relation between the immediate memory span and the memory search rate. *Psych. Rev., 79,* 525–530.

CERASO, J. (1967). The interference theory of forgetting. *Scientific American, 217,* (October), 117—124.

CHERKIN, A. (1969). Kinetics of memory consolidation: Role of amnesic treatment parameters. *Proceedings of the National Academy of Science, 63,* 1094—1101.

CHERRY, C. (1953). Some experiments on the recognition of speech with one and two ears. *J.A.S.A., 23,* 915—919.

CHOMSKY, N. (1957). *Syntactic Structures.* The Hague: Moulton.

CLARK, S. E. (1969). Retrieval of colour information from preperceptual memory. *J.E.E., 82,* 263—266.

CLIFTON, C. and BIRENBAUM, S. (1970). Effects of serial position and delay of probe in a memory scan task. *J.E.P., 86,* 69—76.

CLIFTON, C. and TASH, J. (1973). Effect of syllabic word length on memory search rate. *J.E.P., 99,* 231—235.

COHEN, G. (1973). How are pictures registered in memory? *Q.J.E.P., 25,* 557—564.

COLE, R. A. (1973). Different memory functions for consonants and vowels. *Cog. Psych., 4,* 39—54.

COLE, R. A., COLTHEART, M., and ALLARD, F. (1974). Memory of a speaker's voice: Reaction time to same- or different-voiced letters. *Q.J.E.P., 26,* 1—7.

COLLINS, A. M. and LOFTUS, E. F. (1975). A spreading excitation theory of semantic processing. *Psych. Rev., 82,* 407—428.

COLLINS, A. M. and QUILLIAN, M. R. (1969). Retrieval time from semantic memory. *J.V.L.V.B., 8,* 240—248.

COLLINS, A. M. and QUILLIAN, M. R. (1972). How to make a language user. In: *Organization of Memory,* edited by E. Tulving and W. Donaldson. New York: Academic Press.

COLTHEART, M. (1972). Visual information processing. In: *New Horizons in Psychology 2,* edited by P. C. Dodwell, Harmondsworth: Penguin.

CONRAD, C. (1972). Cognitive economy in semantic memory. *J.E.P., 92,* 149—154.

CONRAD, C. (1974). Context effects in sentence comprehension: A study of the subjective lexicon. *Memory and Cognition, 2,* 130—138.

CONRAD, R. (1964). Acoustic confusions in immediate memory. *B.J.P., 55,* 75—84.

CONRAD, R. and HULL, A. J. (1968). Input modality and the serial position curve in short-term memory. *Psychon. Sci. 10,* 135—136.

CORBALLIS, M. C. (1967). Serial order in recognition and recall. *J.E.P., 74,* 99—105.

CORBALLIS, M. C. (1969). Patterns of rehearsal in immediate memory. *B.J.P., 60,* 41—49.

CORBALLIS, M.C., KIRKBY, J., and MILLER, A. (1972). Access to elements of a memorized list. *J.E.P., 94,* 185—190.

CORBALLIS, M. C. and LOVELESS, T. (1967). The effect of input modality on short-term serial recall. *Psychon. Sci., 7,* 275—276.

CORCORAN, D. W. J. (1966). An acoustic factor in letter cancellation. *Nature, 210,* 658.

CORTEEN, R. S. and WOOD, B. (1972). Automatic responses to shock associated words in an attended channel. *J.E.P., 94,* 308—313.

CRAIK, F. I. M. (1968). Two components in free recall. *J.V.L.V.B., 7,* 996—1004.

CRAIK, F. I. M. (1970). The fate of primary memory items in free recall. *J.V.L.V.B., 9,* 143—148.

CRAIK, F. I. M. (1971). Primary memory. *British Medical Bulletin, 27,* 232–236.

CRAIK, F. I. M. and BIRTWISTLE, J. (1971). Proactive Inhibition in free recall. *J. E. P., 91,* 120–123.

CRAIK, F. I. M., GARDINER, J. M. and WATKINS, M. J. (1970). Further evidence for a negative recency effect in free recall. *J.V.L.V.B., 9,* 554–560.

CRAIK, F. I. M. and LEVY, B. A. (1970). Semantic and acoustic confusions in primary memory. *J.E.P., 86,* 77–82.

CRAIK, F. I. M. and LOCKHART, F. S. (1972). Levels of processing: A framework for memory research. *J.V.L.V.B., 11,* 671–684.

CRAIK, F. I. M. and TULVING, E. (1975). Depth of processing and the retention of words in episodic memory. *Journal of Experimental Psychology: General, 104,* 268–294.

CRAIK, K. H. W. (1948). Theory of the human operator in control systems: II, Man as an element in the control system. *B.J.P., 38,* 142–148.

CROWDER, R. G. (1967). Prefix effects in immediate memory. *C.J.P., 21,* 450–461.

CROWDER, R. G. (1969). Behavioural strategies in immediate memory. *J.V.L.V.B., 8,* 524–528.

CROWDER, R. G. (1970). The role of one's own voice in immediate memory. *Cog. Psych., 1,* 157–178.

CROWDER, R. G. (1971). The sound of vowels and consonants in immediate memory. *J.V.L.V.B., 10,* 587–596.

CROWDER, R. G. (1973). Representation of speech sounds in precategorical acoustic storage (PAS). *J.E.P., 98,* 14–21.

CROWDER, R. G. and MORTON, J. (1969). Precategorical acoustic storage (PAS). *P. and P., 5,* 365–373.

CROWDER, R. G. and RAEBURN, V. P. (1970). The stimulus suffix effect with reversed speech. *J.V.L.V.B., 9,* 342–345.

CUTTING, J. E. (1973). A parallel between encodedness and the magnitude of the right ear effect. *J.A.S.A., 53,* 358.

DALE, H. C. A. and GREGORY, M. (1966). Evidence of semantic coding in short-term memory. *Psychon. Sci., 5,* 75–76.

DALLETT, K. (1965). "Primary memory": The effects of redundancy upon digit repetition. *Psychon. Sci. 3,* 237–238.

DARWIN, C. J. (1969). Auditory perception and cerebral dominance. Unpublished PhD Thesis, University of Cambridge.

DARWIN, C. J. (1971). Ear differences in the recall of fricatives and vowels. *Q.J.E.P., 23,* 46–62.

DARWIN, C. J. and BADDELEY, A. D. (1974). Acoustic memory and the perception of speech. *Cog. Psych., 6,* 41–60.

DARWIN, C. J., TURVEY, M. T., and CROWDER, R. G. (1972). An auditory analogue of the Sperling partial report procedure: Evidence for brief auditory storage. *Cog. Psych., 3,* 255–267.

DAVIS, J. C. and SMITH, M. C. (1972). Memory for unattended input. *J.E.P., 96,* 380–388.

DEUTSCH, J. A. (1969). The physiological basis of memory. *Annual Review of Psychology, 20,* 85–104.

DEUTSCH, J. A. (1973). *The Physiological Basis of Memory,* (Editor). London: Academic Press.

DEUTSCH, J. A. and DEUTSCH, D. (1963). Attention: Some theoretical considerations. *Psych. Rev.,70*, 80–90.

DEUTSCH, J. A. and DEUTSCH, D. (1967). Comments on "Selective attention: Perception or response?" *Q.J.E.P., 19*, 362–363.

DUNLAP, K. (1900). The effect of imperceptible shadows on the judgement of distance. *Psych. Rev., 7*, 435–453.

ECKSTRAND, B. R. (1972). To sleep, perchance to dream (about why we forget). In: *Human Memory: Festschrift in Honor of Benton J. Underwood*, edited by C. P. Duncan, L. Sechrest, and A. W. Melton, New York: Appleton-Century Croft.

EFRON R. (1970). Effects of stimulus duration on perceptual onset and offset latencies. *P. and P., 8*, 231–234.

EGAN, J. P., CARTERETTE, E. C. and THWING, E. J. (1954). Some factors affecting multi-channel listening. *J.A.S.A., 26*, 774–782.

ELLIOT, L. L. (1967). Development of auditory narrow-band frequency contours. *J.A.S.A., 42*, 143–153.

ELMES, D. G., ADAMS, C., and ROEDIGER, H. L. (1970). Cued forgetting in short-term memory: Response selection. *J.E.P., 86*, 103–107.

EPSTEIN, W. (1969). Recall of word lists following learning of sentences and of anomalous and random strings. *J.V.L.V.B., 8*, 20–25.

EPSTEIN, W. and WILDER, L. (1972). Searching for to-be-forgotten material in a directed forgetting task. *J.E.P., 95*, 349–357.

ERDMANN, B. and DODGE, R. (1898). *Psychogishe Untersuchungen uber das Lesen.* Halle: M. Neimeyer.

ERIKSEN, C. W. and BROWNE, C. T. (1956). An experimental and theoretical analysis of perceptual defence. *Journal of Abnormal and Social Psychology, 52*, 224–230.

ERIKSEN, C. W. and JOHNSON, H. J. (1964). Storage and decay characteristics of non-attended auditory stimuli. *J.E.P., 68*, 28–36.

FECHNER, G. T. (1889). *Elements der Psychophysik.* Leipzig: Breitkopf and Hartell.

FISCHLER, I. RUNDUS, D., and ATKINSON, R. C. (1970). Effects of overt rehearsal processes on free recall. *Psychon. Sci. 19*, 249–250.

FORRIN, B. and CUNNINGHAM, K. (1973). Recognition time and serial position of probed item in short-term memory. *J.E.P., 99*, 272–279.

FRY, D. B., ABRAMSON, A. S., EIMAS, P. D., and LIBERMAN, A. M. (1962). The identification and discrimination of synthetic vowels. *Language and Speech, 5*, 171–189.

FUJUSAKI, J. and KAWASHIMA, T. (1968). The roles of pitch and higher formants in the perception of vowels. *Institute of Electrical and Electronic Engineers Transactions, AV–16*, 73–77.

GERSCHWIND, N. (1972). Language and the brain. *Scientific American, 226 (April).* 76–83.

GLANZER, M. and CUNITZ, A. R. (1966). Two storage mechanisms in free recall. *J.V.L.V.B., 5*, 351–356.

GLANZER, M. and MEINZER, A. (1967). The effects of intralist activity on free recall. *J.V.L.V.B., 6*, 928–935.

GLUCKSBERG, S. and COWEN, G. N. (1970). Memory for nonattended auditory material. *Cog. Psych., 1*, 149–156.

GLUCKSBERG, S. and DANKS, J.H. (1969). Grammatical structure and recall: A function of the space in immediate memory or of recall delay? *P. & P., 6,* 113–117.

GRAY, J. A. and WEDDERBURN, A. A. (1960). Grouping strategies with simultaneous stimuli. *Q.J.E.P., 12,* 180–184.

GREEN, D. M. (1964). Detection of auditory sinusoids of uncertain frequency. In: *Signal Detection and Recognition by Human Observers,* edited by J. A. Swets. New York: Wiley.

GREGORY, R. L. (1970). *The Intelligent Eye.* London: Weidenfeld and Nicolson.

GUTTMAN, N. and JULESZ, B. (1963). Lower limits of auditory periodicity analysis. *J.A.S.A., 35,* 610.

HABER, R. N. and HERSHENSON, M. (1973). *The Psychology of Visual Perception.* New York: Holt, Rinehart, and Winston.

HAGGARD, M. P. (1971). Encoding the REA for speech signals. *Q.J.E.P., 23,* 34–45.

HAMILTON, P. and HOCKEY, G. R. J. (1970). Recency/primacy ratio: A short test of task orientation. *Psychon. Sci., 21,* 253–254.

HAMILTON, W. (1859). *Lectures on Metaphysics and Logic.* Edinburgh: Blackwood.

HEBB, D. O. (1949). *The Organization of Behaviour.* New York: John Wiley.

HEBB, D. O. (1961). Distinctive features of learning in the higher animal. In: *Brain Mechanisms and Learning,* edited by J. F. Delafresnaye. London: Oxford University Press.

HEDE, A. J. (1973). Stimulus array and recall method as variables in audio-visual split-span memory. *Q.J.E.P., 25,* 130–137.

HENDERSON, L. and PARK, N. (1973). Are the ends of tachistoscopic arrays processed first? *C.J.P., 27,* 178–183.

HERNANDEZ-PEON, R., SCHEERER, H. and JOUVET, M. (1956). Modification of electrical activity in the cochlear nucleus during 'attention' in unanaesthetised cats. *Science, 123,* 331–332.

HERSHENSON, M. (1969). Stimulus structure, cognitive structure, and the perception of letter arrays. *J.E.P., 79,* 327–335.

HINTZMAN, D. L., BLOCK, R. A., and INSKEEP, N. R. (1972). Memory for mode of input. *J.V.L.V.B., 11,* 741–749.

HINTSMAN, D. L., CARRE, F. A., ESKRIDGE, V. L., OWENS, A. M., SHAFF, S. and SPARKS, M. E. (1972). "Stroop" effect: Input or output phenomenon? *J.E.P., 95,* 458–459.

HOCK, H. S. and EGETH, H. (1970). Verbal interference with encoding in a perceptual classification task. *J.E.P., 83,* 299–303.

HOCKEY, G. R. J. (1972). Attentional strategies in memory. Paper read at meeting of the Experimental Psychology Society, held in London.

HOCKEY, G. R. J. (1973). Rate of presentation in running memory and direct manipulation of input processing strategies. *Q.J.E.P., 25,* 104–111.

HOLDING, D. J. (1970). Guessing behaviour and the Sperling store. *Q.J.E.P., 22,* 248–256.

HOLDING, D. H. (1973). Recognition tests of visual information storage. *B.J.P., 64,* 9–16.

HOWARTH, C. I. and ELLIS, K. (1961). The relative intelligibility threshold for one's own and other people's names. *Q.J.E.P., 13,* 236–240.

HOWES, D. H. and SOLOMAN, R. L. (1951). Visual duration threshold as a function of word probability. *J.E.P., 41,* 401–410.

HUNT, E. and LOVE, T. (1972). How good can memory be? In: *Coding Processes in Human Memory*, edited by A. W. Melton and E. Martin. Washington, D.C.: Winston.

INGLIS, J. (1965). Dichotic listening and cerebral dominance. *Acta Oto-laryngologica, 60*, 231–237.

JACOBSON, J. Z. (1973). Effects of association upon masking and reading latency. *Canadian Journal of Psychology, 27*, 58–69.

JACOBY, L. L. (1973). Encoding processes, rehearsal and recall requirements. *J.V.L.V.B., 12*, 302-310.

JAMES, W. (1890). *The Principles of Psychology.* New York: Holt.

JEVONS, W. S. (1871). The power of numerical discrimination. *Nature, 3,*281–282.

JOHNSON-LAIRD, P. N. (1975). Meaning and the mental lexicon. In: A. KENNEDY and A. WILKES (Eds.), *Studies in Long Term Memory.* London: Wiley.

JOHNSTON, W. A., GREENBERG, S. N., FISHER, R. P., and MARTIN, D. W. (1970). Divided attention: A vehicle for monitoring memory processes. *J.E.P., 83*, 164–171.

JOYNSON, R. B. (1970). The breakdown of modern psychology. *Bulletin of the British Psychological Society, 23*, 261–269.

JOALA, J. F., FISCHLER, I., WOOD, C. T., and ATKINSON, R. C. (1971). Recognition time for information stored in long-term memory. *P. & P., 10*, 8–14.

KAHNEMAN, D. (1973). *Attention and Effort.* Englewood Cliffs: Prentice-Hall.

KATZ, J. J. and POSTAL, P. M. (1964). *An Integrated Theory of Linguistic Descriptions.* Cambridge, Mass.: M.I.T. Press.

KAY, H. (1968). Learning and aging. In: *Theory and Methods of Research on Aging,* edited by K. W. Schrie. Morgantown: West Virginia University Press.

KAY, H. and POULTON, E. C. (1951). Anticipation in memorizing. *B.J.P., 42*, 34–41.

KEELE, S. W. (1973). *Attention and Human Performance.* Pacific Palisades: Charles Goodyear.

KELLY, G. A. (1955). *The Psychology of Personal Constructs.* New York: Norton.

KEPPEL, G. and UNDERWOOD, B. J. (1962). Proactive inhibition in short-term retention of single items. *J.V.L.V.B., 1*, 153–161.

KIMBLE, G. A. and PERLMUTER, L. C. (1970). The problem of volition. *Psych. Rev., 77*, 361–384.

KIMURA, D. (1961). Cerebral dominance and the perception of verbal stimuli. *C.J.P., 15*, 166–171.

KIMURA, D. (1964). Left-right differences in the perception of melodies. *Q.J.E.P., 14*, 355–358.

KIMURA, D. (1967). Functional asymmetry of the brain in dichotic listening. *Cortex, 3*, 163–178.

KING, F. L. and KIMURA, D. (1972). Left-ear superiority in dichotic perception of vocal nonverbal sounds. *C.J.P., 26*, 111–116.

KINTSCH, W. (1970). *Learning, Memory, and Conceptual Processes.* New York: John Wiley.

KINTSCH, W. and BUSCHKE, H. (1969). Homophones and synonyms in short-term memory. *J.E.P., 80*, 403–407.

KLAPP, S. T. and LEE, P. (1974). Time-of-occurrence cues for "unattended" auditory material. *J.E.P., 102*, 176–177.

KLEIN, G. A. (1972). Temporal changes in acoustic and semantic confusion effects. *J.E.P., 86,* 236—240.

KLEIN, G. S. (1964). Semantic power measured through the interference of words with colour naming. *A.J.P., 77,* 576—588.

LaBERGE, D. and SAMUELS, S. J. (1974). Toward a theory of automatic information processing in reading. *Cog. Psych., 6,* 293—323.

LANDAUER, T. K. (1962). Rate of implicit speech. *Perceptual and Motor Skills, 15,* 646.

LAWSON, E. (1966). Decisions concerning the rejected channel. *Q.J.E.P., 18,* 260—265.

LAZARUS, R. S. and McCLEARY, R. A. (1951). Autonomic discrimination without awareness: A study of subception. *Psych. Rev., 58,* 113—122.

LEWIS, J. L. (1970). Semantic processing of unattended messages using dichotic listening. *J.E.P., 85,* 225—228.

LIBERMAN, A. M., COOPER, F. S., SHANKWEILER, D. P., and STUDDERT-KENNEDY, M. (1967). Perception of the speech code. *Psych. Rev., 74,* 431—461.

LIBERMAN, A. M., HARRIS, K., HOFFMAN, H., and GRIFFITH, B. (1957). The discrimination of speech sounds within and across phoneme boundaries. *J.E.P., 54,* 358—368.

LIBERMAN, A. M., MATTINGLY, I. G., and TURVEY, M. T. (1972). Language codes and memory codes. In: *Coding Processes in Human Memory,* edited by A. W. Melton and E. Martin. New York: Winston.

LINDSAY, P. H. (1970). Multichannel processing in perception. In: *Attention: Contemporary Theory and Analysis,* edited by D. I. Mostofsky. New York: Appleton-Century-Crofts.

LISKER, L. and ABRAMSON, A. S. (1964). A cross-language study of voicing in initial stops: acoustical measurements. *Word, 20,* 384—422.

LOESS, H. (1968). Short-term memory and item similarity. *J.V.L.V.B., 7,* 87—92.

LOFTUS, E. F. (1973). Activation of semantic memory. *A.J.P., 86,* 331—337.

LOFTUS, E. F. (1974). On reading the fine print. *Q.J.E.P., 27,* 324.

LURIA, A. R. (1969). *The Mind of a Mnemonist.* London: Cape.

MACKAY, D. G. (1973). Aspects of the theory of comprehension, memory and attention. *Q.J.E.P., 25,* 22—40.

MACKWORTH, J. F. (1964). Auditory short-term memory. *C.J.P., 18,* 292—303.

MACKWORTH, N.H. and MORANDI, A. J. (1967). The gaze selects informative details within pictures. *P. and P., 2,* 547—552.

MANDLER, G. (1967). Organization and memory. In: *The Psychology of Learning and Motivation, Vol. 1,* edited by K. W. Spence and J. T. Spence. New York: Academic Press.

MANDLER, G. and MANDLER, J. M. (1964). Serial position effects in sentences. *J.V.L.V.B., 3,* 195—202.

MANDLER, G. and WORDEN, P. E. (1973). Semantic processing without permanent storage. *J.E.P., 100,* 277—283.

MARCEL, T. (1974). The effective visual field and the use of context in fast and slow readers of two ages. *B.J.P., 65,* 479—492.

MARTIN, D. W. (1970). Residual processing capacity during verbal organization in memory. *J.V.L.V.B., 9,* 391—397.

MARTIN, D. W., MARSTON, P. T., and KELLY, R. T. (1973). Measurement of organizational processes within memory stages. *J.E.P., 98,* 387–395.

MARTIN, E. and ROBERTS, K. H. (1966). Grammatical factors in sentence retention. *J.V.L.V.B., 5,* 211–218.

MASSARO, D. W. (1970a). Preperceptual auditory images. *J.E.P., 85,* 411–417.

MASSARO, D. W. (1970b). Perceptual processes and forgetting in memory tasks. *Psych. Rev., 77,* 557–567.

MASSARO, D. W. (1971). Effect of masking tone duration on preperceptual auditory images. *J.E.P., 87,* 146–148.

MASSARO, D. W. (1972a). Preperceptual images, processing time, and perceptual units in auditory perception. *Psych. Rev., 79,* 124–145.

MASSARO, D. W. (1972b). Stimulus information vs. processing time in auditory pattern recognition. *P. and P., 12,* 50–56.

MASSARO, D. W. and KAHN, B. J. (1973). Effects of central processing on auditory recognition. *J.E.P., 97,* 51–58.

McGAUGH, J. L. and DAWSON, R. G. (1971). Modification of memory storage processes. *Behavioural Science, 16,* 45–63.

McGEOCH, J. A. (1932). Forgetting and the law of disuse. *Psych. Rev. 39,* 352–370.

McGHIE, A. and CHAPMAN, J.(1961). Disorders of attention and perception in early schizophrenia. *British Journal of Medical Psychology, 34,* 103–116.

McGILL, W. J. (1961). Loudness and reaction time. *Acta Psych., 19,* 193–199.

McGINNIES, E. (1949). Emotionality and perceptual defence. *Psych. Rev., 56,* 244–251.

MEHLER, J. (1963). Some effects of grammatical transformations on the recall of English sentences. *J.V.L.V.B., 2,* 346–351.

MELTON, A. W. (1963). Implications of short-term memory for a general theory of memory. *J.V.L.V.B., 2,* 1–12.

MELTON, A. W. and IRWIN, J. M. (1940). The influence of degree of interpolated learning on retroactive inhibition and the overt transfer of specific responses. *A.J.P., 53,* 173–203.

MERIKLE, P. M. and COLTHEART, M. (1972). Selective forward masking. *C.J.P., 26,* 296–302.

MERIKLE, P. M., COLTHEART, M., and LOWE, D. G. (1971). On the selective effects of a patterned masking stimulus. *C.J.P., 25,* 264–279.

MEUNIER, G. F., RITZ, D., and MEUNIER, J. A. (1972). Rehearsal of individual items in short-term memory, *J.E.P., 95,* 465–467.

MEWHORT, D. J. K. (1967). Familiarity of letter sequences, response uncertainty and the tachistoscopic recognition experiment. *C.J.P., 21,* 309–321.

MEWHORT, D. J. K. (1973). Retrieval tags and order of report in dichotic listening. *C.J.P., 27,* 119–126.

MEWHORT, D. J. K., MERIKLE, P. M., and BRYDEN, M. P. (1969). On the transfer from iconic to short-term memory. *J.E.P., 81,* 89–94.

MEWHORT, D. J. K., THIO, H., and BIRKENMAYER, A. C. (1971). Processing capacity and switching attention in dichotic listening. *C.J.P., 25,* 111–129.

MEYER, D. E. and SCHVANEVELDT, R. W (1971). Facilitation in recognising pairs of words: Evidence of a dependence between retrieval operations. *J.E.P., 90,* 227–234.

MILLER, G. A. (1956). The magical number seven, plus or minus two: Some limits on our capacity for processing information. *Psych. Rev., 63,* 81–97.

MILLER, G. A. (1962). Some psychological studies of grammar. *American Psychologist, 17*, 748–762.

MILLER, G. A. and CHOMSKY, N. (1963). Finitary models of language users. In: *Handbook of Mathematical Psychology, Vol. 3*, edited by R. D. Luce, R. R. Bush, and E. Galanter. New York: John Wiley.

MILLER, G. A., GALANTER, E., and PRIBRAM, K. H. (1960). *Plans and the Structure of Behaviour.* New York: Holt, Rinehart, and Winston.

MILNER, B., BRANCH, C., and RASMUSSEN, T. (1964). Observations on cerebral dominance. In: *Ciba Foundation Symposium on Disorders of Language*, edited by A. V. S. deReuck and M. O'Connor, London: Churchill.

MOORE, J. J. and MASSARO, D. W. (1973). Attention and the processing capacity in auditory recognition. *J.E.P., 99*, 49–54.

MORAY, N. (1959). Attention in dichotic listening: Affective cues and the influence of instructions. *Q.J.E.P., 11*, 56–60.

MORAY, N. (1967). Where is capacity limited? A survey and a model. *Acta Psych., 27*, 84–92.

MORAY, N. (1969). *Attention: Selective Processes in Vision and Hearing.* London: Hutchinson.

MORAY, N., BATES, A., and BARNETT, T. (1965). Experiments on the four-eared man. *J.A.S.A., 38*, 196–201.

MORTON, J. (1969). Interaction of information in word recognition. *Psych. Rev., 76*, 165–178.

MORTON, J., CROWDER, R. G., and PRUSSIN, H. A. (1971). Experiments with the stimulus suffix effect. *J.E.P. Monographs, 91*, 169–190.

MORTON, J. and HOLLOWAY, C. M. (1970). Absence of a cross-modal "suffix effect" in short-term memory. *Q.J.E.P., 22*, 167–176.

MOWBRAY, G. H. (1964). Perception and retention of verbal information presented during auditory shadowing. *J.A.S.A., 36*, 1459–1464.

MURDOCK, B. B. (1960). The distinctiveness of stimuli. *Psych. Rev., 67*, 16–31.

MURDOCK, B. B. (1964). Proactive inhibition in short-term memory, *J.E.P., 68*, 184–189.

MURDOCK, B. B. (1968). Serial order effects in short-term memory. *J.E.P. Monographs, 76*, (Part 4, 2), 1–15.

MURDOCK, B. B. (1972). Short-term memory. In: *The Psychology of Learning and Motivation, Vol. 5*, edited by G. Bower. London: Academic Press.

MURDOCK, B. B. and WALKER, K. D. (1969). Modality effects in free recall. *J.V.L.V.B., 8*, 665–676.

MURPHY, E. H. and VENABLES, P. H. (1970). Ear asymmetry in the threshold of fusion of two clicks: A signal detection analysis. *Q.J.E.P., 22*, 288–300.

MURRAY, D. J. (1966). Vocalization-at-presentation and immediate recall, with varying recall methods. *Q.J.E.P., 18*, 9–18.

MURRAY, D. J. and HITCHCOCK, C.H. (1969). Attention and storage in dichotic listening. *J.E.P., 81*, 164–169.

NAUS, M. J., GLUCKSBERG, S., and ORNSTEIN, P. A. (1972). Taxonomic word categories and memory search. *Cog. Psych., 3*, 643–654.

NEISSER, U. (1963). The multiplicity of thought. *B.J.P., 54*, 1–14.

NEISSER, U. (1967). *Cognitive Psychology.* New York: Appleton-Century-Crofts.

NEISSER, U. (1969). The role of rhythm in active verbal memory: Serial intrusions. *A.J.P. 82*, 540–546.

264   Attention and Memory

NICKERSON, R. S. (1965). Short-term memory for complex meaningful visual configurations, a demonstration of capacity. *C.J.P., 19*, 155–160.
NICKERSON, R. S. (1972). Auditory codability and the short-term retention of visual information. *J.E.P., 95*, 429–436.
NORMAN, D. A. (1968). Toward a theory of memory and attention. *Psych. Rev., 75*, 522–536.
NORMAN, D. A. (1979a). *Memory and Attention.* New York: John Wiley.
NORMAN, D. A. (1969b). Memory while shadowing. *Q.J.E.P., 21*, 85–93.
NORMAN, D. A. (1970). *Models of Human Memory,* (Editor). London: Academic Press.
NORMAN, D. A. (1973). What have the animal experiments taught us about human memory. In: *The Physiological Basis of Memory,* edited by J. A. Deutsch. London: Academic Press.
OSWALD, I., TAYLOR, A., and TREISMAN, M. (1960). Discriminative responses to stimulation during human sleep. *Brain, 83*, 440–453.
PAIVIO, A. (1969). Mental imagery in associative learning and memory. *Psych. Rev., 76*, 241–263.
PAIVIO, A. (1971). Imagery and deep structure in the recall of English nominalizations. *J.V.L.V.B., 10*, 1–12.
PAVLOV, I. P. (1927). *Conditioned Reflexes.* London: Oxford University Press.
PERFETTI, C. A. (1969). Lexical density and phrase structure depth as variables in sentence retention. *J.V.L.V.B., 8*, 719–724.
PERFETTI, C. A. and GOODMAN, D. (1971). Memory for sentences and noun phrases of extreme depth. *Q.J.E.P., 23*, 22–33.
PETERSON, L. R. and KROENER, S. (1964). Dichotic stimulation and retention. *J.E.P., 68*, 125–130.
PETERSON, L. R. and PETERSON, M. J. (1959). Short-term retention of individual verbal items. *J.E.P., 58*, 193–198.
PISONI, D. B. (1973). Auditory and phonetic memory codes in the discrimination of consonants and vowels. *P. and P. 13*, 253–260.
POLLACK, I., JOHNSON, L. B., and KNAFF, P. R. (1959). Running memory span. *J.E.P., 57*, 137–146.
POSNER, M. I. (1969). Abstraction and the process of recognition. In: *The Psychology of Learning and Motivation, Vol. 3,* edited by G. H. Bower and J. T. Spence. New York: Academic Press.
POSNER, M. I. and BOIES, S. J. (1971). Components of attention. *Psych. Rev., 78*, 391–408.
POSNER, M. I., BOIES, S. J., EICHELMAN, W. H. and TAYLOR, R. L. (1969). Retention of visual and name codes of single letters. *J.E.P. Monographs, 79*, (Part 1, 2), 1–16.
POSNER, M. I. and KEELE, S. W. (1967). Decay of information from a single letter. *Science, 158*, 137–139.
POSNER, M. I. and KLEIN, R. (1972). On the functions of consciousness. In: *Attention and Performance IV,* edited by S. Kornblum. New York: Academic Press.
POSNER, M. I. and MITCHELL, R. F. (1967). Chronometric analysis of classification. *Psych. Rev., 74*, 394–409.
POSNER, M. I. and TAYLOR, R. L. (1969). Subtractive method applied to separation of visual and name components of multi-letter arrays. *Acta Psych., 30*, 104–114.

POSTMAN, L. (1969). Mechanisms of interference in forgetting. In: *The Pathology of Memory*, edited by G. A. Talland and N. C. Waugh London: Academic Press.

POSTMAN, L. and UNDERWOOD, B. J. (1973). Critical issues in interference theory. *Memory and Cognition, 1*, 19–40.

PRIBAM, K. H. and BROADBENT, D. E. (1970). *The Biology of Memory*, (Editors). London: Academic Press.

QUILLIAN, M. R. (1967). Word concepts: A theory and simulation of some basic semantic capabilities. *Behavioural Science, 12*, 410–430.

QUILLIAN, M. R. (1969). The Teachable Language Comprehender: A simulation program and theory of language. *Communications of the Association for Computing Machinery, 12*, 459–476.

RAYMOND, B. (1969). Short-term storage and long-term storage in free recall. *J.V.L.V.B., 8*, 567–574.

REED, G. (1972). *The Psychology of Anomalous Experience*. London: Hutchinson.

REICHER, G. M. (1969). Perceptual recognition as a function of meaningfulness of stimulus material. *J.E.P., 81*, 275–281.

REYNOLDS, D. (1964). Effects of double stimulation: Temporary inhibition of response. *Psych. Bull., 62*, 333–347.

ROBINSON, C. E. (1973). Reaction time to the offset of brief auditory stimuli. *P. and P., 13*, 281–283.

ROEDIGER, H. L. and CROWDER, R. G. (1972). Instructed forgetting: Rehearsal control or retrieval inhibition (repression)? *Cog. Psych., 3*, 244–254.

ROZENWEIG, M. R. (1951). Representations of the two ears at the auditory cortex. *American Journal of Physiology, 167*, 147–158.

RUBINSTEIN, H., LEWIS, S. S., and RUBINSTEIN, M. A. (1971). Evidence for phonemic recoding in visual word recognition. *J.V.L.V.B., 10*, 645–657.

RUMELHART, D. E. (1970). A multicomponent theory of the perception of briefly exposed visual displays. *Journal of Mathematical Psychology, 7*, 191–218.

RUNDUS, D. (1971). Analysis of rehearsal processes in free recall. *J.E.P., 89*, 63–77.

SALTER, D. (1973). Shadowing at one and at two ears. *Q.J.E.P., 25*, 549–556.

SAVIN, H.B. and PERCHONOCK, E. (1965). Grammatical structure and the immediate recall of English sentences. *J.V.L.V.B., 4*, 348–353.

SCHONFIELD, D. and ROBERTSON, B. (1966). Memory storage and aging. *C.J.P., 20*, 228–236.

SEGAL, E. (1969). Hierarchical structure in free recall. *J.E.P., 80*, 59–63.

SHAFFER, L. H. (1971). Attention in transcription skill. *Q.J.E.P., 23*, 107–112.

SHAFFER, L. H. (1973). Some determinants of a success and failure of multiple attention. Paper read at joint meeting of the Experimental Psychology Society and the Netherlands Psychonomic Foundation, held in Amsterdam.

SHAFFER, W. O. and SHIFFRIN, R. M. (1972). Rehearsal and storage of visual information. *J.E.P., 92*, 292–296.

SHALLICE, T. (1972). Dual functions of consciousness. *Psych. Rev., 79*, 383–393.

SHANKWEILER, D. P. and STUDDERT-KENNEDY, M. (1967). Identification of consonants and vowels presented to left and right ears. *Q.J.E.P., 19*, 59–63.

SHEPARD, R. N. (1967). Recognition memory for words, sentences, and pictures. *J.V.L.V.B., 6*, 156–163.

SHULMAN, H. G., (1972). Semantic confusion errors in short-term memory. *J.V.L.V.B., 11*, 221–227.

SKINNER, B. F. (1972). *Beyond Freedom and Dignity*. London: Cape.

SMITH, E. E., SHOBEN, E. J., and RIPS, L. J. (1974). Comparison processes in semantic memory. *Psych. Rev., 81*, 214–241.

SMITH, G. J. W. and HENRIKSSON, M. (1955). The effect on an established percept of a perceptual process beyond awareness. *Acta Psych., 11*, 346–355.

SMITH, G. J. W., SPENCE, D. P. and KLEIN, G. S. (1959). Subliminal effects of verbal stimuli. *Journal of Abnormal and Social Psychology, 59*, 167–176.

SPERLING, G. (1960). The information available in brief visual presentations. *Psychological Monographs, 74*, (Whole No. 498).

SPERLING, G. (1963). A model for visual memory tasks. *Human Factors, 5*, 19–31.

SPERLING, G. (1967). Successive approximations to a model for short-term memory. *Acta Psych., 27*, 285–292.

SPRINGER, S. P. (1971). Ear asymmetry in a dichotic listening task. *P. and P., 10*, 239–241.

STANDING, L. (1973). Learning 10000 pictures. *Q.J.E.P., 25*, 207–222.

STERNBERG, S. (1966). High speed scanning in human memory. *Science, 153*, 652–654.

STEVENS, S. S. and DAVIS, H. (1938). *Hearing*. New York: John Wiley.

STROOP, J. R. (1935). Studies of interference in serial verbal reactions. *J.E.P., 18*, 643–662.

STUDDERT-KENNEDY, M., SHANKWEILER, D. P., and PISONI, D. B. (1972). Auditory and phonetic processes in speech: Evidence from a dichotic study. *Cog. Psych., 3*, 455–466.

SUTHERLAND, N. S. (1969). Outlines of a theory of visual pattern recognition in animals and men. In: *Animal Discrimination Learning*, edited by R. M. Gilbert and N. S. Sutherland. London: Academic Press.

SWETS, J. A., TANNER, W. P., and BIRDSALL, T. G. (1961). Decision processes in perception. *Psych. Rev., 68*, 301–340.

TAYLOR, M. M., LINDSAY, P. H., and FORBES, S. M. (1967). Quantification of shared capacity processing in auditory and visual discrimination. *Acta Psych., 27*, 223–229.

TELFORD, C. W. (1931). The refractory phase of voluntary and associative responses. *J. E. P., 14*, 1–36.

THEIOS, J., SMITH, P. G., HAVILAND, S. E., TRAUPMAN, J., and MOY, M. C (1973). Memory scanning as a serial self-terminating process. *J.E.P., 97*, 323–336.

TITCHENER, E. B., (1908). *Lectures on the Elementary Psychology of Feeling and Attention*. New York: Macmillan.

TREISMAN, A. M. (1960). Contextual cues in selective listening. *Q.J.E.P., 12*, 242–248.

TREISMAN, A. M. (1964a). Selective attention in man. *British Medical Bulletin, 20*, 12–16.

TREISMAN, A. M. (1964b). Verbal cues, language, and meaning in selective attention. *A.J.P., 77*, 206–219.

TREISMAN, A. M. (1969). Strategies and models of selective attention. *Psych. Rev., 76*, 282–299.

TREISMAN, A. M. and FEARNLEY, S. (1969). The Stroop test: Selective attention to colours and words. *Nature, 222*, 437–439.

TREISMAN, A. M. and FEARNLEY, S. (1971). Can simultaneous speech stimuli be classified in parallel? *P. and P., 10*, 1–7.

TREISMAN, A. M. and GEFFEN, G. (1967). Selective attention: Perception or Response? *Q.J.E.P., 19*, 1–17.

TREISMAN, A. M. and RILEY, J. G. A. (1969). Is selective attention selective perception or selective response? A further test. *J.E.P., 76*, 27–34.

TREISMAN, A. M., SQUIRE, R., and GREEN, J. (1974). Semantic processing in dichotic listening: A replication. *Memory and Cognition, 2*, 641–646.

TREISMAN, M. and ROSTRON, A. B. (1972). Brief auditory storage: A modification of Sperling's paradigm applied to audition. *Acta Psych. 36*, 161–170.

TULVING, E. (1966). Subjective organization and effects of repetition in multi-trial free-recall learning. *J.V.L.V.B., 5*, 193–197.

TULVING, E. (1968). Theoretical issues in free recall. In: *Verbal Behaviour and General Behaviour Theory*, edited by T. R. Dixon and D. L. Horton. Englewood-Cliffs: Prentice-Hall.

TULVING, E. (1970). Short- and long-term memory: Different retrieval mechanisms. In: *The Biology of Memory*, edited by K. H. Pribram and D. E. Broadbent. London. London: Academic Press.

TULVING, E. (1972). Episodic and semantic memory. In: *Organization of Memory*, edited by E. Tulving and W. Donaldson. New York: Academic Press.

TULVING, E. and COLOTLA, V. A. (1970). Free recall of trilingual lists. *Cog. Psych., 1*, 86–98.

TULVING, E. and GOLD, C. (1963). Stimulus information and contextual information as determinants of tachistoscopic recognition of words. *J.E.P., 66*, 319–327.

TULVING, E. and MADIGAN, S. A. (1970). Memory and verbal learning. *Annual Review of Psychology, 21*, 437–484.

TULVING, E. and PATTERSON, R. D. (1968). Functional units and retrieval processes in free recall. *J.E.P., 77*, 239–248.

TULVING, E. and PEARLSTONE, Z. (1966). Availability versus accessability of information in memory for words. *J.V.L.V.B., 5*, 381–391.

TURVEY, M. T. and KRAVETZ, S. (1970). Retrieval from iconic memory with shape as the selection criterion. *P. and P., 8*, 171–172.

UNDERWOOD, B. J. (1948). Retroactive and proactive interference after five and after forty-eight hours. *J.E.P., 38*, 29–38.

UNDERWOOD, B. J. (1957). Interference and forgetting. *Psych. Rev., 64*, 49–60.

UNDERWOOD, G. (1972). Response organization in attention control and a perceptual serial position effect. *Q.J.E.P., 24*, 340–351.

UNDERWOOD, G. (1973a). Control of selective attention and interference of processing in memory. *J.E.P., 99*, 28–34.

UNDERWOOD, G. (1973b). Concerning the role of perceptual factors in the serial position effect. *P. and P., 13*, 344–348.

UNDERWOOD, G. (1973c). Transition probability and dichotic listening. *Nature, 241*, 134–135.

UNDERWOOD, G. (1974a). Moray vs. the rest: The effects of extended shadowing practice. *Q.J.E.P., 26*, 368–372.

UNDERWOOD, G. (1974b). Searching through categorical memory. Unpublished Ms.

UNDERWOOD, G. (1975). Perceptual distinctiveness and proactive interference in the primacy effect. *Q.J.E.P., 27*, 289–294.

UNDERWOOD, G. (1976a). Semantic interference from unattended printed words. *B.J.P., 67*, in press.

UNDERWOOD, G. (1976b). Attention, awareness, and hemispheric differences in word recognition. *Neuropsychologia, 14*.

UNDERWOOD, G. and MORAY, N. (1971). Shadowing and monitoring for selective attention. *Q.J.E.P., 23*, 284–295.

UNDERWOOD, G. and SWAIN, R. A. (1973). Selectivity of attention and the perception of duration. *Perception, 2*, 101–105.

VINCE, M. A. (1948). The intermittency of control movements and the psychological refractory period. *B.J.P., 38*, 149–157.

VON WRIGHT, J. M. (1968). Selection in visual immediate memory. *Q.J.E.P., 20*, 62–68.

WANG, M. D. (1970). The role of syntactic complexity as a determiner of comprehensibility. *J.V.L.V.B., 9*, 398–404.

WARREN, R. E. (1972). Stimulus encoding and memory. *J.E.P., 94*, 90–100. *ental*

WARREN, R. M. and WARREN, R. P. (1970). Auditory illusions and confusions. *Scientific American, 223 (June)*, 30–36.

WATKINS, M. J. and WATKINS, O. C. (1973). The postcategorical status of the modality effect in free recall. *J.E.P., 99*, 226–230

WAUGH, N. C. (1969). Free recall of conspicuous items. *J.V.L.V.B., 8*, 448–456.

WAUGH, N. C. and NORMAN, D. A. (1965). Primary memory. *Psych. Rev., 72*, 89–104.

WEARING, A. J. (1972). Remembering complex sentences. *Q.J.E.P., 24*, 77–86.

WEARING, A. J. and CROWDER, R. G. (1971). Dividing attention to study sentence acquisition. *J.V.L.V.B., 10*, 254–261.

WEISS, M. S. and HOUSE, A. S. (1973). Perception of dichotically presented vowels. *J.A.S.A., 53*, 51–58.

WEISKRANTZ, L. (1966). Experimental studies of amnesia. In: *Amnesia*, edited by C. W. M. Whitty and O. L. Zangwill. London: Butterworth.

WEIST, R. M. (1972). The role of rehearsal: Copy or reconstruct? *J.V.L.V.B., 11*, 440–450.

WEIST, R. M. and CRAWFORD, C. (1973). Sequential versus organized rehearsal. *J.E.P., 101*, 237–241.

WELFORD, A. T. (1952). The psychological refractory period and the timing of high speed performance: A review and a theory. *B.J.P., 43*, 2–19.

WELFORD, A. T. (1958). *Ageing and Human Skill.* London: Oxford University Press.

WHEELER, D. D. (1970). Processes in word recognition. *Cog. Psych. 1*, 59–85.

WHITMORE, M. G. (1972). Stimulus meaning as a variable in dichotic listening. *Psychon. Sci., 26*, 207–208.

WICKELGREN, W. A. (1965). Acoustic similarity and retroactive interference in short-term memory. *J.V.L.V.B., 4*, 53–61.

WICKELGREN, W. A. (1970). Multitrace strength theory. In: *Models of Human Memory*, edited by D. A. Norman. New York: Academic Press.

WICKENS, D. D., BORN, D. G., and ALLEN, C. K. (1963). Proactive inhibition and item similarity in short-term memory. *J.V.L.V.B.*, *2*, 440–445.

WICKENS, D. D. and ECKLER, G. R. (1968). Semantic as opposed to acoustic encoding in short-term memory. *Psychon. Sci.*, *12*, 63.

WILLOWS, D. M. and MacKINNON, G. E. (1973). Selective reading: Attention to the "unattended" lines. *C. J. P.*, *27*, 292–304.

WOOD, G. (1972). Organization processes and free recall. In: *Organization of Memory* edited by E. Tulving and W. Donaldson. New York: Academic Press.

WOODWARD, A. E. and BJORK, R. A. (1971). Forgetting and remembering in free recall: Intentional and unintentional. *J.E.P.*, *89*, 109–116.

WOODWORTH, R. S. and SCHLOSBERG, H. (1954). *Experimental Psychology*. New York: Holt, Rinehart and Winston.

WRIGHT, P. (1969). Two studies of the depth hypothesis. *B.J.P.*, *60*, 63–69.

YNGVE, V.H. (1960). A model and a hypothesis for language structure. *Proceedings of the American Philosophical Society*, *104*, 444–466.

YNGVE, V. H. (1962). Computer programs for translation. *Scientific American*, *206 (June)*, 68–76.

YNTEMA, D. B. and TRASK, F. P. (1963). Recall as a search process. *J.V.L.V.B.* *2*, 65–74.

ZUCKERMAN, M. (1960). The effects of subliminal and supraliminal suggestion on verbal productivity. *Journal of Abnormal and Social Psychology*. *60*, 404–411.

AUTHOR INDEX

SUBJECT INDEX